Foundations of the Everyday

Philosophical Projections

Series Editor: Andrew Benjamin, Distinguished Professor of Philosophy and the Humanities, Kingston University, UK, and Professor of Philosophy and Jewish Thought, Monash University, Australia

Philosophical Projections represents the future of Modern European Philosophy. The series seeks to innovate by grounding the future in the work of the present, opening up the philosophical and allowing it to renew itself, while interrogating the continuity of the philosophical after the critique of metaphysics.

Titles in the Series

Foundations of the Everyday, Eran Dorfman

Foundations of the Everyday

Shock, Deferral, Repetition

Eran Dorfman

ROWMAN & LITTLEFIELD
INTERNATIONAL

London • New York

Published by Rowman & Littlefield International, Ltd.
16 Carlisle Street, London, W1D 3BT
www.rowmaninternational.com

Rowman & Littlefield International, Ltd. is an affiliate of Rowman & Littlefield
4501 Forbes Boulevard, Suite 200, Lanham, Maryland 20706, USA
With additional offices in Boulder, New York, Toronto (Canada), and Plymouth
(UK)
www.rowman.com

British Library Cataloguing in Publication Information Available
A catalogue record for this book is available from the British Library

ISBN: HB 978-1-78348-049-4
ISBN: PB 978-1-78348-050-0

Library of Congress Cataloging-in-Publication Data

Dorfman, Eran.
Foundations of the everyday : shock, deferral, repetition / Eran Dorfman.
pages cm — (Philosophical projections)
Includes bibliographical references and index.
ISBN 978-1-78348-049-4 (cloth : alk. paper) — ISBN 978-1-78348-050-0 (pbk. : alk.
paper) — ISBN 978-1-78348-051-7 (electronic)
1. Life. 2. Experience. 3. Events (Philosophy) 4. Civilization. I. Title.
BD311.D58 2014
111'.1—dc23
2014003659

♾™ The paper used in this publication meets the minimum requirements of
American National Standard for Information Sciences Permanence of Paper for
Printed Library Materials, ANSI/NISO Z39.48-1992.

Printed in the United States of America

Contents

Acknowledgements

"One of the pleasures of working on everyday life is that everyone has a view on the matter", affirms Michael Sheringham. I must confess, however, that for me this pleasure has also been a source of trouble. The confusion surrounding the concept of the everyday challenges the usual solidity of academic writing. What is the everyday? Is there just one everyday or as many different everydays as the number of people who have told me how they perceive theirs? These questions have haunted me during the years in which I have worked on this book. Indeed, they have not made my life easy, but they have also obliged me to find my own way to think of the matter and write on it.

I therefore wish to thank all the people—friends, family and colleagues—who have shared their thoughts with me and helped me better understand mine. Havi Carel, Monique David-Ménard, Fabrice Lébely, Liran Razinsky, Hili Razinsky and Nimrod Reitman read earlier versions of the manuscript and gave me insightful comments that significantly contributed to the clarity and vigor of this book.

Among the people with whom I discussed different themes of the book, I would particularly like to thank the following: Nir Avissar, Michal Bril, Cyrille Deloro, Aïm Deüelle Lüski, Baruch Dorfman, Sara Dorfman, Ilit Ferber, Yona Fischer, Tahel Frosh, Arik Glasner, Assaf Gruber, Itamar Hacohen, Martin Hershenzon, Roni Hirsh-Ratzkovsky, Aurélia Kalisky, Adam Kaplan, Nehama Kaplan, Hagi Kenaan, Boaz M. Levin, Michael Lewis, Claudio Oliveira, Abigail Saggi, Shaul Setter, Nir Ratzkovsky, Sara Raz and Philippe Roepstorff Robiano.

During the years of research leading to this book I benefitted from several generous fellowships. The Alexander von Humboldt Foundation allowed me to spend two years at the Freie Universität Berlin, and I wish to thank Georg W. Bertram, who was a most welcoming host in the Institute of Philosophy. A Pratt Fellowship at Ben Gurion University and a post-doctoral fellowship at Tel Aviv University enabled me to launch my research on the everyday, and I am grateful to Dalia Drai, Yakir Levin, Anat Matar and Yaron Senderowicz, who were so helpful and friendly during those first years. I finally thank wholeheartedly my colleagues from the Department of French Studies at Tel Aviv University, and especially Michèle Kahan Bokobza and Hava Bat-Zeev Shyldkrot, who have helped me find an academic home, without which I cannot imagine how my everyday life would now look.

I am grateful to Sarah Campbell at Rowman & Littlefield International for her devoted and professional hospitality, as well as to Andrew Benjamin for the encouragement that made all this possible. Alice Lagaay and Uri Landesberg contributed considerably to the final form of the manuscript and gave me invaluable intellectual stimulation and assistance.

I finally wish to thank my students in the various seminars I have taught on the everyday at Tel Aviv University, Ben Gurion University, Bezalel Academy of Art, the Freie Universität Berlin and the Collège International de Philosophie, Paris. Without them, this work would feel much more lonesome.

Introduction

The "Everyday" Versus "Experience"

"Out of the Everyday, into Experience!"[1] So runs a recent slogan of Deutsche Bahn, the German Rail Company, revealing one of the presuppositions of our time: the "everyday" and "experience" are conceived as opposites. One has to get out of the former to attain the latter. It is only by taking a train, real or metaphorical, that one can escape the prison of everyday life and gain "experience". The everyday, as implied by the word, is what happens every day, what repeats itself, again and again. Experience, on the other hand, is the unique, the new, what goes beyond repetition.

This book aims to challenge the distinction between the everyday and experience. More precisely, it aims to show that this distinction is modern and stems from various historical, sociological and theoretical factors that will be examined throughout this book. My basic claim is that the everyday cannot be conceived of without reference to the different actions and events that are founded upon it. The everyday is not the ordinary within which the extraordinary is allegedly concealed,[2] but rather a constant process through which what goes beyond the ordinary may be absorbed and reintegrated into the global movement of the day-to-day. It is a meeting point between old and new, allowing both stability and openness, continuation and change.

I propose the notion of *foundation* to capture the way the everyday functions. The everyday as foundation is the background against which any significant activity occurs. It is the physical and mental, bodily and cognitive basis upon which life constantly takes place. Accordingly, the everyday is not a static, motionless and frozen ground, necessary for "real" activity which is separate from it, since it is constantly influenced and changed by every activity. My theory is thus anything but foundationalist, since the foundation of the everyday acts as both a *noun* and a *verb*: it is a foundation that constantly founds itself, a moving complex which accompanies every one of our activities and enables its progress while transforming itself throughout this very process.

The most basic instance of such a foundation of the everyday is the body. My body is what accompanies me at all times, which under normal circumstances seems a stable, unchangeable basis. And yet, it is constantly in flux, as I notice, not without certain unease, when I look at old photos of me, or when I fall ill. The changeability, fragility and plasticity of the body usually go without notice in everyday life, and yet without them I would not have any life at all. The vulnerability of the body is the price I must pay for the ability to act upon reality, the price for a life that is not static and mechanical, but dynamic and organic. My body gives me continuity, a general and relatively solid framework in which endless transformations and adaptations take place. It is this combination of an evident, stable presence together with a concealed underlying plastic, elastic or even liquid nature, that is also true of all foundations of the everyday, be they language, habits, self-identity or relationships with others.

THE MOVEMENT OF FOUNDATION: SHOCK, DEFERRAL, REPETITION

Any founding act of the everyday combines change with stability. It emerges *out* of the old foundation and then collapses *back* into it, changing something in it and eventually becoming itself a part of the foundation. However, this movement is never singular; it must repeat itself over and over again, until the new is eventually integrated into the old. We can think, for instance, of how we make new friends: the hesitation or the excitement of the beginning gradually gives way; after re-interacting with the new friend several times, a more evident and solid friendship is established. The repetition gradually transforms the texture of the everyday in a blend of conservation, creation and destruction, since each new habit or friend both revalidates and changes the everyday (see figure 1).[3]

In order to outline this double movement of foundation, three interrelated mechanisms are called upon: *shock, deferral* and *repetition.* Every action or event that attempts to go "outside" the global movement of the everyday (the smaller arrow) is regarded as *shock.* This term is to be conceived literally—that is, as a strike, an attack on the everyday, which is nonetheless the very condition of the double movement of foundation: conservation (the larger arrow) and self-transcendence (the smaller arrow). Indeed, most of the time shocks are too small to be perceived. For instance, when brushing my teeth, I may touch a painful tooth and, as a result, slightly change the angle of my brushing—that is, change something in the everyday. The shock is a more or less extraordinary event that goes out of the global movement of the everyday, but the degree to which it affects the everyday depends

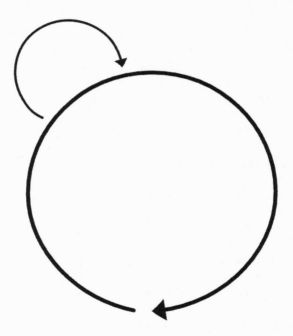

Figure 1. The Double Movement of Foundation: Global and Particular (the smaller arrow indicates particular action of foundation, and the larger arrow indicates global movement of the everyday)

on various factors and involves the two other everyday mechanisms I mentioned above: deferral and repetition.

When my toothbrush encounters an aching tooth, I usually pause for a minute, halt and put off the everyday movement of brushing my teeth. Similarly, when shock occurs, the everyday in which I am engaged is somehow suspended through a mechanism of *deferral*. The deferral may vary in quantity (from a very short to a very long lapse of time) and in quality (from an imperceptible deferral to a self-conscious and reflective one). Moreover, deferral may either concern the shock itself, by parrying or quarantining it (for instance, skipping the painful tooth each time I brush my teeth), or operate a more global scission in the everyday (for instance, if I decide not to brush my teeth until I find a solution to the problem).

In what follows, I will present several forms of deferral and attempt to show how they deal with shocks such that the latter are parried from or integrated into the everyday. I will argue that *late modernity* marks a radical change in the quantity, quality and object of deferral, such that shocks are either hardly deferred or deferred too much.

Deferral is not the only mechanism that processes shocks. *Repetition* is another such mechanism which complements it. After the tooth-brushing is interrupted, for example, I may gently repeat the brushing movement around the aching tooth in order to better understand where exactly the pain is coming from; alternatively, I may engage in a new form of brushing that avoids the sore area and will proceed in this way from now on. Finally, I may try to ignore the pain for fear of its significance, stubbornly repeating the same movement of the brush without any change.

I suggested earlier that any action or event goes "out" of the every-day and eventually returns to it through a certain form of repetition. Indeed, repetition constitutes a key element in the foundation of the everyday, in so far as through it the new is integrated into the old. But repetition, too, has various forms and rhythms, which are moreover conditioned by deferral: when a shock is slightly deferred, its eventual repetition will be very different from a shock which is repeated imme-diately. The reenactment of the suspended action or event will affect the everyday according to the amount of time passed and the events that took place meanwhile. Different deferrals entail different repeti-tions and vice versa, creating together a complex everyday movement that processes actions and events (shocks) in various ways.

We may thus conclude that these three basic everyday mechanisms—shock, deferral, repetition—are intimately interlinked, such that any change in the structure of one implies a change in the structure and shape of the two others. In this book I will try to elucidate these mechanisms, their multiform interconnections and the transformations they have undergone in late modernity. I thus hope not only to provide a better theory of the everyday but also to propose how to deal with shocks in a way that might attenuate the split between the everyday and experience.

MODERNITY AND THE CRISIS OF THE EVERYDAY

The model I have presented so far may offer a good picture of the ideal movement of the everyday, with every repetition, every day, taking something from and bringing something new to the foundations of life, changing them slightly and making the everyday a plastic, endless adventure. Yet what happens when this double movement no longer functions as it is supposed to? What happens when the number of shocks is so high that one has no ability to acquire anything new? This is when one enters the era of what I call the crisis of the everyday.

I have hinted above that this book is about the modern everyday and the transformations it has undergone. My claim throughout this book is that late modernity brings with it a crisis of the everyday. The crisis lies precisely in the separation between the everyday and experience, a separation which can be represented by the figure above as a disjunction between the movements of the two arrows: between the global movement of the everyday and the particular action or event which is founded upon it. It is as if the small arrow has detached itself from the global movement without managing to come back to it—and the same goes for numerous other small arrows, all aiming outside the everyday, at the open, adventurous world. In other words, it is in late modernity that the actions and events that transcend the everyday become shocks. These are simultaneously sought for and feared, and in both cases the shocks are parried from rather than integrated into the everyday. My choice to call these actions and events "shocks" is thus not incidental. Indeed, a sore tooth may not necessarily be perceived as a shock, but I will argue and show throughout this book that the unprecedented number of possible actions and events in modernity makes everything

that presents itself as new be considered as a potential threat: an attack
or a strike—that is, a shock.

Consequently, the everyday that is supposed to be the background
and home of any meaningful action finds itself detached from it, resulting in a life in which all sorts of things occur, but nothing really "happens".[4] The more one acts in the world, the less this action manages to
be integrated into the texture of the everyday and to receive a long-
lasting meaning. The everyday thus becomes an adaptation, an automatic pilot which cannot take off or land. This is why I sometimes
sense that it is not exactly my life that I'm living, but the life of
"another"; that I am not exactly "at home". I am constantly on the
lookout for things to happen, places to go, all sorts of solutions that
may give me my life back, but when things finally happen I have the
feeling, once more, that they are not happening *to me*, so that the
restless pursuit goes on *ad infinitum*.

The everyday, I claim, is the necessary condition for a meaningful
experience, but in late modernity its mode of functioning is deficient.
This combination of necessity and deficiency has led many thinkers to
characterise the everyday as an ambiguous notion.[5] And indeed, when
we think about the everyday, two seemingly contradictory images
come to mind. According to the first, the everyday is the trivial, grey
and insignificant element of life, opposed to the real events that are to
be remembered. In the second, the everyday is life in its most homely,
familiar and safe element. From this perspective, the everyday is *my
own* life, in contrast to the imagined, wished-for one, filling my fantasies and nourished by Hollywood fairy tales. It is rather the concrete,
sometimes harsh life of the here-and-now, enduring unceasingly, day
upon day, from the moment I am born until the moment I die. The
everyday thus provokes an uneasy mixture of repulsion[6] and intimacy,
depending on the relationship between the global movement of the
everyday and the concrete actions and events it allows. Any investigation of the everyday should consequently take into account these two
poles.

AGAINST ANONYMITY

While preparing the manuscript of the present book, I was struck by a
common graphic feature shared by many contemporary books dealing
with the everyday: the cover tends to be a photograph or an illustration

of an urban *street*, busy with anonymous passersby.[7] What makes the anonymous street such an appealing everyday figure? The answer lies, to my view, in a short text which is nonetheless one of the most influential in the current research on the everyday—namely, Maurice Blanchot's "Everyday Speech" (1962), originally entitled "Street Man" (*"L'homme de la rue"*).[8] A short analysis of this text will help clarify what I borrow from Blanchot and where I depart from him.

"The everyday escapes. Why does it escape? Because it is without a subject. When I live the everyday, it is any man, anyone at all who does so" (245). This declaration of Blanchot clearly states the *anonymous* character of the everyday, its being neither subjective nor properly objective—an in-between layer or dimension which is best figured by the street: "If it is anywhere, [the everyday] is in the street" (242).[9] But what happens in the street that makes it the prime location of such a notion of the everyday? Nothing. Or rather, nothing in particular, since the "everyday is without event" (243). The everyday, according to Blanchot, is the uneventful, but as such it is split from experience—that is, from the sphere of the events.

Blanchot is silent about the place of experience with regard to the everyday,[10] probably because he would have to admit that the insignificance he attributes to the everyday entails an insignificance of experience as well. But he does say something important about modernity and the place it gives to the everyday: "Man (the individual of today, of our modern societies) is at once engulfed within and deprived of the everyday. And a third definition: the everyday is also the ambiguity of these two movements, the one and the other hardly graspable" (239).[11] This is indeed a difficult passage to understand, since it succinctly evokes three different definitions of the modern everyday. The first portrays the everyday as that in which one is engulfed. It is "the everyday with its tedious, painful, and sordid side (the amorphous, the stagnant)" (239). I suggest that one might see it as the global movement of the everyday, presented in figure 1 (the larger arrow): a self-enclosed circle that moves around itself with apparently no escape, no outside.

Yet there *is* escape from the everyday, only that when one actually transcends the everyday, one suddenly feels deprived of it. This is described in Blanchot's second definition of the everyday: "the inexhaustible, irrecusable, constantly unfinished everyday that always escapes forms or structures" (239). The everyday is always open to changes, always transcending itself. It is never "finished". But the problem is that when an action actually transcends the everyday, at least in late modernity, it does not find its way back into it, making one feel deprived of the everyday.

These two movements of the everyday as self-enclosure and self-transcendence form together Blanchot's third definition of the everyday as ambivalent. He states that "the two sides always meet" (239), but he nonetheless considers them as opposite. This, I argue, reflects the above-mentioned ambiguous attitude towards the everyday, seeing it both as a prison (first definition) and as a (lacking) home (second definition). In order to clarify this point, it would be helpful to address the work of Henri Lefebvre, who published in 1958 the second edition of his *Critique of Everyday Life* (Vol. 1),[12] to which Blanchot refers several times.[13]

Lefebvre sees ambiguity as a category of the everyday, a category which, according to him, is "perhaps essential" (18) and which he attributes to the *source* of actions and events: "from the ambiguity of consciousnesses and situations spring forth actions, events, results, without warning. These, at least, have clear-cut outlines. They maintain a hard, incisive objectivity which constantly disperses the luminous vapours (*la brume lumineuse*) of ambiguity—only to let them rise once again" (18–19). If we return to the diagram above, we may say that the big circle—that is, the "pure" or "eventless" everyday—is the source of actions which is in itself undefinable and ambiguous. The arrow that goes from it outwards, on the other hand, is an objective action or event that disperses the ambiguity, but then falls back to the everyday such that ambiguity reigns again. In other words, it is only by going "out" of the everyday that one can gain some clarity with regard to it; yet when the journey is over, when the action or event is absorbed in the everyday, it becomes obscure once more.

So, according to Lefebvre, one can only clearly view the actions that are based upon the everyday, but not the everyday "itself" (if there is such a thing). This does not mean that the everyday is anonymous, as Blanchot argued, but rather, on the contrary, that only personal actions and events can disperse the ambiguity of the everyday. It would not make sense for Lefebvre to try to isolate a pure layer of the everyday as Blanchot attempts to do (at least in the first definition he gives), since the everyday is the source of actions and events, a source that should not and cannot be considered in isolation from them.[14]

On this ground, it is easier to understand Blanchot's following statement: "The everyday escapes. In this consists its strangeness—the familiar showing itself (but already dispersing) in the guise of the astonishing" (240). What escapes here, however, is only the everyday in its pure and isolated form, figured in the category of the "familiar" as opposed to the "astonishing" (*l'étonnant*). This is why both Lefebvre and Blanchot argue that it is only through a more or less extraordinary event that one can see the everyday, at least for a short moment until it disperses.[15] Any vision of the everyday—be it "illusionary" or "true"— is possible only through an action or an event that transcends the everyday and yet belongs to it.

This is moreover the link between the ambiguity *of* the everyday (its dependence on the event in order to be seen and somehow grasped) and the ambiguity *towards* the everyday (that is, the tendency to view it as both prison and home). Both ambiguities, I argue, stem from the split between the "everyday" (as eventless sphere) and "experience" (the realm of events). Whereas the first ambiguity can be resolved theoretically, understanding the everyday and the event as maintaining a dialectical unity, the second ambiguity attests to a cultural deadlock that is much more difficult to overcome. This cultural ambiguity considers the everyday only as the eventless sphere of self-enclosure and forgets that it is equally characterised by self-transcendence—otherwise it would not be the everyday, but rather death.

In order to promote a theoretical and a cultural change in the notion of the everyday, this book will aim to show the fluctuations and intertwining of both aspects of the everyday—self-enclosure and self-transcendence. It should therefore be stated that I am not trying to defend a notion of the everyday as *against* the event (as some contemporary authors tend to do[16]) or to praise the ordinary *against* the extraordinary.[17] These attempts only accentuate the split that I am trying to overcome, or at least problematise. My aim is rather to investigate the mechanisms that are involved in the integration of actions and events into the global movement of the everyday: shock, deferral, repetition—mechanisms which have gone through various transformations in the course of modernity.

So far I have presented the general conceptual framework of this book, without entering into details. I now wish to present a more historical account of the modern everyday, and the way the different categories it involves (e.g., the ordinary and the extraordinary) have been shaped and reshaped from the mid-nineteenth century onwards. I will delineate an itinerary that goes from Flaubert to the writings of contemporary French author Michel Houellebecq, showing that the everyday has

undergone in late modernity a process of both mechanisation and liberation. This paradoxical process is incarnated in Charlie Chaplin's film
Modern Times, which I will analyse here with the help of Lefebvre. I
will then draw on Georg Simmel and Émile Durkheim to claim that the
extraordinary has become an everyday possibility, yet one which is too
shocking to be integrated into the everyday. I will end this part of the
introduction with Catherine Malabou's theory of plasticity as a possible
solution to the crisis of the everyday.

MODERN TIMES

One of the most famous scenes in the history of cinema is that in which
Charlie Chaplin, playing the hero of *Modern Times*, who works in a
monstrous futuristic factory, is asked to eat his lunch from an experi-
mental feeding machine. The machine starts off well with the soup, but
soon, when it comes to the corncob, it begins to lose control, speeding
up, throwing the food all over Chaplin and finally hitting him frantical-
ly. The automatic machine, a symbol of rational industrialisation, fails
to adjust itself to the anatomy and patterns of the human body, and the
experiment is brought to an end with the words of the factory president:
"It's no good—it isn't practical".

Indeed, modernity equates the good and the practical, morality and
utility, but the film emphasises something else—namely, the incompat-
ibility between human being and machine. The machine is automatic
and regulated, whereas the human being is spontaneous and free. By
switching roles between the machine and the human being, by making
the machine dominant and capricious and the human being weak and
docile, the film shows both how machines try to normalise people and
how this attempt must fail. The human being cannot become a machine; something in him or her will always resist this. In another scene,
Chaplin desperately tries to unite with the machine when he jumps into
the opening at the end of an assembly line, literally letting himself be
swallowed by the machine, passing through its various cogs. But he has
gone too far, and the chief mechanic rushes in, halts the machine and
starts it running in reverse, such that it vomits the worker back into the
assembly line. From this moment on, having intimately known the
machine from within, the worker develops a peculiar hostility towards
it, and tries to interrupt, turn it on backwards or sabotage it whenever
he can. He seems to forget his material need to earn money and yield to

his desire to bring to an end the diabolic cycle of automatic production in favor of a peaceful oasis.

Many years have passed since the making of *Modern Times* in 1936, and one may wonder whether the film has lost its relevance. Contemporary machines are, after all, significantly different from machines made almost eighty years ago. No longer mere work-tools, they have become the apparatus of domestic leisure and entertainment, and they have overcome—or at least give the impression of having overcome—their original repetitious and automatic character. Machines now offer multiple functions and modes so as to create a sensation of novelty, stimulating one's interest and curiosity, at least until the next model comes out on the market. And yet *Modern Times* makes us laugh—not only at the old and cranky machinery of the past but also at something which still prevails in our own modern times. What exactly is it?

In his *Critique of Everyday Life*, Lefebvre gives us a hint, characterising the figure of Chaplin as the Tramp (*Vagabond*), which is the *reverse image* of modern times.[18] Chaplin "comes as a stranger into the familiar world" (11) and, precisely as a stranger, exposes this familiarity as consisting of nothing but "people and things with fixed patterns of behavior" (10). Through his rebellious awkwardness, the hero defeats "machines and men-machines" (12), defying modern alienation and finally overcoming it through a laughter that "denies, destroys, liberates" (13). Chaplin thus suspends the mechanical repetition of everyday modern life, and yet, once the laughter is over, it is not clear what we are left with or what alternative is proposed. This is why Lefebvre is worried about Chaplin becoming a modern myth, as if he could magically transform the ordinary into the extraordinary. This transformation is possible only in films, and the belief in it may lead to a mystification of both the everyday and the fantasised sphere of the extraordinary, resulting finally in only deeper alienation. Alienation stems not only from the separation between the worker and his or her work, as in *Modern Times*, but also from the fantasy that there is an easy escape out of work—and out of the everyday. A critique of the everyday, according to Lefebvre, should therefore begin with an analysis of what pretends to lie beyond the everyday, what tempts one to elude it, only to fall back into alienation.

Indeed, one of the main targets of Lefebvre's first *Critique* is the demystification of the extraordinary or the marvelous, since the "most extraordinary things are also the most everyday" (13). Consequently, one should extract the extraordinary from the ordinary rather than separate the two (259, n22), but the problem is that this separation is not only a theoretical construct but also a prevailing factor of modern culture. What does the separation stem from? Lefebvre locates its emergence in the mid-nineteenth century and finds evidence of it first in the literary work of Baudelaire and Flaubert, then in Rimbaud and finally culminating with Breton and the surrealists, who devaluated the real in the name of the surreal (103–29).

I do not intend to restitute here Lefebvre's genealogy of the ordinary-extraordinary opposition nor to fully analyse his suggestion to engage in a Marxist critique of the everyday.[19] What I borrow from Lefebvre is his diagnosis of the crisis of the everyday as stemming from its opposition with a rival category. Lefebvre names it "the extraordinary", a realm I described above as attributed to (real) "experience", and in what follows I will try to analyse and rethink these different categories. My main divergence from Lefebvre lies in the fact that, whereas he insists (following the Marxist tradition) on the illusionary character of the extraordinary, I argue that the extraordinary is in fact one of the foundations of the everyday, represented by the figure of shock. A short comparison between Flaubert's *Madame Bovary* and the works of Houellebecq will help clarify this point.

FROM *MADAME BOVARY* TO MONSIEUR HOUELLEBECQ

The publication of *Madame Bovary* in 1856 was not only a literary event but also a scandal that led to Flaubert's accusation of immorality in a trial in which he was finally acquitted. The heritage of the novel is attested to by the term "Bovarysme", defined by The *Oxford Dictionary of Literary Terms* as "a disposition towards escapist day dreaming in which one imagines oneself as a heroine or hero of a romance and refuses to acknowledge everyday realities".[20] Indeed, Emma Bovary had an everyday life she disliked: too rigid, too grey, too stifling. But she was able, *upon this background*, to imagine a different, fantastical life, and even try to live it for a while. The novel thus bears witness to the upsurge of the separation between the everyday and experience, the latter being traditionally described as a forbidden love affair, an extraordinary adventure that would break the ordinary laws of the everyday.

Whereas in *Madame Bovary* the ordinary and the extraordinary are still clearly distinguished from each other, if we turn to the work of

Houellebecq, we encounter a different picture. Although the protagonists of *The Elementary Particles*, *Platform* and *The Map and the Territory* are not satisfied with their everyday lives, whenever they try to escape they just fall even deeper into them. Imagining or living a stormy love affair would do no good, since they have already had too many of them; they have already tried too many possible ways out.[21] Certainly they persist in their quest for those small satisfactions, repeating their daily pursuit, but this repetition only reminds them that there is really no point in even trying. In this sense they present the contemporary consequences of Emma Bovary's separation between the everyday and experience. Freed from Emma Bovary's moral constraints, the truth does not take long to reveal: a romance without an everyday is a fiction, a fiction in which we are trapped and try in vain to live. Madame Bovary could believe in that fiction only because romance was so extraordinary for her. But when the extraordinary becomes ordinary, when the sweet taste of transgression is gone, the ability to escape the everyday also disappears.

In order to appreciate the shift from Flaubert to Houellebecq, it would be useful to recall Arthur Rimbaud's famous lament from 1873: "True life is absent. We are not in the world".[22] Almost a century later, Emmanuel Levinas inverted this phrase, declaring, "True life is absent. But we are in the world".[23] In both cases, life is absent; dissatisfaction, absence and deficiency characterise the everyday. However, in the first case there is still a world waiting to be found (and indeed both Rimbaud and Emma Bovary *did* make every effort to look for it), but in the second case we are "stuck" in an unsatisfying world with no way out.[24] According to Houellebecq, the only escape from the existing, actual world is achieved through its eradication.

Now, while Emma Bovary's everyday is too rigid, that of Houellebecq's heroes is *both* too rigid and too flexible or liquid.[25] This is why these modern (anti-)heroes are, above all, tired, exhausted and weary, whereas Emma Bovary was bored or suffocated. In an essay entitled "Approaches to Disarray",[26] Houellebecq vividly describes what he terms "general and authentic lassitude" invading all aspects of life, from the political to the aesthetic, from the commercial to the sexual. Any attempt to dissipate lassitude by engaging in an extraordinary adventure only accentuates it, such that everyday life presents no way out. What could be done to change this situation? Houellebecq evokes the possibility of a "pure and simple refusal" (70) and exemplifies it with two autobiographical stories, two islands in the chaotic ocean of life, two oases in its desert.

The first story dates to the *events* of May 1968 in France. Houellebecq, who was ten years old at the time, went with his aunt to pick up his older cousin from high school. However, a strike had been called, and the school gates were closed. As his aunt went to gather some information about this sudden interruption of normal affairs, the young Houellebecq walked calmly into the schoolyard, which, until that day, had always been filled with boys frighteningly bigger than himself. This peaceful and aimless walk into the suddenly empty space was to remain engraved in Houellebecq's memory as a "marvelous moment" (77).

The second story takes place eighteen years later. Houellebecq, who was staying in Avignon, had to return to Paris at short notice due to some "sentimental complications whose narration would be tedious to perform". But, just as in the former story, upon arrival at the train station he discovered that a strike had been declared. Once more, instead of being annoyed by the situation, Houellebecq found it to be liberating, since "the operational succession of sexual exchange, adventure and lassitude was suddenly broken" (78).

Houellebecq accordingly characterises modern everyday life as a "gigantic and oppressive machine" (78), salvation from which is only achieved through occasional disruptive events such as a strike. Yet, contrary to Chaplin's *Modern Times*, the halting of the machine always comes from without, is always initiated by someone or something else, so that one can but passively follow the evolution of events. Houellebecq does not propose an active method of refusing, resisting or transforming the everyday, but rather evokes the "possibility of an island", which is, by no coincidence, the title of one of his novels. The island is a precarious place of silence, a momentary refuge from the merciless dazzling machine of daily life. But how long can one remain on such an island?

SIMMEL'S SOCIOLOGY OF SHOCK

The movement from Flaubert to Houellebecq should be seen, I propose, as a process through which the extraordinary has become an ordinary possibility, yet one which is meaningless and dissatisfying, a foreign body that the everyday does not manage to integrate. On the one hand, *everything* is the everyday—thousands of daily adventures and possibilities. On the other hand, *nothing* is the everyday—nothing seems to really happen, to have a long-lasting meaning, which only pushes one to look for more adventures and try to escape the all-too-open everyday. In order to better understand what process the everyday has undergone, it is helpful to turn here to sociology, a discipline that was developed at the end of the nineteenth century in order to depict and conceptualise the rapid changes in modern life and society. These changes had their roots in two major phenomena: industrialisation and urbanisation. Sirens of the factories began to replace church bells. The everyday life of the small, rural community, with its weekly mass, seasonal feasts and yearly rituals, gradually gave way to urban everyday life, with its mechanical regulation of time according to the capitalist laws of civil society.

It is tempting to describe this process as an uprooting and loss of grounding, as can be seen, for instance, in the work of German sociologist Ferdinand Tönnies. In 1887 he published a book depicting the decline of Community (*Gemeinschaft*, the place of familiarity, warmth and an enduring sense of belonging) and the rise of Society (*Gesellschaft*, the cold, superficial and "foreign land").[27] But the complexity and ambiguity of this process is best illustrated by French sociologist Émile Durkheim, who, in his groundbreaking 1893 book, *The Division of Labor in Society*,[28] developed the notion of *mechanical solidarity*, which he contrasted to *organic solidarity*. One might expect organic solidarity to correspond to traditional community, and mechanical solidarity to industrialised society. But Durkheim surprisingly inverses this scheme, since, according to him, it is rather in traditional societies that "our personality vanishes" (130), being trapped in a well-defined rigid role attributed at birth. No mobility is possible in such societies of mechanical solidarity. Organic solidarity, by contrast, has become possible with the rise of the division of labor. Work is no longer carried out homogeneously according to the community's needs, and the times of harvest, for instance, when the entire community of the village came out to work in the fields, are gone. With the industrialisation of society, labor has become specialised, and every individual, according to his or her skills, is attributed a function that is not equal to, but rather dependent on, those of the others. This dynamic net is equivalent, says Durkheim, to a living body which maintains an organic solidarity between its different organs (129–32).

Durkheim's vision of pre-modernity is thus far from nostalgic, but he, too, acknowledges the dangers that modern, organic solidarity must face. He contrasts "healthy" to "pathological" societies, suggesting that in the same way that a body can suffer from cancer or tuberculosis, so organic solidarity is threatened by internal and external attacks on its organisation (353). What are these attacks and how should they be treated? Durkheim tries to answer this question in some of his subsequent works. In a course on moral education he gave at the Sorbonne in 1902–1903, he speaks of "this malady of infiniteness which torments our age".[29] The origin of this "malady" lies in the vast field of previously unheard-of possibilities introduced by the division of labor, combined with a loosening of moral laws due to the decline of tradition and religion. Durkheim's proposed "cure" is to construct a moral system, and in his 1897 book *Suicide*, he postulates that desires, paradoxically, can only be fulfilled, and consequently freedom and happiness attained, if they are limited by morality: "Unlimited desires are insatiable by definition and insatiability is rightly considered a sign of morbidity. . . . Inextinguishable thirst is constantly renewed torture".[30]

We see here a close link between the freeing of desire and the "malady of infiniteness", a link that I shall further explore in chapter 3 with the help of Freudian theory. It is interesting, however, to notice a parallel investigation of this question by German sociologist Georg Simmel, who published his magnum opus *Philosophy of Money*[31] in the same year Freud published his *Interpretation of Dreams*.[32]

Simmel viewed modernity in general and the city in particular as the site of intensified nervous stimulation.[33] In his famous 1903 essay "The Metropolis and Mental Life",[34] he gives striking descriptions of the modern city and the everyday life it entails.[35] Simmel's initial hypothesis is that the human being is "a differentiating creature" (175), which means that one constantly looks for differences and tends to skip repetitions. What repeats itself or lasts long enough (the ordinary) does not catch our attention. We take for granted our routine surroundings: the more or less stable and habitual images, noises and smells around us. This is the zero degree of perception, and only when something differs from it (that is, only when something extraordinary appears) do we pay attention to it at all.

However, this fundamental human tendency of differentiation encounters serious difficulties in the modern city. The tempo of the metropolis is fast, proposing and imposing a huge variety of changes and novelty in any given moment, compelling one to remain constantly alert. Durkheim's "malady of infiniteness" is thus articulated in the city through the inexhaustible number of shops, cafés, restaurants and bars, as well as the countless events that are available to choose from. However, contrary to Durkheim, Simmel does not place the accent on the unlimited desire as much as on the alertness, attention and consciousness which the city demands. Not only does the city propose possibilities, but it also contains a huge number of dangers and things to be attentive to and conscious of: vehicles and pedestrians on the street, and all of the infinite daily interactions and frictions which city life involves. The extraordinary no longer belongs to a distinguished and rare category but rather constantly pokes one in the form of multiple shocks.

What happens when the extraordinary becomes shocking on a daily basis? Simmel suggests that the attention and consciousness which are needed in order to protect one from shocks are located in the higher layers of mental life and involve the *intellect*, whereas *emotion* comes from the deep, unconscious layers of mental life. The intellect is "the most adaptable of our inner forces". It is not overwhelmed or shocked by the rapid stimuli of the city, but rather accommodates itself to them easily and smoothly. The intellect is the "protective organ" of urban people, defending them against the discrepancies of external environment which would otherwise uproot them (176). Yet the price inhabitants of the city have to pay for this protection is high: it is their ability to develop a profound emotional life. According to Simmel, emotions need time, long-term habits and routine in order to safely and slowly grow. But time is lacking in the city, and the stimuli change too fast for a stable routine to be acquired. This results in the indifference and reserve with which people in the city treat one another, a "*blasé* attitude" which consists of "the blunting of discrimination" and the appearance of the world "in an evenly flat and gray tone; no one object deserves preference over any other" (178).

The large number of stimuli in the metropolis thus changes the way in which one perceives. Quantity affects quality. People's nerves are so agitated and confused that the emotional value of the world diminishes. The stimuli are perceived only by the indifferent and cold intellect, which measures them externally on a quantitative basis: we walk in the street, shop in the supermarket or sit in a café; yet we *measure* everything around us rather than *feel* it. But what are the criteria for this measurement? It is here, says Simmel, that the realm of *money* reveals its mutual dependence upon the realm of the intellect, the combination of the two allowing the individual to retain his or her differentiating capacity: we begin to consider people and objects first and foremost according to the way they look and the subsequent market value they represent.[36]

The result is a "coloration, or rather discoloration of things through their money equivalence" (178), a sentence which Houellebecq would wholeheartedly endorse. City people treat each other as measurable objects, but this, in turn, leaves them empty, since they fall prey to the very same judgement they pass upon others, ending up trapped in a Foucauldian prison: "The individual has become a mere cog in an enormous organization of things and powers which tear from his hands all progress, spirituality and value in order to transform them from their subjective form into the form of a purely objective life" (184).

Simmel thus helps us understand how the intensification of stimuli necessitates rapid and adequate reactions in an ever-changing environment. The everyday has become encircled by an objective layer controlled by what Simmel calls the intellect, with shocks parried from the deeper level of emotions. Every event thus takes place only on the surface, and its integration into the texture of the everyday can only be conducted through a mechanical repetition, as we saw in *Modern Times*: on the objective or mechanical level, reality is very well organised, but this is so only to protect one from the chaos incarnated by the feeding machine, a kind of reverse image of rational society. On the one hand, one repeats the old in order to protect oneself from the overwhelming new; on the other hand, one desperately tries to produce well-controlled extraordinary adventures, as Houellebecq's protagonists do, and yet these do not manage to break the walls of everyday life either.[37] The modern everyday consists of countless voluntary and involuntary shocks and "extraordinary" events, but none of these seem to mean much and they only add another link to the repetitive chain of everyday life.[38]

In this book I will present several forms of repetition that function as a response to shocks in modern everyday life. Simmel himself only sketches some of these forms, such as money or objective measurement,[39] but he does not engage in a systematic investigation of them precisely as repetitions which stem from shocks. This also applies to Alvin Toffler's popular 1970 book *Future Shock*, which expands many of Simmel's observations, diagnosing modern society as being caught in a state of over-stimulation, leading to a growing danger of shock. The shock of modernity shows itself, according to Toffler, in feelings of confusion, exhaustion, irritability, apathy, irrationality, anxiety and aggressiveness.[40] But we should notice that all these reactions equally characterise the hero of *Modern Times*, who is not exactly confronted with *over*-stimulation, but rather with *under*-stimulation—that is, a monotonous and repetitive routine. The mechanical everyday (the too ordinary) is the complementary counterpart of the chaotic and shocking everyday (the too [much] extraordinary), and in order to overcome this artificial and yet existing opposition we need to further understand the mechanisms that play a role in them.

BETWEEN PLASTICITY AND FLEXIBILITY

With Houellebecq, Durkheim and Simmel we gradually begin to grasp the difficulties with which the modern everyday is confronted. I wish to conclude the historical part of this introduction with Catherine Malabou's suggestion that modernity is characterised by a disregard of *plasticity*, which is taken over and superimposed by *flexibility*.[41] Plasticity, according to Malabou, is the ability to create but also to annihilate, the two rather complementing each other, since only on the background of destruction can one conceive anything new (5–6, 71–77). Flexibility, on the other hand, is "plasticity minus its genius" (12)—that is, not an ability to create but rather to adapt oneself to the surroundings, to change in a reactive, conciliatory and docile way. Whereas plasticity is a dialectical notion, moving between its "positive" (creation) and "negative" (annihilation) poles, flexibility has no internal dialectic. It neither creates nor destroys; it just adapts. Therefore, in modern capitalist society, flexibility is externally contrasted with rigidity, which is precisely the inability to adapt, and the fate of the excluded: the ill, the old, the marginal.

Malabou's aim is to reawaken plasticity, to show how creation and destruction actually constitute two poles of the same activity. She calls upon us to "refuse to be flexible individuals" (78) by overcoming the anxiety of explosion and destruction inherent to plasticity. She examines the plasticity of the brain and its neuronal synapses and proposes to take from it the appropriate personal and political lesson—namely, how to resist the "neuronal ideology" (11) that talks about plasticity, but secretly promotes the idea of flexibility, which is "the ideological avatar of plasticity, its diversion, and its confiscation" (12).

If we apply Malabou's concepts to the question of the everyday and experience, we can say that only plasticity allows a dialectical every-

day, in which the repetitive and the new, the ordinary and the extraordinary, would maintain the right balance needed to appropriate one's
experience. According to Malabou, plastic creation alone permits the
creator to become the subject of his or her history (13). In other words,
plasticity allows one not only to act but also to incorporate the action
and its context—that is, to acquire experience. The crisis of the everyday and experience thus stems from a crisis of plasticity.

Malabou attributes this crisis to contemporary neo-liberalism, with
its use of flexibility to perpetuate its ideology, imprisoning us in a
suffocating everyday life. Yet we saw with Simmel that the tendency of
measurement stems from both economical or ideological processes and
perceptual difficulties in an overwhelming reality. It is therefore not
enough to criticise or dismiss flexibility on ideological grounds, and
one should rather explain what permits it to play such a major role in
modern everyday life in the first place. Indeed, Malabou takes some
steps in this direction, citing Alain Ehrenberg's *The Weariness of Being
Oneself* (a title which echoes both Houellebecq's lassitude and Durkheim's malady of infiniteness): "Self-control, flexibility of mind and
feeling, and the capacity for action meant that each individual had to be
up to the task of constantly adapting to a changing world, that was
losing its stable shape, becoming temporary, consisting of ebb and
flow, something like a snakes-and-ladders game".[42]

Modern flexibility is thus not something which can be got rid of
easily, since it is a response to a general state of instability and lack of
continuity. In these circumstances, one cannot afford anymore to be
plastic; one needs, first and foremost, to adapt and survive. Plasticity
may be defined as the ability to link the old to the new, to act and create
upon a solid enough background, such that this background is transformed and partly annihilated during the act of creation. But how can
one create in a state of alertness, upon a background which constantly
changes? This unstable background necessarily affects the link between
the old and the new, repetition and change.[43] But stating this is only the
beginning of the inquiry. The question is not how to avoid flexibility,
but rather how to play on the huge variety the modern everyday offers,
how to constitute a routine—an everyday—which would permit emotion, personal value and meaningful identity.[44]

One of my claims throughout this book will be that the inability to
admit negativity (absence, lack and loss)—that is, the inability to be
plastic—goes hand in hand with a reality which is experienced as too
overwhelming (not only because it does not provide *enough* experi-

ence, but also because it provides *too much*). A second claim will be that this inability to be plastic is articulated by various types of repetition and the consequent values they acquire.

If we take the discourse of flexibility, for instance, we can see that it does not promote repetition. On the contrary, it rather encourages one to be constantly updated, to adapt oneself to quickly changing surroundings, to never allow oneself to be left behind and repeat the old. In fact, flexibility goes hand in hand with an *aversion* to repetition. Yet hostility towards certain forms of repetition also seems to be present in thinkers who are fervent opponents of flexibility and adaptation, such as Gilles Deleuze. In his 1968 monumental *Difference and Repetition*,[45] he goes to great pains to show that repetition is never mechanical. It is rather multilayered and relates to a difference which permits its creativity. In Malabou's terms, repetition is plastic. But is it always so? Aren't Deleuze's attempts to rehabilitate repetition rather an avowal of the modern difficulty to address repetition on its surface?

I propose that one cannot reconnect the everyday and experience, repetition and difference, without first scrutinising modern attempts—and failures—to bypass the repetition of everyday life. In order to do so, we need to find what components are involved in repetition and to what other mechanisms it is related. One of these mechanisms is deferral, and throughout this book I will present deferral as a form of *suspension* either of the everyday itself or of the different shocks it consists of.

HOW TO INVESTIGATE THE EVERYDAY: STRUCTURE OF THE BOOK

In order to develop my thesis, I will engage in an interdisciplinary study, drawing on several methodologies and theories, most of which were developed in Europe in the first half of the twentieth century. One might rightly wonder what relevance these theories have to *contemporary* everyday life, the explicit object of the present book. The answer will be revealed as one progresses in the reading of this book, but as I have already started to argue, our current era is living the consequences and symptoms of a modern split between the everyday and experience. In order to understand the causes of the split and possible ways to overcome it, we first need to linger on the split and make it explicit once more. This, I argue, can only be done by going back to the moment of its creation, which is the period between the mid-nineteenth and the mid-twentieth centuries.

I start the investigation with phenomenology as an attempt to under-stand the everyday through a certain suspension of it. In the first chap-ter I analyse the phenomenological approach of both Husserl and Hei-degger. I focus on the phenomenological reduction as a suspension of the natural attitude of everyday life, a suspension that nonetheless aims to better understand it. I claim that this suspension or deferral is not only a methodological tool, as Husserl presents it, but also a mecha-nism that functions within the everyday itself to deal with its various shocks. I reflect upon Bill Viola's artwork, *Room for St. John of the Cross*, and question phenomenology's ability to defer but also to pene-trate the everyday. Husserl's notion of the Life-world is presented as an attempt to reconcile the everyday with experience, and yet he fails to do so due to his reluctance to concretise the Life-world and introduce objective categories into it. I argue that objectivity stabilises experience in a chaotic world, so that the problem is not so much the mere exis-tence of objective categories, but rather their ability or inability to change and be renovated within the everyday.

I then go on to examine Heidegger's descriptions of everydayness (*Alltäglichkeit*) in order to further develop the mechanisms involved in it. According to Heidegger, the everyday consists of repetitive encoun-ters with lack, absence and obstacles within everyday entities, which engender a momentary halt of the movement of the everyday through what I call "immersed reflection". This reflection is a founding action that helps integrate new practices and events into the everyday through a constant confrontation with moments of "small negativity". However, Heidegger subsequently develops the notion of the Falling, which I interpret as the (modern) difficulty of engaging oneself in the work of immersed reflection due to the negativity that underpins it. The im-mersed suspension of the everyday is thus no longer possible, and Heidegger turns to anxiety as a figure of *radical negativity* that reminds one of the need to relaunch the movement of the everyday and return to "authenticity". I argue, however, that authenticity and inauthenticity are only two extreme poles between which lies a wide spectrum of ways to repeat and renew the old through a recognition of the "small" figures of negativity—that is, daily deficiency, absence and obstacles.

In the second chapter I use Merleau-Ponty's phenomenology of perception to show the *body* as a focal point in the foundation of the everyday. The body is ambiguous: it is both subjective and objective, interior and exterior, static and dynamic, and as such it exemplifies the way the global movement of the everyday meets and integrates into it particular movements. However, the everyday body tends to be objectified, such that, again, the movement of foundation becomes deficient. To illustrate this concept, I analyse the case of amputated patients who suffer from a phantom limb, and I follow Merleau-Ponty's interpretation of this as a *repression of loss* which leads to an imprisonment in rigid objective representations. I then generalise this case by comparing it to Heidegger's descriptions of the Falling, and claim that the inability of the amputated persons to assume their situation is equivalent to the (modern) everyday inability to acknowledge the finitude and lack that are inherent to the body as such. Such an acknowledgement is possible only through immersed or embodied reflection that uses negativity within the everyday in order to renew and re-found it. However, Merleau-Ponty's stress on ecstatic corporal activities and super-creative figures such as the child or the artist makes it difficult to understand how to engage in an embodied reflection within the everyday. I argue that this reflection is related to certain forms of shock, deferral and repetition, and propose to further investigate these through a more historically sensitive analysis with the help of Freud and Benjamin.

In the third chapter I follow Freud's model of the psychic apparatus as a defensive mechanism that receives stimuli while simultaneously protecting against them. I show how Freud gradually moved from a theory of particular sexual *trauma* to a theory of multiple and indefinite *shocks*. Repetition is thus attributed a crucial role in everyday life, such that it is no longer possible to retrace a "primal scene" that would resolve the traumatic aspect of life. In order to illustrate this idea, I compare two works of Marguerite Duras, *Hiroshima mon amour* and *The Ravishing of Lol Stein*, arguing (against Caruth's theory of trauma) that whereas in the first work there is still a possibility of locating an original trauma, the latter employs too many displacements, so that repetition ultimately overshadows its presumed origin. The result is a theory of the modern everyday as constituted by imperceptible internal and external shocks, a term that is plural in opposition to the presumed singularity of trauma. The repetition of shocks is immediate and automatic, avoiding any kind of deferral (*Nachträglichkeit*)—that is, an interval or delay between the trauma and its retroaction. I finally argue that in Freud it is only the child who can maintain deferred retroaction through playful repetition, whereas the adult is condemned to mechanically and immediately repeat and reproduce his or her everyday shocks.

The fourth and fifth chapters further develop the idea of everyday repetition as a response to and prolongation of shocks, drawing on Benjamin's analysis of modernity's impoverished experience. Shock, according to Benjamin, needs to be immediately registered and warded off, thus further accentuating the modern impossibility of deferral. I propose that what Benjamin describes as long experience (*Erfahrung*) involves deferred retroaction, whereas what he calls immediate experience (*Erlebnis*) is an instantaneous reaction to shock. I argue that the famous decline of the aura declared by Benjamin does not solely stem from mechanical reproduction but is rather intrinsically related to the difficulty of accessing the mechanism of deferred retroaction. In the fifth chapter I develop the notion of "the aura of the habitual", which may result from an everyday practice of deferral and retroaction of shocks. To illustrate this idea, I analyse Cindy Sherman's early works as an invitation to engage in such a practice of deferral, regaining and retroacting the aura of the everyday whilst remaining within it.

NOTES

1. *Raus aus dem Alltag—rein ins Erlebnis.* I will analyse in chapter 4 the meaning of the word *Erlebnis* (immediate experience) as opposed to *Erfahrung* (long experience).

2. Stanley Cavell, for instance, claims that the everyday conceals an uncanny strangeness, to be awakened by romanticism. See Stanley Cavell, *In Quest of the Ordinary: Lines of Skepticism and Romanticism* (Chicago and London: University of Chicago Press, 1988), 158–78. As Simon Critchley puts it, for Cavell "the world must be romanticized, the quotidian must be made fantastic and the human made strange" (Critchley, *Very Little . . . Almost Nothing: Death, Philosophy, Literature* [London and New York: Routledge, 1997], 119).

3. My model shares some similarities with the theory of Agnes Heller, but whereas she distinguishes the everyday as a sphere of immanence from the non-everyday as a sphere of transcendence, I conceive the two as internally connected from the outset. This does not mean that the everyday is *everything*, as Henri Lefebvre tends to argue, but rather that the everyday has no significance without the movement of (self-)transcendence. See Agnes Heller, *Everyday Life* (London: Routledge, 1984). See also Michael Sheringham, *Everyday Life: Theories and Practices from Surrealism to the Present* (Oxford: Oxford University Press, 2006), 34–39; Michael Gardiner, *Critiques of Everyday Life: An Introduction* (London and New York: Routledge, 2000), 127–56.

4. It is this aspect that Georg Lukács famously characterised as "the anarchy of the chiaroscuro of the everyday". Cited by Michel de Certeau, *The Practice of Everyday Life*, trans. Steven Rendall (Berkeley: University of California Press, 1984), 199.

5. See, among others, Sheringham, *Everyday Life*, 22–39; Ben Highmore, *Everyday Life and Cultural Theory: An Introduction* (London and New York: Routledge, 2002), 1–3; and the works of Henri Lefebvre and Maurice Blanchot that I will analyse below.

6. When I ask students to describe their everyday lives, they sometime succinctly (and perhaps sarcastically) use the word "shit", which nonetheless reveals the almost abject aspect of the repetitive and humdrum.

7. See, among others, Bruce Bégout, *La Découverte du quotidien* (Paris: Allia, 2005); Highmore, *Everyday Life and Cultural Theory*; Ben Highmore, *The Everyday Life Reader* (London and New York: Routledge, 2002); John Roberts, *Philosophizing the Everyday: Revolutionary Praxis and the Fate of Cultural Theory* (London and Ann Arbor, MI: Pluto Press, 2006); Sheringham, *Everyday Life*. A recurrent alternative image is an interior scene with everyday objects (dishwasher, clothes dryer rack, table, etc.), which presents the same idea of objective anonymity. See Ben Highmore, *Ordinary Lives: Studies in the Everyday* (London and New York: Routledge, 2010); Joe Moran, *Reading the Everyday* (London and New York: Routledge, 2005); Sarah Pink, *Situating Everyday Life: Practices and Places* (London: Sage, 2012). Following Naomi Schor, Highmore affirms that there is a contrast between two types of everyday: one that lies in the *inner* space, and another that lies in the *public* sphere. He attributes this contrast to feminist and masculinist approaches to the everyday, with the masculinist approach dominating the scene until recently (Highmore, *Everyday Life and Cultural Theory*, 11–12). I do not contest this observation, but my claim is that both approaches, at least as they are represented on book covers, share the same presupposition regarding the anonymous nature of the everyday.

8. Maurice Blanchot, "Everyday Speech", in *The Infinite Conversation*, trans. S. Hanson (Minneapolis and London: University of Minnesota Press, 1993), 238–45.

9. It is not simply the street, but rather the modern, urban street, since everydayness "belongs first of all to the dense presence of the great urban centers" (242).

10. He attributes to newspapers the task of telling all that is "strange, sublime, abominable" (243) but does not say where "normal" experience is. It is noteworthy that this text on the everyday appears in the second part of *The Infinite Conversation*, entitled "The Limit-Experience".

11. It is interesting to note the similarity between Blanchot's statement and Giorgio Agamben's provocative declaration from 1978: "The question of experience can be approached nowadays only with an acknowledgement that it is no longer accessible to us. For just as modern man has been deprived of his biography, his experience has likewise been expropriated" (Giorgio Agamben, *Infancy and History: The Destruction of Experience*, trans. Liz Heron [London and New York: Verso, 1993], 13). We see here how closely connected are the themes of the everyday and experience, the expropriation of one affecting the other.

12. Henri Lefebvre, *Critique of Everyday Life*, vol. 1, trans. John Moore (London and New York: Verso, 1991).

13. On the relationship between Blanchot's and Lefebvre's texts, see Sheringham, *Everyday Life*, 16–22.

14. This is probably why the covers of the English translation of Lefebvre's three volumes of *Critique of Everyday Life* have the merit of showing individual human beings within their daily actions, rather than anonymous streets.

15. In a typical act of appropriation, Blanchot takes the verb used by Lefebvre, *disperse* (*dissiper*), and inverts its meaning: instead of the event dispersing the ambiguity of the everyday, for Blanchot the everyday is "already dispersing". Moreover, according to Blanchot "the everyday is what we never see for a first time but can only see again (*revoir*), having always already seen it by an illusion that is constitutive of the everyday" (240). Any vision of the everyday is illusionary, but it is a *constitutive* illusion.

16. See, for example, Michael Sayeau, *Against the Event* (Oxford: Oxford University Press, 2013).

17. For an excellent critique of this sometimes naive tendency to defend the sphere of the ordinary in the price of losing its dimension of openness, see Sheringham, *Everyday Life*, 28–30.

18. Lefebvre, *Critique of Everyday Life*, 1:12.

19. For an investigation that goes in this direction, see Roberts, *Philosophizing the Everyday*, esp. 100–123. See also Gardiner, *Critiques of Everyday Life*, 71–101.

20. As Elissa Marder puts it in her superb reading of the novel, "If Flaubert's *Madame Bovary* remains so timely, it is because its heroine, Emma, suffers from a quintessential malady of modernity, the inability to incorporate time into experience" (Marder, *Dead Time: Temporal Disorders in the Wake of Modernity [Baudelaire and Flaubert]* [Stanford, CA: Stanford University Press, 2001], 131). In many respects, my reading in chapter 3 of Marguerite Duras's novel *The Ravishing of Lol Stein* is a response to Marder's reading of *Madame Bovary*.

21. On love in the age of capitalism, see Eva Illouz, *Cold Intimacies: The Making of Emotional Capitalism* (Cambridge: Polity Press, 2007); Eva Illouz, *Why Love Hurts: A Sociological Explanation* (Cambridge: Polity Press, 2012).

22. Arthur Rimbaud, "A Season in Hell", in *A Season in Hell and The Drunken Boat*, trans. L. Varèse (New York: New Directions, 1961), 37.

23. Emmanuel Levinas, *Totality and Infinity: An Essay on Exteriority*, trans. A. Lingis (The Hague, Boston and London: Martinus Nijhoff, 1969), 33. Levinas's idea, however, has taken him in a quite different direction to that of this book.

24. This point is equally articulated by Michel de Certeau: "Tactics are more and more frequently going off their tracks. Cut loose from the traditional communities that circumscribed their functioning, they have begun to wander everywhere in a space which is becoming at once more homogeneous and more extensive" (Certeau, *The Practice of Everyday Life*, 40). In other words, tactics, which are supposed to be everyday subversive acts, no longer have solid enough rivals (strategies, proper places) against which they can fight. The everyday now reigns everywhere—and thus nowhere—and Certeau himself invites us to rethink his theory of the everyday as composed of subversive practices.

25. See Zygmunt Bauman's works on this theme, such as *Liquid Modernity* (Cambridge: Polity Press, 2000) and *Liquid Life* (Cambridge: Polity Press, 2005).

26. Michel Houellebecq, "Approches du désarroi", in *Interventions* (Paris: Flammarion, 1998), 57–80. My translation.

27. Ferdinand Tönnies, *Community and Civil Society*, trans. José Harris and Margaret Hollis (Cambridge: Cambridge University Press, 2001), 17–91.

28. Émile Durkheim, *Division of Labor in Society*, trans. G. Simpson (New York: The Free Press, 1947).

29. Émile Durkheim, *Selected Writings*, ed. Anthony Giddens (Cambridge: Cambridge University Press, 1972), 173.

30. Émile Durkheim, *Suicide*, trans. John A. Spaulding and George Simpson (New York: The Free Press, 1951), 246.

31. Georg Simmel, *The Philosophy of Money*, trans. Tom Bottomore and David Frisby (London: Routledge, 1978).

32. Sigmund Freud, *The Interpretation of Dreams*, ed. James Strachey, *The Standard Edition of the Complete Psychological Works of Sigmund Freud* (London: Hogarth Press, 1953–1974), vols. 4–5. Henceforth, references to this edition will be abbreviated SE followed by the volume and the page numbers. *The Interpretation of Dreams* actually came out in 1899, but Freud, convinced of its importance, asked the publisher to insert the symbolic number 1900. It is noteworthy that both Simmel and Freud encountered serious problems in achieving a distinguished academic status, due not only to their Jewish background but also to their having challenged the traditional concept of

science as detached observation. They dared to transgress the limits between the everyday and theory, and paid a heavy professional and personal price for this choice.

33. The nervous system as a model for mental life was popular at the end of the nineteenth century, due to the rapid industrialisation of society and technological inventions such as electricity. See, for instance, Durkheim, *Selected Writings*, 143. For an analysis of the question of nerves and shock in Germany at the end of the nineteenth and the beginning of the twentieth century as related to social and structural developments of the time, see Andreas Killen, *Berlin Electropolis: Shock, Nerves, and German Modernity* (Berkeley, Los Angeles and London: University of California Press, 2006). On the role of the laws of thermodynamics in nineteenth-century thinking, see Anson Rabinbach, *The Human Motor: Energy, Fatigue, and the Origins of Modernity* (New York: Basic Books, 1990).

34. Georg Simmel, "The Metropolis and Mental Life", in *Simmel on Culture: Selected Writings*, ed. David Frisby and Mike Featherstone (London: Sage, 1997), 174–85. For an analysis of this text through an interesting comparison between Simmel, Tönnies and Durkheim, see Deena Weinstein and Michael A. Weinstein, *Postmodern(ized) Simmel* (London and New York: Routledge, 1993), esp. 101–14, 118–23.

35. These descriptions have furthermore influenced the thought of Walter Benjamin, which I will examine below in chapters 4–5. On this theme, see Frederic Jameson, "The Theoretical Hesitation: Benjamin's Sociological Predecessor", *Critical Inquiry* 25, no. 2 (1999): 267–88, and David Frisby, *Fragments of Modernity: Theories of Modernity in the Work of Simmel, Kracauer and Benjamin* (Cambridge, MA: MIT Press, 1988).

36. Simmel's entire *Philosophy of Money* is dedicated to the analysis of money as a tool of measurement, and the Metropolis essay can be seen as an appendix to this book, as Simmel himself signals. See Simmel, "The Metropolis", 185 n2.

37. It is interesting to compare this with the figure of adventurer portrayed by Simmel in his 1911 article "The Adventure" (in *Simmel on Culture*, 221–32). Indeed, adventure seems to make the impossible possible: on the one hand, it "occurs outside the usual continuity of this life" (that is, outside the everyday), but, on the other hand, it is integrated into it as "a foreign body in our existence which is yet somehow connected with the centre; the outside, if only by a long and unfamiliar detour, is formally an aspect of the inside" (222). Adventure is like "an island in life"—an island in which "the whole of life is somehow comprehended and consummated" (223). The problem is that the only figure of adventurer that Simmel cites is the eighteenth-century Casanova. In order to become adventurer, he says, one must have a "unifying core of existence from which meanings flow" (224), and "one must sense above its totality a higher unity, a super-life, as it were" (225). Indeed, Simmel claims that we are all adventurers to a certain extent. Yet I would argue that the basic conditions of adventure are no longer valid in modernity, such that adventure remains a foreign body within the everyday *without* being connected to its centre.

38. Guy Debord supplies similar descriptions in his 1967 *The Society of Spectacle* (trans. Donald Nicholson-Smith, [New York: Zone Books, 1995]). I will cite here only one of them: "Our epoch, which presents time to itself as essentially made up of many frequently recurring festivities, is actually an epoch without festival. Those moments when, under the reign of cyclical time, the community would participate in a luxurious expenditure of life, are strictly unavailable to a society where neither community nor luxury exists. Mass pseudo-festivals, with their travesty of dialogue and their parody of the gift, may incite people to excessive spending, but they produce only a disillusion— which is invariably in turn offset by further false promises. The self-approbation of the time of modern survival can only be reinforced, in the spectacle, by reduction in its use value. The reality of time has been replaced by its *publicity*" (113).

39. Other than money and objective measurement, Simmel mentions *fashion* as a mechanism that allows one to both repeat and renew everyday life: the fashion leaders

try to distinguish themselves and become "extraordinary"; yet they are immediately imitated by "ordinary" people, such that fashion needs to change again and so on. See Georg Simmel, "The Philosophy of Fashion", in *Simmel on Culture*, 187–206.

40. Alvin Toffler, *Future Shock* (New York: Random House, 1970), 344–48. The recent book by media theorist Douglas Rushkoff, *Present Shock: When Everything Happens Now* (New York: Current, 2013), continues Toffler's line of thought and situates it in an "accelerated present". However, Rushkoff takes the notion of shock for granted and focuses on the symptoms of presentness rather than its causes. This leads him to a somewhat disappointing concluding remark: "The solution, of course, is balance. Finding the sweet spot between storage and flow, dipping into different media and activities depending on the circumstances" (265).

41. Catherine Malabou, *What Should We Do with Our Brain?*, trans. Sebastian Rand (New York: Fordham University Press, 2008), 12.

42. Alain Ehrenberg, *The Weariness of the Self: Diagnosing the History of Depression in the Contemporary Age* (Montreal: McGill-Queen's University, 2010), 185.

43. Malabou claims that "the formation of each identity is a kind of resilience, in other words, a kind of contradictory construction, a synthesis of memory and forgetting, of constitution and effacement of forms" (77). I cannot agree more with this phrase, but rather propose to focus on the question of why it is so difficult to accept this resilience and use it as a motor of creation.

44. To a large extent, this is the critique which Michel de Certeau has directed at Foucault and (implicitly) Baudrillard, claiming that both focus on how certain objects (Baudrillard) or dispositions (Foucault) are imposed, while ignoring the subjective and subversive play on them. See Certeau, *The Practice of Everyday Life*, 43–49.

45. Gilles Deleuze, *Difference and Repetition*, trans. Paul Patton (New York: Columbia University Press, 1994).

Chapter One

Figures of Suspension

Husserl and Heidegger on the Everyday

You enter a dark space, with a large screen at the back, showing snow-covered mountains. The images are jittery, shifting rapidly from one mountain to another. An unpleasant sound, probably the wind, adds to the feeling of unease, which makes you want to turn away from the screen. In the middle of the dark space stands a cubicle, a small chamber. Through its only window you can see a wooden table with a metal jug, a glass of water and a small video monitor showing another snow-covered mountain. Yet this time the mountain is calm and stable, and beautiful, peaceful murmurs in Spanish issue from the room. After the tiring experience of the agitated mountains outside, listening to the murmurs and observing the interior of the room with its image of a majestic mountain is a welcome relief, an enchanting experience of calm and stability.

Bill Viola's 1983 installation *Room for St. John of the Cross* provides a contemporary glimpse of what St. John of the Cross experienced in 1577, during the nine months he spent in a Toledo prison after his arrest by the Spanish Inquisition. Far from being discouraged by his daily torture or by the impossibly small size of his windowless cell, the Spanish mystic and poet wrote in prison some of his most beautiful poems, which we can hear as they burst out of the tiny room in the middle of the dark space. Here is the beginning of one of them:

Figure 2. Bill Viola, *Room for St. John of the Cross*, 1983. (Courtesy of the Museum of Contemporary Art, Los Angeles)

> I went out seeking love
> and with unfaltering hope
> I flew so high, so high,
> that I overtook the prey.
>
> That I might take the prey
> of this adventuring in God
> I had to fly so high
> that I was lost from sight;
> and though in this adventure
> I faltered in my flight,
> yet love had already flown so high
> that I took the prey.[1]

What is the prey the poet is looking for? What is the love he went out to seek? The restless movement of the mountains on the big screen might remind us of a flight high in the mountains, but this particular flight is

aimless: the flyer or pilot is apparently never satisfied with any mountaintop, and he or she is therefore repetitively and tediously in quest of
a different one. I said earlier that Bill Viola's work is contemporary,
and indeed, the hectic search for new achievements characterises everyday life in modernity much more than in St. John of the Cross's
times. Every action, event and object are today immediately followed
by a need to look further, to reach another peak, with no time to integrate them into the global texture of everyday life. In other words, they
are perceived as shocks. Why is it so?

Every action or event consists to a large extent of repetition. I might
go to a foreign and exotic country, but even if I acquire a new identity, I
will generally keep the same name, body and habits. I might learn a
new language, but it will be incorporated into my native language, and
in any case, the novelty soon ceases to be novel and becomes a part of
the everyday—that is, a part of repetition. Modernity, however, has
brought with it an aversion to repetition. As we saw in the introduction,
the unprecedented amount of stimuli and possibilities for action create
a paradoxical situation in which one tends to forget the inevitability of
the everyday and think that repetition can be overcome. Nonetheless, it
would seem that repetition is needed for order to be created in an
otherwise chaotic world. *Room for St. John of the Cross* reminds us that
it is in trying to avoid repetition, aiming at new achievements and
peaks, that I finally find myself trapped in a repetitious life which is not
satisfactory or homely. It is precisely by giving up the "rat race" of
everyday life and turning to solitary concentration, as St. John of the
Cross was forced to do, that I may not only reach the mountaintop but
also be able to remain there—if not in reality, then at least in my
imagination.

In his poem St. John suggests that in order to seize my "prey"—any
goal that I might wish to attain for good—I need to get so high that I
become "lost from sight". It is a certain detachment from everyday
perception that permits a different, sharper vision. It is only through a
suspension of everyday experience that a deeper, steadier, but also
more creative experience can emerge. Indeed, St. John of the Cross, in
his prison, had lost his free everyday life, but in this way he was able to
contemplate it and to arrive at a different form of reality. He acquired a
new, lasting presence precisely by succumbing to absence; he achieved
an unexpected freedom precisely by fully accepting his imprisonment.
In other words, he managed to turn the stifling repetition of everyday
life into a repetition which is peaceful and harmonious.

To a certain extent, this is also the aim of the phenomenological enterprise: giving up life in order to reclaim it differently. In this chapter I will examine phenomenology's use of suspension as a way to achieve a better understanding of the everyday. I will first present Edmund Husserl's notion of suspension as a methodological tool, and I will then show how Martin Heidegger largely broadens it to introduce suspension into the everyday itself. I will claim that suspension is a form of deferral of both the everyday and the shocks of which it consists, and that this deferral is accompanied by repetition. Repetition can be, according to Heidegger, both authentic and inauthentic, and I will therefore try to clarify these attributes with regard to the modern situation of the everyday.

PHENOMENOLOGY AND THE RETURN TO
THE THINGS THEMSELVES

Phenomenology is commonly identified with Husserl's maxim "back to the things themselves!"[2] And yet, more than a century after this enthusiastic and appealing call, not only do we seem to remain quite distant from the things themselves, but we also hardly understand what these things really are. Are they everyday things or rather extraordinary ones? Are they empirical or transcendental?

One of Husserl's favorite examples in order to illustrate his method is the process of looking at a cube.[3] When I look at a cube in my everyday life, I have no difficulty whatsoever in claiming that it has six sides. But I would be more hesitant if I were asked to stop any other activity and just look attentively at the cube, concentrating on what I *actually* see. The basic phenomenological move, named *epoché* ("suspension" in Greek),[4] consists of bracketing all everyday beliefs, judgements and activities in favor of pure observation and reflection upon what offers itself to perception. Thus, when I suspend for a minute my constant engagement within the world, when I take the time to focus on the cube reflectively, what exactly do I see? I must now admit that what presents itself to my visual perception is not six faces, but only three.

But this is only the beginning of the procedure named "phenomenological reduction", since while I should bracket all my everyday beliefs concerning the cube (namely, that it has six faces), this does not mean that I should completely forget these beliefs. On the contrary, my task now is to find out how in the first place I made the move from the actual perception of three faces to my neglectful perception of six faces. I should try to examine the cube from every possible point of view, effecting what Husserl named "free variation",[5] in order to arrive at the essence of the cube. This essence, according to Husserl, is what remains identical to itself throughout the changing perspective. What, then, is the stable character of the cube? What never changes itself? The answer is quite simple: it is precisely that it shows three faces and hides three others.

The phenomenological reduction thus suspends the everyday only to better understand it. This understanding is achieved through the work of perception combined with reflection. Reflection here guides perception, obliging it, contrary to its natural tendency, to constantly alter its perspective on the perceived object. Perception, in turn, gives reflection material to reflect upon; it provides it with multiple sensory data from numerous points of view. The result of this shared and concentrated effort is what Husserl describes as the upsurge of the thing, the birth of phenomena—namely, the appearance of the things themselves to which we have been called to return.

Returning to *Room for St. John of the Cross*, I would claim that the installation illustrates this phenomenological procedure. I suggested earlier that the twitchy mountains stand for our nervous, contemporary everyday reality, but now this claim should be refined. If the mountains figured truly in our everyday reality, we would be incapable of noticing them, since the everyday, as we saw with Lefebvre and Blanchot, is characterised precisely by the fact that it hides itself: we are far too accustomed to it and immersed in it in order to understand the everyday explicitly. I am therefore aware of my own everyday only at its transitional moments—for instance, in the morning, when I need to wake up, or at the end of the day, when I get back home and feel tired and frustrated or, alternatively, lively and satisfied. In order to have a clearer insight into the everyday, I need to assume a distance from it, and it is this distance that both phenomenology and art use and explore.

Bill Viola's installation magnifies and accentuates images, sounds and feelings that form the everyday. By constantly and rapidly changing the perspective on the mountains, and accompanying it with an unpleasant windy sound, Viola reveals the contemporary everyday as an aimless yet shocking repetition. He shows how one is constantly looking for something new, while actually repeating the same thing, the same movement, which consequently yields nothing. The artwork thus uncovers the everyday perception, but at the same time it reveals its object: we see not only the movement from one mountain to another but also the mountains themselves, or, more exactly, their summits. The mountaintops can be regarded as St. John's "prey"—namely, the things we are looking for in life and which we can never fully attain due to their shocking appearance and the consequent move to other mountaintops, objects and preys. But here a second phenomenological and artistic move takes place. Whereas the big screen shows everyday perception's repeatedly failed attempt to grasp the mountains, the interior room contains a stable, tranquil mountain. It seems, then, that the elusive "prey" is finally achieved only inside the room: this is the secret goal of perception, its lost and ultimately found object. Does this mean that the "prey" can never be achieved in everyday life, but only through an artistic, poetic, mystic or philosophical perception?

LIVED EXPERIENCE, NATURALISM AND OBJECTIVISM

Throughout his career, from the *Logical Investigations* onwards, Husserl maintained that phenomenology describes the essence of *lived experience (Erlebnis)* and its correlate (its "object") in the world.[6] Lived experience is the concrete, present and spontaneous experience of perceiving, feeling, moving and speaking. It is a rich and multi-perspectival experience, revealing the deeper layers of our everyday experience. If we refer to Bill Viola's artwork, it is a combination of the moving mountains and the abiding image seen in the monitor: a combination of the outside and the inside, of world and consciousness, of multiplicity and unicity, of variation and essence. But one difficulty remains unresolved in Husserl, which I propose to elaborate on here: If lived experience, as it is described by phenomenology, actually differs from the everyday pre-reflective experience, then who exactly lives it?

A clarification of the term "lived experience" is called for in order to grasp the difficulty. But when we examine Husserl's writings, we find that in order to explain what lived experience is, he tends to start by naming what it is *not*. Parallel to his discovery of the phenomenological reduction, at the beginning of the twentieth century, Husserl developed a systematic criticism of the philosophical movements which, according to him, had overlooked the essence of lived experience: first psychologism,[7] then naturalism[8] and finally objectivism.[9] I will focus here on the last two attitudes, which tend to be merged by Husserl.[10]

Objectum in Latin means "that which lies in front". It is a self-enclosed, well-defined, detached and independent entity, which we can observe whenever we wish, since it does not change: it is frozen in a timeless space. This does not mean that it *never* changes, but rather that it is understood as if it were an autonomous entity, regardless of its development in time (evolution, historicity) and in space (interactions with the environment). Both objectivist and naturalistic attitudes do not recognise the relativity of their present perception and therefore lose the ability to transform it and its objects. They neglect the dynamic, environmental, subjective and cultural aspects which are constitutive to any perception of any object, although they remain hidden behind its apparently stable appearance. As a result, the objects are taken for granted and do not incite a perception which may transcend or transform them.

I asked above: *Who lives lived experience?* But the question now seems to have become: *Who holds the objectivist and naturalistic tendencies?* Husserl's main critical target was scientific naturalism, and his original answer seems therefore to be simple: the naturalistic attitude is held by *science* and by the philosophy influenced by it. Modern science, since Galileo,[11] has concentrated on creating geometric-like artificial structures, measured and quantified according to fixed rules, which led to the "mathematisation of nature".[12] Indeed, one could respond that this critique concerns only classic mathematics and physics, whereas today far more dynamic models are used in other domains of science.[13] But Husserl's emphasis is less on the scientific method as such and more on its blind use, particularly on its dangerous extrapolation from the natural sciences to other domains and especially psychology—that is, the science of the psyche. It is not possible, he argues, to understand what a human being is and what it is for him or her to have a world by quantifying and measuring perception and objects. It is rather subjective experience that should be at the centre of the humanities and social sciences if we wish for them to have any meaning at all. Otherwise they become (and still are) a pure *techné*.[14]

Although Husserl was a contemporary of Simmel, it is not clear that he knew the work of the latter.[15] And yet it is striking to see how his critique of naturalism and objectivism corresponds to what Simmel considered as the modern condition of perception and action in the Metropolis. But does Husserl also believe that the scientific tendency is shared by everyday life? This is implied in his emphatic words: "Merely fact-minded sciences make merely fact-minded people".[16] We have

here an indication that scientific processes affect the everyday life of
women and men who live in our contemporary technological, materialistic and utilitarian society. People in the scientific era have themselves
become "fact-minded": they are preoccupied with exterior, objective
elements without considering the contextual, subjective and cultural
ingredients thereof. [17]

However, as the big screen in *Room for St. John of the Cross* shows,
something in the everyday resists objectivism, since every object, every
mountaintop, is soon abandoned in favor of the next one. The everyday
attitude, I suggest, is paradoxical: it is attracted to objects, but is never
fully satisfied with them, quickly turning from one object to another,
thus confirming and refuting objectivism at the same time. In order to
understand this paradoxical and ambiguous everyday attitude towards
objects, I propose that we conceive it now in the light of what Husserl
names *the natural attitude*. [18]

THE NATURAL ATTITUDE AND
THE PROBLEM OF SUSPENSION

The natural attitude is first mentioned in Husserl's 1907 seminar *The
Idea of Phenomenology*, before being further developed six years later
in *Ideas I*. Husserl does not define the natural attitude as naturalistic or
objectivistic per se but says rather that it consists of our everyday way
of looking only at the *existing* world, believing in "a world that has its
being out there". [19] However, doesn't taking reality as it is also mean
ignoring the other side(s) of the object? What the objectivist, the naturalistic and the natural attitudes all have in common is that they are
satisfied with ready-made categories, names and objects. Phenomenology consequently aims to bracket the natural attitude in order to arrive
at lived experience. The problem, however, is that lived experience
itself is dominated by an objectivist tendency, so it is not at all clear
what would be left over if we suspended it.

Husserl gradually becomes aware of this problem, and in order to
solve it, in *Ideas II* he makes a distinction between the natural
(*natürlich*) and naturalistic (*natural/naturalistich*) attitudes. [20] The natural attitude refers to the Life-world (*Lebenswelt*), the spontaneous
world of praxis, whereas the naturalistic attitude characterises the natural sciences, referring to the causal, objective and mechanistic world.
Husserl says that only the natural attitude is primordial, and he calls it

personalistic—that is, an attitude of a person relating to his or her surrounding world, contrary to the attitude of the scientist, who is not affected by what he or she analyses and treats it from a distance.

Husserl thus suggests that the natural attitude is not naturalistic but equivalent to the looked-for lived experience. Both lived experience and the natural attitude are characterised by a naïveté, but this does not make them impoverished or problematic. However, only a few pages earlier Husserl admits that one can also *live* in the naturalistic attitude,[21] which turns out to be not only theoretical and a part of science but also practical and possibly part of the everyday. Husserl looks for a renewal of objectivist perception which is also a renewal of the everyday. This renewal must be achieved through a certain suspension of the everyday, but it is difficult to understand how to realise this suspension, or who exactly can effect it.

One of the most interesting things about *Room for St. John of the Cross* is not only that it suspends the natural attitude, as phenomenology does, but also that it accentuates this attitude, such that it is understood precisely through its suspension. It shows what kind of lived experience the natural attitude provides (the big screen), and what other life it aims at (the monitor). Now, where in the everyday itself can we find such a combination—suspension *and* accentuation? The notion in Husserl that comes closest to this is the "Life-world", which is introduced in order to solve the crisis of European sciences. I do not intend, however, to elaborate here on the Life-world, since, as some commentators have lamented,[22] when it comes to concretely describing this world, Husserl prefers to offer mostly transcendental descriptions of a purely formal experience.[23] It seems that, for Husserl, any introduction of *concrete* reality into the Life-world runs the risk of accepting objectivist idealisations,[24] which would contaminate it and draw the crisis into it. Despite the need to combine the transcendental and the empirical, the suspension of the everyday and its manifestation, it seems that Husserl finally prefers the inner room to the jittery mountains. The only way to escape humanity's loss of meaning, the only way to escape the chaotic and mechanical everyday, is to turn one's back on it. Husserl thus warns against humanity's crisis, but it seems that his only solution is to construct phenomenology far away from it, on a solid yet abstract ground, turning the Life-world into what Paul Ricœur calls "phenomenology's lost paradise".[25]

This does not mean, however, that we need to dismiss Husserl's phenomenology. Moreover, Husserl himself acknowledged the impossibility of totally bracketing the natural attitude and abandoning it once and for all. Eugen Fink, Husserl's assistant, reveals (in an article approved by Husserl himself) that his master's major text, *Ideas I*, is still situated within the natural attitude and is only a preparation for its bracketing.[26] However, this preparation does not seem to be temporary. Phenomenology is *always* in a state of preparation for the "real thing", which explains why Husserl wrote so many "introductions to phenomenology", each time from a different perspective. This eternal repetition, which is nonetheless not identical to itself, does not stem from an accidental lack of accuracy, but rather defines phenomenology's essential character. To use Husserl's words, the phenomenologist is a "perpetual beginner".[27]

Phenomenology's inability to fully exploit its position regarding the everyday is, I argue, not its weakness, but rather precisely its main point of interest. Phenomenology's "on the way" position manifests an endless, essentially incomplete passage from the empirical to the transcendental world, from the rapidly shifting mountains to the stable peak of the inner room. Perhaps if we focused our attention on this perpetual movement instead of beguiling ourselves with the possibility of effecting the phenomenological reduction once and for all, we would be able to better understand the way the everyday life is founded and repeated.[28] In order to accomplish that, I propose to radicalise the idea of suspension, considering it not only as a methodological tool to understand the everyday "once and for all" but also, and most especially, as an everyday repetitive mechanism that can transform it from within.

OUT OF THE EVERYDAY AND BACK

So far I have presented *Room for St. John of the Cross* as contrasting the everyday with its secret goal, the big screen with the small monitor. In this way the artwork manages to suspend and capture the ordinary, transforming it therefore into the extraordinary. But my aim here is precisely to overcome this distinction, and this is why I wish now to show how suspension as deferral is a crucial element in the everyday itself. Indeed, facing a repetitive and shocking everyday, it is tempting to imagine an enchanted interiority, where the upsurge of things and the birth of phenomena would quietly and calmly take place. A certain tendency in Husserlian phenomenology goes indeed in this direction, trying to realise our yearning for a pure, peaceful and concentrated life, isolated from exterior noise. However, the problem is not only that I am trapped in this noise but also that I actually *need* it. I would not seriously consider, for instance, giving up my mobile phone or Internet connection in favor of a more silent and interiorised environment.[29] Indeed, even in a paradisiacal holiday on a sunny island I find myself working hard to remain connected. Connected to what? I would say: to the everyday. What everyday? The one I wanted to leave behind.

This combination of an explicit will to escape the everyday and an implicit fear or anxiety to abandon it makes *holiday* an interesting case in which to examine the foundations of the everyday. What happens to my everyday life when I am away from home? No matter how comfortable the conditions might be, I tend to experience a certain lack: suddenly I must get used to a variety of unfamiliar elements and surroundings. In the middle of the night, I wake up horrified and ask myself, "Where am I?" After a second or two, the reassuring answer is "on holiday". And yet this brief moment of horror reveals how protective the habits of the everyday are, how much they permit a normal functioning in an otherwise unstable environment.

Like a turtle, I carry a host of everyday elements with me wherever I go. Even when I am away, I still have, for instance, the same body, the same language and the same habits. And yet these cannot always function in the same way. Jet lag may disturb my habitual sleeping hours; the local language may lead to numerous misunderstandings; the foreign environment may give rise to feelings of uncanniness; and the food may be strange or too spicy for my taste. Of course, one might say that this is why I went on holiday in the first place: to "have a break", experience a temporary escape from my routine. And yet I do not wish the change to be too radical. I do not wish to lose all contact with my everyday life. The everyday might be my prison, but it is also my protective structure, and the fragile balance between these two aspects is challenged when the everyday changes, for instance when one is on holiday.

It is no wonder that islands are popular destinations for holidays, providing shelter from everyday pressures. The protective aspect of the everyday is partially replaced here by the self-containment of the island, its secure environment guaranteed by the shield of the sea. And yet modern islands provide various means of remaining in touch with the outside world. Television, telephone, Internet—all are still available, so I can feel at home while I am away. The island offers sea, sun and leisure, but no real isolation. Isolation would cut me off from too many things I left behind, exposing me to the nakedness of time and the wildness of space.

The holiday resort aims to free me from the everyday conceived as a prison, yet without making me lose touch with the everyday conceived as protective stability. This peculiar combination is reflected in the way many holiday resorts are constructed—namely, as an island within an island (see figure 3). The holiday resort duplicates and inverts the natural structure of the island, placing the swimming pool at its centre and replacing the monotonous yet dangerous character of the sea with a controlled overflow of light, music and activities around the clock. Anything that might hint at deficiency, void or lack is hidden, so that *free* time or *leisure* (literally meaning "allowed") must be consumed in accordance with a variety of activities offered by the holiday resort. The term "all included" is thus taken literally—but what remains nonetheless *excluded* in this world? Isn't it precisely the *nothing*?

A good holiday is one from which I return full of energy, but also with a better understanding of my everyday life, thanks to a partial detachment I have had from it. Holiday can thus be regarded as another

Figure 3. Holiday Resort: An Island within an Island.

version of the phenomenological reduction, a procedure which permits one to consider and reconsider the usual, routine life when it, or some of it, is no longer there. However, for the phenomenological reduction to take place, one needs to recognise and assume the detachment from ordinary reality. One needs to engage oneself in a free variation of life possibilities—habits, landscapes, values, language—and put them into question in order to potentially transform them.

It is clear, however, that this recognition is denied by modern holiday resorts. The rhythm of the holiday is so intense that I am immediately carried away, with no need to adjust myself and slowly digest the new environment. Indeed, I hardly have any time to reflect upon my own abandoned everyday—but isn't that precisely because the "normal" everyday is not abandoned at all? I would suggest that the holiday resort provides a symmetrically inverted form of everyday life, only replacing the monstrous machine named "work" by the monstrous machine named "fun".

Holiday is therefore perceived as a moment of total salvation, which only accentuates the rigid opposition between an ever oppressive everyday life ("work") and an all-satisfying holiday-event ("fun"). An example of this is given by the rapidly growing cruise industry, which attracts people to spend their savings on a once-in-a-lifetime cruise once they have retired. This long-awaited event is supposed to compensate for all the sorrows of "ordinary" life, but the disappointment and feeling of deception do not fail to sooner or later arrive, as is beautifully illustrated in Jonathan Franzen's *The Corrections* and David Foster Wallace's *A Supposedly Fun Thing I'll Never Do Again*. Cruises have indeed become both the most sophisticated and most monstrous figures of modern islands, but their artificial luxury seems to do nothing but accentuate the misery of the vast and tedious shore they try to escape.

HEIDEGGER'S BEING AND THE EVERYDAY

The overwhelming saturation offered by the holiday resort hints at what saturation tries to fill in and cover: not simply everyday life, but rather its incompleteness and internal lack. As Malabou argues, no plasticity is possible without negativity. The everyday protects from negativity by its reassuring routine, but on the other hand it is dependent upon it, since otherwise the routine would become completely mechanical without any possible change. Perhaps more closely than

any other phenomenologist, Martin Heidegger investigated the everyday as based upon negativity.[30] In what follows I shall follow his
thought as laid out in the 1927 magnum opus *Being and Time* to see
how negativity shapes and influences the everyday, and how suspension reacts to negativity and permits or blocks a creative use of it
through repetition.

Heidegger opens *Being and Time* with a declaration that the most
burning, yet neglected, question in philosophy is that of the meaning of
Being.[31] Being, he says, has become a too remote and abstract notion to
our modern ears, and we thus need to awaken and rediscover it. How?
Heidegger proposes to analyse Being through the entity which understands it the most: an entity that understands its *own* Being. Heidegger
calls this entity *Dasein*, the being-there, and although we can equate
this term with the human being, he is careful not to do so, keeping this
term to remind one of its essence.

What is Heidegger's methodology in describing Dasein and Being?
We saw that Husserl aimed to bracket the natural attitude in order to
arrive at a purified experience. The question, consequently, was if this
experience characterises everyday life or only a transcendental experience—that is, the condition of the everyday rather than the everyday
itself. Heidegger poses the same question, but his treatment of it is far
from simple. On the one hand, he criticises Husserl for his technique of
epoché, saying that there is no point in suspending the belief in the
Being of the world if this Being is precisely what one wants to understand.[32] Dasein is the being-there, and as such it is always already
"outside"—that is, in the world. Therefore, the inquiry should focus on
this peculiar situation rather than eliminate it. Instead of thematising
the artificial world which results from the bracketing suggested by
Husserl, Heidegger proposes to describe the world with which Dasein
is most familiar—the world of the everyday. In Heidegger's words, one
needs to show Dasein "as it is *proximally and for the most part*—in its
average *everydayness*" (BT, 37–38).[33]

On the other hand, Heidegger's analysis of everydayness is far from
being a goal in its own right. Although the investigation should start
with the natural attitude of everyday life, Heidegger, too, soon finds
ways to suspend it and arrive at a more "authentic" contact with Being.
The important difference between Husserl and Heidegger thus lies not
so much in the mere act of bracketing, but rather in its context. For
Husserl, the bracketing is a theoretical method, carried out by the philosopher in order to better see and understand the world, whereas Hei-

degger considers it a practical activity which takes place within the everyday world itself and transforms it.[34] Let us examine how this peculiar everyday suspension functions and what it arrives at.

In section 16 of *Being and Time*, Heidegger presents everydayness as a pragmatic and spontaneous sphere, the place in which Dasein uses equipment and tools to achieve various goals, mainly material products. According to this picture, Dasein is a craftsman: it makes shoes, clocks and various useful products. As long as it is not finished, the product is conceived as the work to be accomplished, and once it is done it becomes equipment serving for the manufacturing of a different product. The work can thus never be finished, and the infinite chain of equipment-work-products actually constitutes what Heidegger calls "the world": an endless, holistic network of useful things which refer to each other. For instance, a hammer is used in order to fasten nails to a wall; the nails are used in order to hang pictures; the pictures are used in order to decorate the house; the house is used in order to shelter people and make it possible for them to produce other things; and so on. Every such "in order to" constitutes the essence of the thing at the same time as it shows the dependency of this essence on an infinite number of other essences and things (BT, 95–101).

In many ways these descriptions are reminiscent of Husserl's Lifeworld,[35] the home of primordial life in which the balance between *foundation* as a noun and *foundation* as a verb is perfectly maintained. This everyday is the background for every activity at the same time that it is the activity itself, activity which, far from being repetitive and mechanical, consists of continuous work and action involving unreflective understanding of how to use equipment in the right way to achieve the work. Thus, he says, "the less we just stare at the hammer-Thing, and the more we seize hold of it and use it, the more primordial does our relationship to it become, and the more unveiledly is it encountered as that which it is—an equipment" (BT, 98).

Heidegger borrows from Husserl the desire to attain the things themselves, but instead of the complicated procedure of *epoché* and phenomenological reduction, he seems to propose that one stop merely *thinking* about things and start *using* them. The things themselves are just there: lift your hand and touch them.

FIRST SUSPENSION: WHEN EQUIPMENT GOES AWRY

But if this is so, why do we need theory (and Heidegger) in the first place? Why can we not just go on happily with our everyday life, if it is in it that we attain the things themselves anyway? On the one hand, Heidegger warns against vain contemplation: we should not suspend our everyday use of things, nor should we try to look at them from all possible perspectives as Husserl tried to do, since this would surely miss the practical nature of their Being. But on the other hand, he adds, action is not blind; it has its own kind of sight, which he names *circumspection* (BT, 99). Dasein looks around all the time, yet not lazily or theoretically. Its gaze rather continuously seeks how to efficiently accomplish the work. What Dasein sees in the everyday world is what it does not yet use but shall use once it is ready—namely, the work: something to be produced like a shoe or a clock, a piece of future equipment which is made through present equipment. But the present equipment itself is not seen, since its very essence is to withdraw from sight. We do not stare, for instance, at the hammer whilst manipulating it, and if we actually started looking at it attentively, the chances are that this would only slow down and obstruct our use of it. Consequently, Heidegger characterises the Being of equipment as *readiness-to-hand* (*Zuhandenheit*), a definition that stresses the usefulness of equipment and its adaptation to Dasein's hand without further ado.

All this may sound very intuitive or even trivial, and yet, if equipment is ready-to-hand, and if the ready-to-hand is only used and never seen, it is hard to understand how we know what a hammer looks like. Is our everyday gaze directed only at goals ("work") and never at equipment? It is here that things start to become more complicated, since Heidegger reveals that we *do* see equipment in our everyday life, but in a special mode which he calls *presence-at-hand* (*Vorhandenheit*). In order to explain this, he describes three everyday situations in which equipment is discovered to our sight.

In the first situation a piece of equipment becomes unusable after it has been damaged or found unfit for the task. To draw once more on Heidegger's favorite example, let us imagine a woman who wants to hammer a nail, but suddenly the hammer breaks down or is found inadequate (for instance, too small for the task). Until this moment, the woman never thought about the hammer; she simply used it, as it always perfectly functioned. Now, for the very first time, she needs to reflect upon the Being of the hammer, precisely because it is broken or unsuitable. She needs to reflect, for instance, upon the fragility of the hammer, upon its material ingredients or its size. She needs to figure out how to repair or replace it. In this way, says Heidegger, the ready-to-hand becomes *conspicuous*: it is looked at because it can no longer be used. But did we not see earlier that when we just look at the ready-to-hand we miss its Being? This is why Heidegger adds that what we see, in this situation, is no longer the equipment as ready-to-hand, but rather the equipment as present-at-hand or objectively present.[36] The hammer simply lies there; it becomes an object for our gaze, a ready-to-hand discovered as such only when it is no longer ready-to-hand.

This applies equally to the next two situations that Heidegger mentions—namely, equipment as *missing* (the woman, say, wants to hammer a nail but cannot find a hammer) and equipment as *obstructing* (the woman crosses the street and suddenly runs into a hammer that has fallen from a truck and almost causes her to fall over; BT, 102–7). Indeed, all these situations are common in our everyday lives. Things are often discovered to be unsuitable, missing or obstructing, so that we need to figure out what they are made of and how to replace, obtain or remove them. Moreover, if we go back to the scheme I presented in the introduction, we may note that these situations perfectly exemplify the everyday mechanism of foundation. Any founding act is a movement that reaches beyond the everyday and brings something back into it. With Heidegger, we are now in a position to better understand the motivation of this movement—that is, the inadequacy of equipment. Dasein is out there in the world, repeating an activity it masters, when suddenly this activity cannot be accomplished anymore. Dasein then needs to suspend the everyday movement and reflect upon the situation; it needs to carefully look at the unusable equipment and consider how to carry out the interrupted activity. This reflection or vision supplies Dasein with fresh knowledge of how things work in everyday life and how an activity can be fulfilled in more than one way such that the everyday may change. The woman learns, for instance, how to repair or replace a hammer, and in this way her foundation is set into motion, provided that she returns to work and applies in it what she has just learned.

SUSPENSION AS IMMERSED REFLECTION

Heidegger does not mention what *follows* the suspension of the everyday, and how the woman returns from a vision of equipment as present-
at-hand to a use of it as ready-to-hand. I propose to see this movement
of use-suspension-reuse as the circular movement of everyday foundation. Secondly, I propose that the suspension it involves is a form of
immersed reflection—that is, an imperceptible halt of the everyday that
allows a revitalisation of its movement through a better understanding
of its functioning. Immersed reflection is a process at the end of which
the ready-to-hand becomes inconspicuous once more; yet Dasein uses
it slightly differently, perhaps in a more sophisticated way, since it
understands better both how it is structured and what relations it has
with other entities in the world and with the everyday in general.

Heidegger presents only two extreme cases of vision: mere contemplation and practical looking—and I thus propose to add a middle term,
the intermediate kind of vision that I call immersed reflection. Indeed,
vision is an essential part of everyday life (yet not the only one, as we
will see in the next chapter), and although it implies a certain distance
from the things that are seen, it is not necessarily detached from them
or from their practical use. On the contrary, in order to better use
things, we need to consider them from time to time as a part of the
action. Reflection is not necessarily or even mainly an artificial act, nor
even a matter of cold decision, but rather an everyday and spontaneous
procedure.

Suspension as immersed reflection, I propose, is nothing but an
everyday use of the phenomenological reduction.[37] The reduction, let
us recall, suspends the everyday movement of things in order to carefully consider them and find their true essence. This is exactly what
happens to the woman who wishes to hammer a nail and suddenly
cannot do so. She is thus obliged to perform the same suspension of her
activity, but instead of doing it willingly and coldly, she finds herself in
the need to do so within her everyday life. She freezes her everyday
movement for a moment, looks at the hammer, and only after a while
finds a solution to the problem, a sort of "essence" that permits her to
regain her everyday life with a fresh understanding of it, renewing its
foundation.

I examined earlier the phenomenological tension between theory
and praxis through the figure of *Room for St. John of the Cross*. Phenomenology, on the one hand, aims to capture its "prey" in a pure,

inner room, but, on the other hand, it must recognise that the only way to do so is to remain in touch with the exterior—that is, with everyday life. Bill Viola exposes the everyday as a repetitive, hectic and shocking movement from one mountain to another, but the essence of this movement can be discovered only by a certain suspension of it, placing it together with the inner room and its stable mountain. By this he shows us an artistic way to simultaneously defer and attain the everyday, but with Heidegger we can lead this intuition further, applying it not only to artificial or voluntary reflection, like that of art or philosophy, but also to the immersed reflection of the everyday. The transformation of the ready-to-hand into a present-at-hand is, then, a suspension of the everyday, not just in order to be detached from it, as Heidegger is commonly read, but also to better return to it. This return is practical more than theoretical, taking place in Dasein's world of work.[38]

But if this is so, is there really a crisis of the everyday, and if there is, where does it stem from? It is crucial to note that what provokes immersed reflection according to Heidegger is always a certain problem related to equipment that does *not* function as it is supposed to. Therefore, suspension as immersed reflection involves *a moment of negativity*: a moment in which things no longer take their usual course, requiring a new kind of behavior, a new use of the things to be adopted. In what follows I will try to show that negativity is not a rare incident in everyday life but rather its secret rule and force of motivation. At the same time it is a threat to the everyday, a threat that one tends to avoid, resulting in a deterioration of the everyday movement. This, I argue, is the meaning of what Heidegger names the "Falling of Dasein".

THE FALLING OF DASEIN AS THE DENIAL OF LACK

Room for St. John of the Cross presents a repetitive movement from one mountaintop to another, which I interpreted as a sign of dissatisfaction from the everyday. However, the nature and origin of this dissatisfaction remained unexplained in Husserl. Indeed, Heidegger does not mention dissatisfaction either, since Dasein's constant search for goals is related to practical rather than emotional needs. But how does Dasein decide what work to achieve and where to continue? The three situations mentioned above hint that it is rather negativity (that is, disturbance, lack or obstacle) which leads to a suspension of the normal course of things. When Dasein does *not* find a hammer, it is driven to look for a new one or to create one if no ready-made hammer is available. If the hammer obstructs some other task, Dasein needs to clear it away. Negativity leads to reflection, but this reflection does not mark a complete halt of the world. It is rather an immersed reflection that soon motivates a new task within the old one, in a quite harmonious process of foundation of, and within, the everyday.

However, as the example of the holiday resort has shown, admitting negativity, and especially lack and deficiency, seems to present a particular challenge in modernity. Every day things break down, are found inadequate or simply get lost. Every day we are torn from our supposedly harmonious being-in-the-world, since worldly entities have the tendency to not always be there when we need them. But far from seeing this as a happy occasion to renew the foundation of our everyday life, we tend to find this annoying, and we try as hard as we can to avoid or deny lack.

One may say that it is natural to wish to avoid lack, and yet this presupposes that lack is necessarily something painful. The negative judgment of lack, I would claim, depends on cultural and contextual factors. It is rather in Western modern societies—the affluent societies—that lack has become unbearable, and the case of holiday resorts is only an extreme example. Indeed, Heidegger rarely talks in *Being and Time* about modernity.[39] Although he admits that every historical period is characterised by a different attitude towards Being, he insists on the universality and necessity of one characteristic of Dasein which he calls the Falling (*Verfallen*).

Heidegger claims that the Falling is not the result of some original sin but the very condition of Dasein which does not express any negative evaluation (BT, 220). However, it is difficult to ignore the theological connotation of the word.[40] According to Christian theology, original sin came about when fruit was eaten from the forbidden tree of knowledge of good and evil. Until that moment, Adam and Eve lived a peaceful and harmonious life in Paradise. They were in need of nothing, since everything was effortlessly available in abundance. They were, for instance, naked without noticing that they were, since the weather was always fine and shame did not have a place in their world. We can say that it was a life without negativity, a life in which work and artifacts were not needed or missing, since everything was always and already ready-to-hand, without reflection or useless consideration: an age of innocence.[41]

But one fatal day the serpent came to Eve and revealed to her what would happen if she and Adam ate of the forbidden fruit: "Your eyes shall be opened, and ye shall be as gods, knowing good and evil" (Gen. 3:5). The forbidden fruit is thus conceived as an eye-opener. It brings vision, *theoria*, which is equally moral knowledge. And indeed, as soon as Eve and Adam were tempted to eat the fruit, "the eyes of them both were opened, and they knew that they were naked; and they sewed fig leaves together, and made themselves aprons" (Gen. 3:7). The fruit brought vision, but it is crucial to note that the first thing they saw was a *lack*: Adam and Eve noticed that they were naked, so they produced aprons from fig leaves—the first human craft production to appear in the Bible, the first work to be carried out.

The fruit of knowledge made Adam and Eve move from blind and unproductive praxis to a vision immersed in active production. Is this the Falling? According to theology, perhaps, but not according to Heidegger. On the contrary, it is the beginning of an active and creative world. I propose that the Falling does not lie in vision itself, but rather in its rupture from action and the forgetfulness of the constant necessity to renew it. As Heidegger mentions, the ready-to-hand has no being without the present-at-hand, such that a world of pure praxis without theory at all would be a myth.[42] The immediate effect of eating of the fruit of knowledge of good and evil is not vain contemplation, but rather the production of clothes to cover the nakedness of Adam and Eve. More than that, this production does not make them forget their lack. This is why, when God asks Adam "Where art thou?", he replies "I heard thy voice in the garden, and I was afraid, because I was naked; and I hid myself" (Gen. 3:10). Although Adam has an apron, he acknowledges that it does not cover his nakedness completely: nothing could cover it, so he must keep looking for clothes to produce and shelters to hide in for the rest of his life.

But the "real" Falling does eventually take place, and this, I would claim, is when God expels Adam and Eve from Paradise. The Falling consists in that every kind of human production is henceforth accompanied by *sorrow*: the bearing of children for Eve ("In sorrow shalt thou bring forth children") and the production of food for Adam ("Cursed is the ground for thy sake; in sorrow shalt thou eat of it all the days of thy life"). From now on, the production of children, food and equipment are to involve not only visible lack but also sensible sorrow. This sorrow makes one try to overcome the lack as quickly as possible, but it also makes one, at least in modernity, deny it. Why should I work hard to produce aprons if I can simply (provided that I have money) go to the mall and buy them? The comfort with which modernity allows the middle class to avoid lack and sorrow—at least at their superficial level—makes it difficult to use lack or negativity in general as an opportunity to examine the ready-to-hand, understand its functioning and find ways to use it in a more sophisticated way. Rather, one is tempted to flee or negate negativity by looking for a ready-to-hand which has already been produced by someone else. Who is this some-one else? It is both no one and everyone. Heidegger calls this anony-mous entity *das Man*, which serves in German as the neutral form, translated into English as the "they" or the "one".

DISTANCE AND THE REALM OF THE "THEY"

In order to explain the appearance of the "they" within the everyday, Heidegger introduces another figure of negativity to the three men-tioned above—namely, *distance*. We saw that circumspection is a prac-tical gaze which is directed at the work to be produced together with the appropriate equipment to accomplish the task. Heidegger now adds that everyday circumspection has the character of *de-severing* or *de-distancing (Ent-fernung)*. He suggests that Dasein removes distance at the same time that it creates distance, a paradoxical activity which, he admits, is amplified in modernity:

> *In Dasein there lies an essential tendency towards closeness.* All the ways in which we speed things up, as we are more or less compelled to do today, push us on towards the conquest of remoteness. With the "radio" for example, Dasein has so expanded its everyday environment that it has accomplished a de-severance of the "world"—a de-severance which, in its meaning for Dasein, cannot yet be visualized. (BT, 140)

The modern everyday environment expands as distances are more easi-ly crossed, so that I can not only physically move from one place to another on a daily basis but also be in several places simultaneously—for instance, by staying at home and attending a concert listened to on the radio. And yet, as the term *Ent-fernung* implies, making the dis-tance disappear entails deepening the same distance on another level, since I am *not* actually in the concert hall. When I listen to the radio I may get closer to what I hear, but I do not fail to notice my distance from it, a distance which can never be overcome: "This de-severance—

the farness of the ready-to-hand from Dasein itself—is something that Dasein can *never cross over*" (BT, 142).

Heidegger says that it is precisely when Dasein can have a *rest*, when it has finally achieved the work and has free time, that it starts looking for other things to bring close. And this has crucial consequences: Dasein tending "away from what is most closely ready-to-hand, and into a far and alien (*fremde*) world. Care becomes concern with the possibilities of seeing the 'world' merely as it *looks* while one tarries and takes a rest. Dasein seeks what is far away simply in order to bring it close to itself in the way it looks" (BT, 216). Dasein thus abandons the realm of the ready-to-hand in favor of an alien or even alienated world, which is a constitutive aspect of the Falling. Heidegger names this aspect *curiosity*, in German *Neugier*, literally meaning "avidity of the new". This avidity is a vision that concerns itself with only the surface of things. It does not regard their use but rather their novelty, yet in a most gossipy and stereotypical level.

It thus seems that only the working Dasein can maintain the movement of the everyday, movement of immersed reflection motivated by small moments of negativity. However, even work is not conducted in a self-enclosed world; other Daseins are concerned just as much. In chapter IV of Division I in *Being and Time*, immediately prior to the introduction of the Falling, Heidegger describes what he calls *Being-with*. He says that Dasein is in its essence never alone in the world but always with others. Indeed, it is these others who lead to the Falling, yet not due to the state of Being-with as such, but rather from a certain mode of it—namely, that of the "they".

Heidegger characterises the "they" as a basic and unavoidable characteristic of Dasein, a part of an "everyday Being-with-one-another", in which "Being is taken over by someone else" (BT, 163). But it is important to note that what permits this taking over is precisely *distance*. Dasein perceives a distance between itself and the others, a distance whose "disturbance is one that is hidden from it" (BT, 164). This unconscious feeling of distance makes Dasein succumb to the "they", but although this point seems crucial, Heidegger does not provide much detail on the affective or existential state of Dasein in this situation.

I presented further above lack as one of the negative moments that are constitutive of Dasein's everyday life. With the notion of distance we may now connect lack to *otherness*. The distance between Dasein and the others is a form of lack that remains unconscious most of the time. Dasein, then, finds itself in a curious situation in which it needs to overcome an unacknowledged distance. Dasein therefore quickly borrows from the "they" ready-made categories that would make it closer to all other Daseins, and in this way it becomes *average.* The result, according to Heidegger, is the dictatorship of the "they": "The 'they', which is nothing definite, and which all are, though not as the sum, prescribes the kind of Being of everydayness" (BT, 164).

To sum up, Dasein no longer recognises lack, distance or obstacles in order to move from the practical ready-to-hand to a more reflective present-at-hand, and vice versa. It is rather the "they" which has already accomplished this task for it. In this way Dasein is dis-burdened of its Being—that is, from the laborious cycle of producing-seeing-producing. Dasein is rather tempted by the "they" and is led to "a leveling down of all possibilities of Being" (BT, 165). It finds itself in a shallow, yet comfortable and reassuring, everyday existence, where it only needs to follow well-known possibilities, without any personal reflection and decision making. Consequently, Dasein itself becomes a part of the "they", so that "the Self of everyday Dasein is the *they-self,* which we distinguish from the authentic Self" (BT, 167).

"I wanted only to try to live in accord with the promptings which came from my true self. Why was that so very difficult?" This is the epigraph of Hermann Hesse's highly influential novel *Demian* from 1919.[43] The search for authenticity has been a major theme in the first half of the twentieth century in literature, art and philosophy.[44] The wars and horrors of that period only served to emphasise how the public sphere regularly invades one's inner life and prevents the individual from realising itself. But parallel to this, and all the more so in the second half of the twentieth century, one began to wonder whether such a thing as the "self" really exists, and what selfhood might be all about. This is why Heidegger is presented by some critics as a naïve philosopher, believing in a pure authentic self which should overcome its inauthentic everyday existence.[45]

However, Heidegger insists that the Falling is not a derived or a secondary state; it is not a deterioration from some ideal and primordial realm, in which the self would have been truer and the contact with Being stronger. We have always fallen and will always fall, he declares, so that, due to its very nature, the self cannot be pure or authentic. And yet Heidegger does admit that different historical periods have different forms and degrees of control of the "they" upon Dasein (BT,

167). Modernity thus seems to be an era in which the reign of the "they" is particularly powerful, precisely because Dasein needs to choose from such a wide array of possibilities. Durkheim's "malady of infiniteness" is articulated here as well; yet in Heidegger all possibilities are soon taken over by someone else, as a quick and easy solution for the problem of infinite choice. What is, then, Heidegger's solution to the problem? Let us continue to follow the path he delineates: a path that goes first from Dasein's everyday work to the realm of the "they" and then back to Dasein's self.

SECOND SUSPENSION: ANXIETY AND
THE NOTHINGNESS OF THE WORLD

During my adolescence I used to take the bus back home from school. Several bus stops were located on the sidewalks around a spacious parking lot, and the area was mostly full of cars and kids waiting for the bus. But I remember that on certain occasions, for an unexplained reason, the parking lot and the sidewalks around it would suddenly seem to me to be completely empty. It would suddenly strike me that I was all by myself, and when this happened I was overcome with panic: Where was everyone? Was I all alone on earth? Did the world still exist? These questions would fill me with anxiety, and there would be nothing I could do except wait for the feeling of unprompted emptiness to fade away. After a while, some people would arrive or the bus would come, and I would be drawn back into the world and myself again. "It was nothing", I would say to myself, but traces of these uncanny incidences have remained long with me, and still linger today.

So what was it all about? For Heidegger, the important phrase in my story would be the "it was nothing". The radical negativity, the nothingness of the world was suddenly revealed to me, and with it disappeared the homey everyday appearance of the world. Perhaps I had perceived what the German language beautifully expresses with the word *Unheimlich*, the uncanny. *Heim* means "home", but *heimlich* means both "homey" and "secret".[46] Being at home means hiding a secret from yourself and from others, and it is only when you no longer feel at home—when you feel *unheimlich*—that the secret can be revealed.

I remember that during these uncanny incidences, despite my panic, I also felt a kind of peculiar pleasure, as suddenly all the school pressure, all my efforts to follow rules (and I only now clearly understand how alienating they were), gave way to an infinite emptiness. It was a pleasure quite similar to that which Michel Houellebecq describes having felt as a child when he walked into an empty schoolyard during the 1968 strike. To use Heidegger's vocabulary, in these moments of emptiness beings gave way to Being. All the worldly objects, feelings, thoughts and efforts disappear, and in their place pure Being shines and reigns in the figure of pure Nothingness.

It is only in the second division of *Being and Time* that Heidegger further develops the notion of anxiety as bringing Dasein back to itself. Until now, anxiety has been presented as an uncanny encounter with Being *as* nothingness, but here Heidegger adds that anxiety is actually *death* anxiety. Does this mean that panic invaded me because of a dread of death? It depends how we consider the word "death": as a concrete and empirical event in the world, or (as Heidegger suggests) an imminent possibility of the impossibility of Dasein—a deep understanding that sooner or later I and all my possibilities will perish (BT, 307).

Even if we follow Heidegger, we ought to still ask whether close contact with the nothing that anxiety brings about necessarily entails a taste of my own perishing. Jean-Paul Sartre, for instance, developed a philosophy of *Being and Nothingness* without equaling nothingness to death. For Sartre, death is only one (though extreme) manifestation of negativity. Negativity stands at the limit of each object, since the limit says what the object is *not* and extracts it from the opaque mass of Being. Being and Nothingness are thus two complementary terms which belong to the same world.[47] For Heidegger, too, the emphasis is not on death as such, but rather on the anxiety that acquaints me with the radical lack of any possibility. Heidegger calls this radical lack "nullity", whose understanding is the only way for me to become "resolute", being able to take a proper decision, made upon my own (null) possibilities, and not upon those dictated by the "they".

But how can I take a decision if all my possibilities disappear? For Heidegger, resoluteness is not the concrete act of deciding something, but rather an existential lucidity which is the a priori condition for an authentic decision. In Heidegger's words, "When Dasein is resolute, it takes over authentically in its existence the fact that it is the null basis of its own nullity" (BT, 354). Resoluteness is thus the understanding that every decision or act of foundation is not based upon something steady and solid. It is an understanding that the foundation is rather in a constant movement, and as such it can never stop and pretend, as the "they" does, to have arrived "home", at a calm, static and tranquilised sphere of a cozy everyday life. For a decision to be authentic, Dasein must understand that nothing grounds it—or, more accurately, that the ground is to be founded in the act itself of decision.

We saw earlier that negativity may serve as a motivation for the continuous foundation of the everyday, and we learn now that negativity—in its most radical form—is also what stands at the basis of any foundation. Dasein's decisions, behaviors, habits or routines do not have a basis outside themselves, lacking external or transcendental justification. The sudden understanding of Dasein that it is doomed to die—or rather, "is dying", in the words of Heidegger—only emphasises that whatever Dasein acquires during its lifetime is ephemeral. Heidegger names this condition of being in a foreign, arbitrary and finite world "throwness" (*Geworfenheit*) or "abandonment" (*Überlassenheit*). However, it seems to be very difficult to grasp this situation in everyday life, in the realm of the "they" where all sorts of urgent demands and unquestioned beliefs are the rule. Only when Dasein understands its ownmost nullity, only when it realises that nothing is stable and that every ready-made and easy possibility is an illusion introduced by the "they", does it have a chance to resume the authentic foundation of the everyday as based on negativity.

This is why Heidegger adds that, in order to become resolute, anxiety itself does not suffice. One has first to listen to the "call of conscience". This is a mysterious, silent voice, coming from myself ("before" the Falling?) to myself ("after" the Falling?), having only one word to say: "Guilty!" Am I guilty for my acts, having forgotten the need to found and re-found my everyday life constantly, without turning to the "they" for support? Am I guilty for my having become one of the "they" and having failed to help my close surroundings to get over it? Or am I finally guilty because of the very structure of Being, there being no basis for my decisions and my everyday life? All these meanings of the word *guilty* are valid, according to Heidegger, and he mentions that the German word for guilt, *Schuld*, also means being indebted, being responsible for, coming to owe something to others, as well as lacking something (BT, 327–28).

The last meaning of guilt as lack sends us back to the moments of "small" negativity, in which a piece of equipment is found to be unsuitable, missing or obstructing. Can Dasein understand its guilt in these moments? Can I, for instance, get in touch with my "guilt" when something breaks off in my routine in a sort of electricity failure which throws light on Being through the sudden darkness? Can I understand it when I go on holiday to a new environment, feel all of a sudden abandoned, deprived of solid ground which would make existence evident? Heidegger rather stresses that Dasein does not lack anything concrete or empirical, since only *things* can lack and be missing, not Dasein. Contrary to things, Dasein exists, and "in existence there can be nothing lacking" (BT, 329). Indeed, we saw earlier that it is equipment and not Dasein that may show itself as unusable. But if a thing is missing, it is necessarily missing *to* Dasein, which therefore lacks it. It seems that when Heidegger says that in existence there can be nothing lacking, he means that Dasein is a holistic entity, which can either be or not be, without intermediate options.[48] Thus, only when Dasein is affected by death anxiety does it become acquainted with negativity: "When Dasein is resolute, it takes over authentically in its existence the fact that it *is* the null basis of its own nullity" (BT, 354).

I would therefore claim that it is precisely Heidegger's reluctance to attribute "small" negativity to Dasein that makes it difficult to understand how one can regain one's everyday life once the anxiety is gone. Heidegger seems to worry that the empirical and concrete negativity might conceal the more primordial and radical negativity, and he therefore locates the discovery of original nullity only in the rare moments of anxious resoluteness. But even if we accept that "small" negativity only characterises entities other than Dasein, can they not remind it of its primordial nullity and the need to re-found the everyday?

Many commentators have consequently pointed out that anxiety, the call of conscience and resoluteness are only momentary situations in Dasein's life, in which authenticity is achieved through the annihilation of all worldly possibilities. The question remains open whether Dasein can return to its everyday life without losing authenticity and without succumbing again to the "they".[49] Indeed, Heidegger speaks of an *action* that should be taken on the basis of anxiety, and of a new state of mind which consequently appears and which he calls *joy* (BT, 358). But he does not say much about this action and this joy. We can only assume that joy results from the resumption of the foundation of the everyday, seeing negativity no longer as necessarily linked to sorrow, but rather as a prior condition for any action in the world. In other words, joy occurs through the passage from the local, concrete lack to a more primordial absence, understanding that existence itself lacks nothing. As long as I exist, I am one with the world, and only the things around me are missing and lacking, not me.

Yet my interest in this book lies not in pure existence but in the everyday itself. Indeed, in the moment of anxiety all possibilities are annihilated, so that Dasein attains pure Being, but this purity, as we already saw in Husserl, is artificial: it may belong to the transcendental level but not to the empirical realm of the everyday. This is no doubt the real danger of Heideggerian philosophy, for whereas in Husserl purity always goes hand in hand with a theoretical procedure, in Heidegger it receives a more accessible allure, suggesting that it can in fact be part of life itself. If we remain on a superficial level, without reflecting upon the mutual dependence between "pure" Being and "impure" everyday, we risk falling prey to the fascist temptation, as happened to Heidegger himself.[50]

The fascist temptation is the implicit or explicit wish to achieve purity within everyday life— that is, to clear life of everything which would damage wholeness and completeness. One may attain this state personally (for instance, through an ascetic way of life), but when one tries to generalise this personal effort and find social and political conditions which may enable it, one may end up adhering to some fascist movement. In fascism the individual and the collective finally become one, as a part of a harmony which imitates the pre-Falling everyday life. But this harmony is imaginary, and it can be achieved only at the price of violently repressing or annihilating anything which threatens to break it, anything that reveals not only the perfect null basis of everyday life but also the imperfect small holes and lacks which constitute its routine. Paradoxically, therefore, it is the wish to get away from the "they" and achieve authenticity which finally gives the "they" an overwhelming power, as it has in fascist regimes.

How can one avoid the temptation of purity? How can one live an everyday life which acknowledges its negativity and absence of basis, without filling it in with ready-made entities and rigid categories? It is difficult to find answers to these questions in Heidegger, because his focus on the everyday is subjected to his investigation of Being, and Being can be attained only in its pure form of nothingness rather than in the tiny lacks and absences which constitute our everyday life.[51] This is moreover why Heidegger prefers to use the more general term "everydayness" rather than the concrete "everyday". However, a hint of the direction to follow is given by Heidegger's notion of *time* as the meaning of Being. Heidegger claims that time can be authentically realised only in anxiously running towards death; yet this anxiety seems to be located outside the everyday. On the other hand, Dasein achieves its temporal self-understanding through something that is at the centre of the everyday—namely, *repetition*.

TIME AND REPETITION

I do not intend to fully analyse Heidegger's complex concept of time here, but to focus, rather, on the relationship between time and repetition, since the movement of the everyday, as I argued in the introduction, is repetitive in its essence. However, Heidegger does not connect repetition to the everyday per se, but rather to anxiety: "Anxiety is anxious about naked Dasein as something that has been thrown into uncanniness. . . . Anxiety brings one back to one's thrownness as something *possible* which *can be repeated*" (BT, 393–94). In anxiety, Dasein finds that it is naked, null and has no basis for its existence. Nevertheless, Dasein is thrown—that is, it is out there, in a world it has not chosen. Thrownness, as we have begun to see, is the passive aspect of Dasein, of which it is unaware most of the time. Dasein finds itself in a world where a variety of things, words, customs and deeds already take place. This world is Dasein's home, and yet it is an uncanny, un-homey home, since the world, no less than Dasein, lacks a basis. More precisely, all the possibilities which the world proposes depend only on Dasein, since Dasein alone can choose and give them a (baseless) basis, precisely by *repeating* them.

What kind of repetition is this? The German word for *repetition* is *Wiederholung*, literally meaning "to catch up or fetch again". Heidegger defines repetition as an authentic "Being-as-having-been" (BT, 388)—that is, going back to the thrown past ("having-been") and catching up its possibilities in the present. This authentic present is defined as "a moment of vision (*Augenblick*) of anticipatory repetition" (BT, 443), combining past, present and future. Repetition thus characterises the authentic temporality, and Heidegger contrasts it with the inauthentic temporality of the "they": "The 'they' evades choice. Blind from possibilities, it cannot repeat what has been, but only retains and receives the 'actual' which is left over" (BT, 443).

The "they" prefers actuality over possibility. It takes thrownness—the given world—as it is, and does not try to re-appropriate it by repeating it. Therefore the "they" is void of history, which is enabled only through repetition: "By repetition, Dasein first has its own history made manifest" (BT, 438). Repetition turns to the past but only in the light of the present and the future, thus making one resolute (BT, 444), allowing a decision to be taken upon the thrown, unchosen past. Repetition is therefore the only way to make something mine, to take the past in charge, re-found and re-appropriate it. This act would not, however, be an exact repetition, but rather a repetition which acknowledges its difference: the passing of time perceived through my approaching death. The understanding of my finitude reminds me of the need to found and re-found my past and present, to find new hidden possibilities in it that I need to repeat and actualise in the light of death, which always threatens to annihilate my possibilities.

Heidegger thus sketches a mechanism of foundation which does not forget the constant need to renew it, and this through the constant reminder of death and death anxiety. But is this mechanism active in the everyday itself or only in rare moments of anxiety? Heidegger only gives some contradictory statements regarding this question in *Being and Time* and other writings from the same period.[52] Once more, my purpose is not so much to understand what Heidegger "really" thought, but rather to borrow from him some elements which might help us understand the functioning of the foundation of the everyday, both in general and in modernity.

We thus realise the crucial role of repetition, which can be engaged by the two variants of the phenomenological reduction: the small moments of negativity and the radical negativity in anxiety. These two types of suspension of the everyday are in fact already part of its foundation, and the question is how to keep using them, maintaining the everyday as a stable yet open enough basis for further halts, actions and events. In the introduction, the *body* was presented as one of the central elements of the everyday, something that gives a solid basis to my acts while simultaneously changing through this very process. Yet the body has a further complication which makes it a particularly interesting case from which to examine the foundations of the everyday. On the one hand, the body is absolutely mine and serves as my private sphere, my interior, but, on the other hand, it is out there in the world, and can be seen and manipulated by others. My body is thus at the same time subjective and objective, mine and not mine, inside and outside, and as such it may bridge these oppositions, which remained unclear in Husserl and Heidegger.

Moreover, the body incarnates both the radical (or "big") negativity and the empirical (or "small") negativity: it is something that comes from nothingness and goes eventually back to nothingness, but it is not nothing itself; it is completely dependent upon its environment, always in a state of deficiency and lack, being hungry, thirsty, tired or ill, and yet it is also an active entity which can shape and influence itself and its surroundings. It is this everyday duality of negativity and positivity, absence and presence, passivity and activity, which I would like now to investigate, and this with recourse to the philosopher who consecrated his life to the phenomenology of the body: Maurice Merleau-Ponty.

NOTES

1. St. John of the Cross, *The Collected Works of St. John of the Cross*, trans. K. Kavanaugh and O. Rodriguez (Garden City, NY: Doubleday, 1964), 721.

2. Edmund Husserl, *Logical Investigations* I, trans. J. N. Findlay (New York: Humanities Press, 1970), 252.

3. See Robert Sokolowski, *Introduction to Phenomenology* (Cambridge: Cambridge University Press, 2000), 17–21. See also Edmund Husserl, *The Crisis of European Sciences and Transcendental Phenomenology*, trans. David Carr (Evanston, IL: Northwestern University Press, 1970), 157–58.

4. The term stems from the skeptic philosophy of Pyrrho (4th–3rd century BC).

5. See Edmund Husserl, *Experience and Judgment*, trans. J. S. Churchill and K. Ameriks (Evanston, IL: Northwestern University Press, 1973), §87.

6. Husserl, *Crisis*, 249.

7. See Husserl, *Logical Investigations* I, §§17–51.

8. See in particular Edmund Husserl, "Philosophy as a Rigorous Science", trans. M. Brainard, in *New Yearbook for Phenomenology and Phenomenological Philosophy* 2 (2002 [1910–1911]), 249–95. In his 1906–1907 lectures on "Introduction to Logic and Theory of Knowledge", Husserl even adopts religious terms in order to characterise naturalism as a "sin against the Holy Spirit of Philosophy". (See Dermot Moran, "Husserl's Transcendental Philosophy and the Critique of Naturalism", *Continental Philosophy Review* 41 [2008]: 413.)

9. Especially in Husserl, *Crisis*.

10. For a more detailed analysis of these two attitudes and their relation to the everyday, see Eran Dorfman, "Naturalism, Objectivism and Everyday Life", *Royal Institute of Philosophy Supplement* 72 (2013): 117–33.

11. In the "Vienna Lecture" Husserl talks more broadly about Western culture since Euclid as detaching itself from lived experience in favor of geometrical models of it (*Crisis*, 269–99).

12. Husserl, *Crisis*, 21–59.

13. See Don Ihde, *Bodies in Technology* (Minneapolis and London: University of Minnesota Press, 2002), 56–57.

14. Husserl, *Crisis*, 56–57.

15. On the affinity between the two thinkers, see Gary Backhaus, "Simmel's Philosophy of History and Its Relation to Phenomenology: Introduction", *Human Studies* 26, no. 2 (2003): 203–8.

16. Husserl, *Crisis*, 6.

17. This criticism is further developed by Martin Heidegger, especially in "The Question Concerning Technology", in *Basic Writings*, ed. David Farrell Krell, trans. William Lovitt (London and New York: Routledge, 1993), 307–41.

18. For an analysis and genealogy of the natural attitude in Husserl, see Sebastian Luft, "Husserl's Phenomenological Discovery", *Continental Philosophy Review* 31 (1998): 153–70, and Moran, "Husserl's Transcendental Philosophy", 401–25.

19. Edmund Husserl, *Ideas: General Introduction to Pure Phenomenology*, trans. W. R. Boyce Gibson (London: Allen & Unwin, 1931), 106.

20. Edmund Husserl, *Ideas Pertaining to a Pure Phenomenology and to a Phenomenological Philosophy*. Second Book: *Studies in the Phenomenology of Constitution*, trans. R. Rojcewicz and A. Schuwer (Dordrecht: Kluwer, 1989), 189.

21. Husserl, *Ideas II*, 183.

22. See Bruce Bégout, *La Découverte du quotidien* (Paris: Allia, 2005), 142–68.

23. For a detailed analysis of this problem, see Eran Dorfman, "History of the Life-world: From Husserl to Merleau-Ponty", *Philosophy Today* 53, no. 3 (2009): 294–303. On Husserl's attempts to introduce history or historicity into the Life-world, see Dan Zahavi, *Husserl's Phenomenology* (Stanford, CA: Stanford University Press, 2003), 133–40.

24. See Husserl, *Experience and Judgment*, 41–51.

25. Paul Ricoeur, *From Text to Action*, trans. K. Blamey and J. B. Thompson (Evanston, IL: Northwestern University Press, 1991), 14. More than any other, it was Alfred Schutz who tried to further develop Husserl's concept of the Life-world. However, he does not go beyond Husserl's transcendental and eidetic model either. See Alfred Schutz and Thomas Luckmann, *The Structures of the Life-World*, trans. Richard M. Zaner and T. Engelhardt (Evanston, IL: Northwestern University Press/London: Heinemann, 1973).

26. Eugen Fink, "The Philosophical Phenomenology of Edmund Husserl and Contemporary Criticism", in *The Phenomenology of Husserl*, ed. and trans. R. O. Elveton (Seattle: Noesis Press, 2000), 115.

27. Husserl, *Crisis*, 291. On the difficulty of delineating the limits of the Husserlian *epoché*, see Jacob Rogozinski, *The Ego and the Flesh: An Introduction to Egoanalysis*, trans. Robert Vallier (Stanford, CA: Stanford University Press, 2010), 123–37.

28. There are two further themes in Husserl that are relevant to the study of the everyday: the first is his notion of temporality, which I will discuss in the next chapter in the light of Merleau-Ponty, and the second is his analysis of passive and active synthesis, which are equivalent to a certain extent to the two movements of the everyday delineated in the introduction. On this theme, see Bruce Bégout, *La Généologie de la logique* (Paris: Vrin, 1999), as well as David Carr's introduction to Husserl, *Crisis*, xl–xlii.

29. The example of the Internet does, however, show a possibility of getting out while staying at home, which makes the Internet an important topic for future research of the modern everyday.

30. See Giorgio Agamben, *Language and Death: The Place of Negativity*, trans. Karen E. Pinkus with Michael Hardt (Minneapolis: University of Minnesota Press, 1991).

31. Martin Heidegger, *Being and Time*, trans. J. Macquarrie and E. Robinson (New York: Harper & Row, 1962), 19. Henceforth abbreviated BT followed by the page number. For the German original, see Martin Heidegger, *Sein und Zeit* (Tübingen: Max Niemeyer, 1927), 1.

32. Martin Heidegger, *History of the Concept of Time*, trans. Theodore Kisiel (Bloomington: Indiana University Press, 1992), esp. 108–14. For an excellent analysis of Heidegger's divergence from Husserl, see Simon Critchley, "Heidegger for Beginners", in Simon Critchley and Reiner Schürmann, *On Heidegger's* Being and Time, ed. Steven Levine (London and New York: Routledge, 2008), 9–55.

33. The translation of Joan Stambaugh (Albany: State University of New York Press, 1996) renders Heidegger's *zunächst und zumeist* into "initially and for the most part".

34. On the status of the phenomenological reduction in Heidegger, see Jacques Ta-miniaux, *Metamorphoses of Phenomenological Reduction* (Milwaukee, WI: Marquette University Press, 2004), and Matheson Russell, "Phenomenological Reduction in Hei-degger's 'Sein und Zeit': A New Proposal", *Journal of the British Society for Phenome-nology* 39, no. 3 (2008): 229–48.

35. On the relationship between Heidegger's *Being and Time* and Husserl's notion of the Life-world, see, among others, Don Ihde, *Technology and the Lifeworld: From Garden to Earth* (Bloomington: Indiana University Press, 1990), esp. 31–38; David Carr, *Interpreting Husserl* (Dordrecht: Martinus Nijhoff, 1987); R. Philip Buckly, *Husserl, Heidegger and the Crisis of Philosophical Responsibility* (Dordrecht: Kluwer, 1992).

36. In German the distinction between the *ready-to-hand* and the *objectively-present* makes more sense: the first is *Zuhanden*, literally "to the hand", and the second is *Vorhanden*, literally "before the hand".

37. For a similar approach to the phenomenological reduction, see Rudolf Bernet, *La Vie du sujet* (Paris: Presses Universitaires de France, 1994). Most interpreters of Hei-degger in the Anglo-Saxon world propose, however, a pragmatist interpretation of Hei-degger, and they consequently do not attribute an important role to the sudden unusabil-ity of tools. See Hubert L. Dreyfus, *Being-in-the-World* (Cambridge, MA: MIT Press, 1991), 99–100; Stephen Mulhall, *Heidegger and* Being and Time (London and New York: Routledge, 1996), 47–49. The problem with these interpretations is that when they come to describe the Falling, which we will soon meet, they cannot relate it to Heidegger's prior descriptions of the world of tools.

38. For an original discussion of Heidegger's conception of the ready-to-hand and the world of tools/objects, see Graham Harman, *Tool-Being: Heidegger and the Meta-physics of Objects* (Chicago: Open Court, 2002).

39. He will do so explicitly later on, starting from the 1930s. It would be interesting to compare his analysis of the everyday in *Being and Time* with his treatment of Van Gogh's *A Pair of Shoes* almost ten years later in "The Origin of the Work of Art" (in *Basic Writings*, trans. Albert Hofstadter, 139–212). In both cases, however, the "real" everyday "thing" seems to be lost to modern perception.

40. In German, the Fall of Man is *Sündenfall*—namely, the sin-fall that is echoed in Dasein's *Verfallen*. For an interesting analysis of Heidegger's Falling as a theological Fall, which goes in a direction different from the one I adopt here, see Stephen Mulhall, *Philosophical Myths of the Fall* (Princeton, NJ: Princeton University Press, 2005), 46–84.

41. On the myth of the archaic as the innocent, see Mircea Eliade, *The Myth of the Eternal Return: Cosmos and History*, trans. Willard Trask (New York: Harper & Row, 1963).

42. "*Readiness to hand is the way in which entities as they are 'in themselves' are defined ontologico-categorially*. Yet only by reason of something present-at-hand, 'is there' anything ready-to-hand" (BT, 101). On the mutual dependence of the ready-to-hand and the present-at-hand, see Eran Dorfman, "La Parole qui voit, la vision qui parle: De la question du Logos dans *Être et temps*", *Revue Philosophique de Louvain* 104, no. 1 (2006): 104–32.

43. Hermann Hesse, *Demian*, trans. Michael Roloff and Michael Lebeck (New York: Bantam, 1968).

44. On the role of authenticity within modern society, see, for example, Marshal Berman, *The Politics of Authenticity: Radical Individualism and the Emergence of Modern Society* (London: Allen & Unwin, 1971), and Charles Taylor, *The Malaise of Modernity* (Toronto: House of Anansi Press, 1991).

45. See Theodor Adorno, *The Jargon of Authenticity*, trans. Knut Tarnowski and Frederic Will (Evanston, IL: Northwestern University Press, 1973), and Michael E.

Zimmerman, *Eclipse of the Self: The Development of Heidegger's Concept of Authenticity* (Athens: Ohio University Press, 1981).

46. For Freud's discussion of the term, see *The Uncanny*, SE 17:217–56. For a broad analysis of the concept in various fields, see Nicholas Royle, *The Uncanny* (Manchester: Manchester University Press, 2003).

47. See Jean-Paul Sartre, *Being and Nothingness*, trans. Hazel Barnes (New York: Simon & Schuster, 1956).

48. The same applies for Sartre, although within a different conceptual structure. For him, there are only two modes of existence: the "for itself" (the human being) and the "in itself" (worldly things). Sartre then plays with the different combinations of the two modes, claiming that the human being aims for the impossible—that is, to be *both* for itself and in itself. Thus, for Sartre as well, the everyday is necessarily the arena of *bad faith*. I would claim, however, that the concept of bad faith stems from Sartre's own rigid dichotomy, which misses the subtle mechanisms of the foundation of the everyday, and especially the possibility to be *simultaneously* within *several* moments of foundation (that is, both *for itself* and *in itself*).

49. See, for example, Jean-Luc Nancy, *The Birth to Presence*, trans. Brian Holmes et al. (Stanford, CA: Stanford University Press, 1993), 82–109, and Rudi Visker, "Dropping: The 'Subject' of Authenticity", in *Deconstructive Subjectivities*, ed. Simon Critchley and Peter Dews (Albany: State University of New York Press, 1996), 59–83.

50. In recent years there has been abundant literature concerning Heidegger's implication with National Socialism and, more generally, with fascist thought. See, notably, Victor Farias, *Heidegger and Nazism* (Philadelphia: Temple University Press, 1989); Richard Wolin, ed., *The Heidegger Controversy: A Critical Reader* (Cambridge, MA: MIT Press, 1993); Johannes Fritsche, *Historical Destiny and National Socialism in Heidegger's* Being and Time (Berkeley and Los Angeles: University of California Press, 1999); Tom Rockmore, *On Heidegger's Nazism and Philosophy* (Berkeley: University of California Press, 1997); Emmanuel Faye, *Heidegger: The Introduction of Nazism into Philosophy in Light of the Unpublished Seminars of 1933–1935* (New Haven, CT: Yale University Press, 2009); Hans Sluga, *Heidegger's Crisis: Philosophy and Politics in Nazi Germany* (Cambridge, MA, and London: Harvard University Press, 1993).

51. Simon Critchley proposes to resolve this problem by "aspect change from a heroics of authenticity to an originary inauthenticity" (Critchley, "Originary Inauthenticity: On Heidegger's *Sein und Zeit*", in Critchley and Schürmann, *On Heidegger's* Being and Time, 143). I adhere to Critchley's suggestion, but whereas he puts the accent on the relationality of Dasein, for me it is through suspensions of (and within) the everyday that "originary inauthenticity" is achieved.

52. See in particular Heidegger's analysis of boredom in *The Fundamental Concepts of Metaphysics: World, Finitude, Solitude*, trans. William McNeill and Nicholas Walker (Bloomington: Indiana University Press, 1995), 74–164, and "What Is Metaphysics?", trans. David Farrell Krell, in *Basic Writings*, 89–110.

Chapter Two

The Ambiguous Body According to Merleau-Ponty

"This body is mine!" These words, accompanied by my finger pointing towards my chest, can be nothing but true. My body belongs to me; my body is mine. But when, or in what situation, might I find myself obliged to pronounce these words? Mostly when someone is trying to get hold of my body. It could be someone concrete who is harassing me and whom I try to push away, crying out, "This is my body, not yours!", or it could be someone or something more abstract—for instance, fashion magazines or TV commercials that dictate a certain model of the body and to whom I may silently reply, "This is my body, and it is for me, not you, to decide how to treat it".

The exclamation "This body is mine!" thus reveals the double face of the body: it is the most private and intimate thing that I have on earth, but it nevertheless remains a *thing*, which can consequently be treated as a mere object by others or even by myself. The body, my innermost everyday belonging, the house and shelter which I always carry with me and upon which everything I have is founded, constantly incarnates the risk of being taken over by someone else.

Indeed, the notion of the everyday I elaborate in this book is not universal, objective or free-floating. It is *someone's* everyday. So far I have discussed it in the light of the thinking-perceiving subject in Husserl, and the practical and engaged Dasein in Heidegger. I now wish to investigate, with Maurice Merleau-Ponty, the everyday of the *embodied* subject.

The entire phenomenological enterprise of Merleau-Ponty (1908–1961) is aimed at extracting the personal dimension of the body from the impersonal one, showing the interactions and movements between the two. Being embodied does not simply add another dimension to the subject, since the body, as Merleau-Ponty insists time and again, radically transforms the entire notion of subjectivity, being both inside and outside, both subject and object. If we wish to fully understand what kind of everyday life the embodied subject may have, we must never neglect this double aspect of the body.

Moreover, Merleau-Ponty proposes a special method of investigation which would correspond to the embodied situation of the subject. The phenomenological reductions proposed by Husserl and Heidegger aimed to suspend the objectified categories of the everyday in order to arrive at a pure Life-world or authentic existence. But Merleau-Ponty's phenomenological reduction cannot go in this direction, since the body, on which it is focussed, is by definition never pure nor fully authentic. The body, according to Merleau-Ponty, is *ambiguous*. Yet ambiguity is not an accidental lack of clarity which can be fixed or got rid of by means of the right treatment. Ambiguity rather characterises human existence as such—that is, as embodied.

Let us take an example which Merleau-Ponty borrows from Husserl.[1] If you put the book down and held your hands together, could you tell which hand touches which?

You would probably be hard pressed to answer this question. Indeed, each hand touches and is touched at one and the same time, but it is as if we needed to choose between the two—as if it were impossible to perceive the same hand touching and being touched *at once*. In other words, it is (almost) impossible to perceive ambiguity in one actual perception. I am thus inclined to see and feel my body *either* as a subject (touching) *or* as an object (touched). Ambiguity tends to hide itself in the everyday world, and therefore needs to be uncovered if I wish to gain a genuine understanding of what the body—my body—is. The main question I wish to develop in this chapter is whether this discovery of ambiguity can take place within the everyday, and what consequences it entails.

Merleau-Ponty's major work, *Phenomenology of Perception* (1945), goes through various aspects of existence such as space, time, sexuality, speech, otherness and freedom. For each of these, Merleau-Ponty shows how it is based and constructed upon the ambiguity of the body, an ambiguity that is concealed in the everyday and needs to be exposed. Could this exposure lead to a different everyday treatment of the body? Merleau-Ponty aims to shed light on a zone where the distinctions between subject and object, the inside and the outside, no longer (or not yet) exist; a zone where I cannot tell which hand touches which. But is this zone a philosophical concept, an extraordinary realm of total immersion or a viable everyday possibility? We saw that Husserl proposed the artificial procedure of *epoché* in order to arrive at the "things themselves", whereas Heidegger placed the suspension within the everyday, whilst connecting it to death-anxiety which is involuntary and whose effects on the everyday seem to be very precarious. Could Merleau-Ponty help us *live* an ambiguous everyday life—that is to say, life which constantly moves between subjectivity and objectivity? Or does he rather discover a zone which lies *beneath* the everyday, so that it can be attained only so long as the everyday is suspended?

Merleau-Ponty does not address these questions directly, but my claim is that his method of investigation aims to tackle them by adopting an ambiguous style of writing. This might frustrate a reader who is eager to find straightforward answers and quick prescriptions, but Merleau-Ponty's style is essential to his philosophy and cannot be simply cleared away in favor of unequivocal assertions. From this point of view, Merleau-Ponty is similar to Heidegger, both trying to turn philosophy itself into a transformative praxis which would not only describe but also create a more genuine mode of existence. This ambition makes both develop their own tone and style of writing, utilising rhetorical elements—repetitions, digressions, neologisms—inherent to the content of their philosophy. Whereas Heidegger's tone is pathetic, evocative and sometimes anxiety provoking, Merleau-Ponty's style oscillates between the scholarly serious, the dreamily poetic and the critically ironic. Simone de Beauvoir, who was an intimate friend of Merleau-Ponty in their youth, wrote in her *Memoirs* that he used to go dancing,[2] and it certainly shows. Merleau-Ponty literally dances within and between several registers and attitudes. And indeed, what other bodily practice is able to blur better the limits between my body and the world?

ONTOLOGICAL VERSUS PSYCHOLOGICAL AMBIGUITY

Many people declare that they do not like to dance, that it makes them feel too embarrassed or self-conscious. They complain that they do not know how to move their bodies in a dance, and they judge themselves to be too awkward and exposed when they finally dare to do so. Others do like to dance, but they need a drink or two in order to loosen up and take to the dance floor. Why is it so difficult to do something as easy as to freely move your body in public? It seems that dancing reveals something that many people, at least in their adult age, prefer to leave in the dark. Could this have something to do with ambiguity? In order to tackle this question, let us first try to understand what dancing consists of.

When I dance I do much more than just move my body. First, I move it for no other apparent goal than the movement itself. Contrary to the utilitarian everyday activity described by Heidegger, in which everything is always for the sake of something, the purpose of dancing is simply to dance. It is a movement which produces nothing but the dance itself. However, this does not mean that it takes place in a void. First, dancing is most often accompanied by music, which provides the rhythmic and melodic framework. To dance well, I must do more than merely listen to the music; I must let it penetrate my body and vibrate with it as if from within. Second, I usually do not dance alone, but with other people. When I dance, these people somehow become an extension of my body, a strange yet natural part of it, and reciprocally I also become a part or an extension of their bodies. It is as if we all created together a big common body, and therefore a good dance party is one in which the dancers manage to bypass the limits of their own bodies and create a new multiple body. This new body would combine the whole and the parts, letting each of its members express itself individually, yet in harmony with the others.

Music and people, two elements that dance usually involves, cease to be external to me when I dance and somehow become an inherent organ of my body—a body which expands and becomes much bigger than the limits of the skin. Music and people touch me and are touched by me, just as in the case of the two hands touching each other. Here, too, it is difficult to say who touches whom. Dancing is thus ambiguous, but do I actually feel this ambiguity while dancing? It seems that only when I *begin* to dance, when there is still a hesitation, when I am not yet sure if I like the music and the crowd—only then do I feel ambiguous. At first my body is not yet resolved to extend itself and lose its safe and distinct frontiers. Only later, after these ambiguous moments have passed, do I gradually get into the dance and let myself become a part of the whole. We can thus distinguish between an ontological ambiguity (a mutual belonging) and a psychological ambiguity (a refusal to merge). The first is realised only when the second disappears, which constitutes the paradox of embodied existence: I can become one with the world only when I forget for a while the troubling contours of my skin which separate me from the world outside.

I dance like a madman, full of joy and love for the world. I am my dance and the dance is me. I am the music and the music is me. I am the dancing crowd and the dancing crowd is me. But sooner or later I get tired. It becomes late and people start to leave. Or perhaps someone has pushed me or stepped on my toes. This suddenly brings me back from the ontological ambiguity to the psychological ambiguity, and I am reminded of my limits. The *interrupted* experience of dance, therefore, makes me realise that although my body may belong to a larger one, most of the time it feels as if it were desperately isolated: from the world, from others and even from myself. So whose body is this?

I would suggest that there are two extreme poles between which my attitude towards the body oscillates: total separation, on the one hand, and total immersion, on the other. In the first I feel my body itself as a thing in the world: an external and rather hostile object that I awkwardly move and which I am sadly doomed to carry until the end of my life. This attitude may come to the foreground due to illness,[3] injury, depression or simply self-alienation. In the second extreme case objectivity disappears and I feel an inseparable and mutual belonging between myself and my body, as well as between my body and the world. When this feeling occurs, it is a powerful moment of inebriated joy and happiness, which I may feel when I dance, make love, engage in sport or am simply at peace with my body.

Merleau-Ponty calls this second realm of mutuality and intertwining *Flesh*, a notion he develops primarily in his last two writings, *Eye and Mind* and the unfinished *The Visible and the Invisible*.[4] In the realm of the Flesh, which is more primordial than the realm of objectivity, only ontological ambiguity rules. In it I fully belong, through my body, to the carnal texture of the world, and the Flesh is defined precisely as this interdependence and mutual belonging: "The flesh we are speaking of is not matter. It is the coiling over of the visible upon the seeing body, of the tangible upon the touching body, which is attested in particular when the body sees itself, touches itself seeing and touching the things, such that, simultaneously, *as* tangible it descends among them, *as* touching it dominates them all and draws this relationship and even this double relationship from itself, by dehiscence or fission of its own mass".[5] We see here clearly how the different poles of the body, but also more generally of the everyday, find their right balance in the Flesh: the touching and the touched, the seeing and the seen, the body as subject and the body as object. The Flesh thus characterises the attitude of immersion, and Merleau-Ponty gives three examples of this—namely, sex, drugs and football[6]—which all follow the same logic I have described with recourse to the experience of dance.[7]

When I make love I desire the body of the other with which I become physically entwined. When I take drugs (Merleau-Ponty gives the example of the then popular hallucinatory drug mescaline), my senses interact with each other, so that I see voices, hear visions and touch odors. When I play football, I become incorporated in the game-field and feel as if the ball becomes an organ of my body. In all cases the limits of the inside and the outside, the body and the world, lose their distinctiveness and therefore express the ontological ambiguity of the body and of existence. But what about the attitude that sees the body as separated from the self and from the world and therefore tends towards psychological ambiguity? And where to locate the everyday in relation to these different attitudes?

EMBODIED REFLECTION AND
THE QUESTION OF NEGATIVITY

I claimed that when I am actually engaged in the ontological ambiguity of the body while dancing, I do not feel ambiguous at all, but rather immersed in the Flesh. The same applies to the examples given by Merleau-Ponty: when I make love, take hallucinatory drugs or play football, I get so absorbed in what I am doing that I do not feel the psychological ambiguity, nor do I have time or feel the need to reflect on it; I just act, or so it seems. It is only the phenomenologist who takes pleasure in regarding retrospectively and analysing, from a comfortable position, what it means for me to make love, take drugs or play football.

However, in the same way Heidegger placed immersed reflection at the heart of the everyday, so, too, does Merleau-Ponty introduce reflection into it. Although at first glance he may seem to be content with the harmonious, "pre-Falling" experiences of dance, sex, drugs and football, I argue that he actually reflects upon them to show that they *already* contain reflection in themselves:

It is true that we discover the unreflected. But the unreflected we go back to is not that which is prior to philosophy or prior to reflection. It is the unreflected which is understood and conquered by reflection. Left to itself, perception forgets itself and is ignorant of its own accomplishments. Far from thinking that philosophy is a useless repetition of life, I think, on the contrary, that it is the agency without which life would probably dissipate itself in ignorance of itself or in chaos. But this does not mean that reflection should be carried away with itself or pretend to be ignorant of its origins. By fleeing difficulties philosophy would only fail in its task.[8]

There is thus a double link between reflection and the unreflected: first, every perception, including one that is unreflected, either accomplishes something or is based upon prior accomplishments. As such, perception is always already a form of foundation that goes back to itself in a reflective yet immersed movement. Second, reflection can also act upon the unreflected from the outside, in a philosophical manner, and in this way help to elucidate the interdependence between the different strata of perception. This philosophical reflection is not immersed, and yet it has a crucial cultural, political and ethical significance, "teaching" perception a form of self-knowledge that would save it from disintegration and chaos.

The experiences of dance, sex, drugs and football may thus be unreflected in themselves, but they do teach us retrospectively to stop considering the body as a mere object, and the others as exterior to myself. Merleau-Ponty's reflection thus calls each one of us to "learn to see the world anew" (PhP, lxxxv/xxiii), to open up perception so that it would join the world and overcome the false opposition between subject and object. However, Merleau-Ponty is aware that everyday perception tends to resist this process of relearning. We are, he says, "obsessed with objective thought" (PhP, 413/457), so that the phenomenological ambition to teach us a better perception must fight a persistent objectivist attitude that governs not only science but also my very own everyday life, as shown already by Husserl.[9]

I dance, I make love, I take drugs, I play football. It is indeed crucial to reflect on the ambiguity hidden in these experiences, but is only philosophy capable of that? We saw in Heidegger, however, that immersed reflection can take place within the everyday. It is a "moment of negativity" that suspends some everyday activity and yet rejoins it after a while. Reflection goes hand in hand with negativity, and if we wish to understand how to reflect on the body, we must first see what role negativity plays in it.

According to Merleau-Ponty, it is not simply that the human being lacks foundation (as in Heidegger), but also that human foundation (namely, the body) is itself lacking. The body is, on the one hand, a solid foundation and the ultimate source of life for every man and woman. As far as I am concerned, there was no world prior to my existence, and there will be no world after it ends. The existence of the world depends on me, and I am its master. But, on the other hand, it is precisely my body that reminds me that I am not only a master but also a servant. The body is organic, a worldly ephemeral entity: it is born, grows up, gets old and finally dies. Moreover, my body is finite not just because it will eventually die but also because it has constant needs. The body practically always lacks something: it is thirsty, hungry, cold, hot, tired, aching, lonely, and so on. In all these various states I am reminded that the body is dependent upon its environment, so my pretension to totally master the world meets infinite obstacles on its way.

This double structure of a total mastery upon the world together with a total subordination to it is reflected in the body's ontological ambiguity. The body is touching and touched, it is constituting and constituted, it is a subject and an object. Ambiguity therefore reveals the force of the human being together with its weakness, and as such it tends to be repressed and transformed into *psychological* ambiguity. The oblivion of ontological ambiguity, according to Merleau-Ponty, is both the share of everyday perception and the share of philosophy (and, more generally, of the Western culture). Ever since Plato, save for a few exceptions which only prove the rule, philosophy has tended to regard the body as the negligible and unessential element of the human being, in contrast to its true and eternal essence—the soul. Merleau-Ponty wishes to rehabilitate the status of the body precisely by refuting the false dichotomy of body and soul. For him, the active mastery of the world does not stem from a pure "soul" or "mind", but rather from the body itself, which serves as both an active agent and a passive entity. The body perceives, acts, constructs, controls, desires. It is not a mere tool, but rather my very own way of being in the world and giving meaning to it. However, my body is simultaneously perceived, acted upon, constructed, controlled and desired. Ambiguity is inherent to the embodied existence in the world, and any attempt to refute or overcome it would be nothing but repression of what it is to be embodied.

When I dance, make love, take drugs or play football, I constitute my environment and am constituted by it. But in these situations I do not lack anything, and this is why I do not feel ambiguous. Instead, I have a strong feeling of mastery upon the world, accompanied by a sense of total belonging to it that effaces all differences between us. I am melted together with the dancing crowd, with my sex partner, with the football field or with the world in general. It is a unity which, when taken as a model of purity and extended towards the political sphere, contains the danger of leading to fascism. *Fascio* in Italian means "bundle": a unity which creates a new whole, erasing the distinctiveness of the individuals. As I argued in the previous chapter, a superficial reading of Heidegger (and Merleau-Ponty) may provoke the fascist temptation, especially in an era in which the everyday is felt as dull or suffocating in comparison with the vehemence of being one with the world. Fascism is thus facilitated by the distinction between the everyday and the extraordinary event, proposing to easily overcome the frustrating dichotomy by making the everyday itself into an arena of continuous and eventful unity.

A certain negativity must therefore be found within the ecstatic experience itself, such that it would relate to other experiences and would not pretend to be self-sufficient. Otherwise, for example, I may live a weekend full of wild experiences of sex and drugs, yet without the ability to connect them to the working week, which now looks ever so miserable. An experience too full goes hand in hand with an experience too dull. Just as I felt that my individuality had been fused into the crowd filling the dance floor, I feel during the week that my individuality is flattened and erased by my impersonal routine. I thus resort to using ready-made categories such as "weekend" and "working week", instead of trying to think of how to transform and overcome them. Is there a way to live ambiguity while still acknowledging negativity—lack, absence and distance?

THE MYSTERY OF THE PHANTOM LIMB

We saw in the previous chapter that Heidegger delineated several moments of "small" negativity as crucial to the foundation of the everyday, but he soon abandoned them in favor of "big" or radical negativity in the form of anxiety. Consequently, it was not clear if and how one can integrate negativity into everyday life. Merleau-Ponty, on the other hand, introduces the body as an archetype of negativity, but he, too, as I will try to show, pays more attention to radical negativity than to minor negativity, since the former is more evident and imposing than the latter. Curiously, however, he does not locate radical negativity in anxiety, but rather in what every body is sooner or later subject to— namely, *pathology*.

Indeed, when one reads the *Phenomenology of Perception*, one is struck by the proportionally large number of pages dedicated to the analysis of pathological cases. The reason for this is simple: pathology shows what everyday normality conceals, the lack and finitude of the body. In order to illustrate this idea, Merleau-Ponty takes a case of pathology inspired by Heidegger. Indeed, Heidegger has often been criticised for having neglected the role of the body in Dasein's exis- tence,[10] but this is not completely true, since there is one bodily organ that stands at the centre of his phenomenology—namely, the *hand*. The hand is the most useful organ for craft production, and as such it is emblematic of our practical attitude towards entities in the world. The worldly entities always need a hand to manipulate them actually and potentially, practically and theoretically. This is why they are charac- terised by Heidegger as ready-to-hand and present-at-hand, and we saw that it is the movement between these two categories that guarantees a harmonious everyday practice. Merleau-Ponty aims to better under- stand the role of the hand in the movement of the everyday, which leads him to ask: What happens when Dasein *loses* its hand? This may seem at first to be a joke at the expense of Heidegger, but Merleau-Ponty is totally serious. In order to understand the function of the body in ac- tions and events, he proposes to carefully examine the case of the loss of the hand, as it is this loss which requires one to confront the negativ- ity of the body and find unusual ways to use it and the world.

When a person loses a limb, one of the following related phenome- na is often found to occur: either the person experiences the feeling of a *phantom limb*—that is to say, a sensation of a real limb coming from the stump—or the person refuses to admit the mutilation in the first place, which is a phenomenon called *anosognosia*, meaning in Greek "unawareness of the disease" (PhP, 78–79/87–88). Merleau-Ponty in- itially evokes these phenomena to show that one cannot clearly distin- guish between the body and the soul, the physiological and the psycho- logical, since they act upon each other, and only their complicated interaction may explain the occurrence of the phantom limb and *ano- sognosia*. In other words, when I have a physiological problem it always has a psychological expression and vice versa, proving the unity—and ambiguity—of existence.

But the phantom limb and *anosognosia* reveal much more than the mere interaction between body and soul. They also reveal my attitude towards the *deficiency* of the body as what underlies my way of living in the world and interacting with it. Let us examine this crucial passage:

> To have a phantom limb is to remain open to all of the actions of which the arm alone is capable and to stay within the practical field which one had prior to the mutilation. . . . In the evidentness of this complete world in which manipulable objects still figure, in the force of movement that goes toward it and where the project of writing or playing the piano still figures, the patient finds the certainty of his [bodily] integrity. But at the very moment that the world hides his deficiency from him, the world cannot help but to reveal it to him. . . . At the same moment that my customary world gives rise to habitual intentions in me, I can no longer actually unite with it if I have lost a limb. Manipulable [*maniable*] objects, precisely insofar as they appear as manipulable, appeal to a hand [*main*] that I no longer have. Regions of silence are thus marked out in the totality of my body. The patient knows his disability [*déchéance*] precisely insofar as he is ignorant of it, and he ignores it precisely insofar as he knows of it. This is the paradox of all being in the world. (PhP, 84/94–95)

The mutilated patient can no longer get along with his or her habitual everyday movement, since the hand, responsible for so many projects and engagements, is suddenly gone. This could have opened him or her to new projects and engagements, inventing new ways of bodily gestures, but the patient cannot face the mutilation, negates it and sticks to the past world and its no-longer-possible projects. In this way the patient is reassured of the stability of the world and the integrity of his or her body, but only at the price of ignoring and passing over in silence every project that would involve the missing hand. The patient's movement in and with the world is consequently degraded, not only because the body has been mutilated, but mostly because the mutilation is not admitted as such. Merleau-Ponty describes this situation as *déchéance*, his French translation of Heidegger's *Verfallen*, the Falling. As we saw in the previous chapter, the Falling does not concern lack or negativity as such, but rather the inability to acknowledge and use them as an essential element in the foundation of the everyday. This mechanism of degradation now becomes more concrete with Merleau-Ponty, and, as he states at the end of the quotation, it does not stem from an accidental or hypothetical deficiency of the body, such as the case of the loss of the limb, but rather from the very condition of embodied being in the world.

Merleau-Ponty thus seems to propose an embodied version of Heidegger's analysis as to how and why one ceases to renew the movement of the everyday. In the same way that it is necessary to acknowledge the non-usability of the ready-to-hand in order to re-found and re-appropriate it by finding new ways to use it, so it is crucial to accept the essential insufficiency of the body in order to renew one's projects. Does this mean that the body is to be considered as an object or a tool? Yes and no. The body, as we already know, is *both* subject and object, both the user of the tool and the tool itself. It is this strange combination that makes the body such an emblematic figure of the foundation of the everyday. Yet the body tends to stick to the old foundation and repeat the same habits even when they are no longer possible:

> It is as though our body comprises two distinct layers, that of the habitual body and that of the actual body. Gestures of manipulation that appear in the first have disappeared in the second, and the problem of how I can feel endowed with a limb that I no longer have in fact comes down to knowing how the habitual body can act as a guarantee for the actual body. How can I perceive objects as manipulable when I can no longer manipulate them? The manipulable must have ceased being something that I currently manipulate in order to become something *one* can manipulate; it must have ceased being something *manipulable for me* and have become something *manipulable in itself.* Correspondingly, my body must be grasped not merely in an instantaneous, singular and full experience, but moreover under an aspect of generality and as an impersonal being. (PhP, 84–85/95)

This passage gives a remarkable account of the bodily foundation of the everyday: on the one hand, the body stands as an apparently stable pole of habits, movements, functions and repetitive projects. On the other hand, it needs to dynamically adjust itself to present reality, looking for new things to manipulate and new work to be done. Ideally, there is a continuous link between the habitual body (static foundation) and the actual body (dynamic foundation), the one permitting the other and vice versa. But in drastic cases of mutilation, such as the loss of one's arm, this link is severely damaged, so that past foundations no longer give place to new foundations. In fact, not only do handy tools become general objects, but the body itself also becomes an object, as everyday language clearly shows. It hides the unpleasant and threatening bodily existence beneath reassuring impersonal and causal phrases like the following: "Do not worry; *one* has a stomach-ache when *one* eats too much"; "Try to do some jogging; *one* feels so good when *one* is doing sport"; and so on. This is the language of the "they" or the "one", which does not regard the body as what ambiguously incorporates me in the world, but rather as a simple and isolated object that obeys physical and social rules. Merleau-Ponty shows that the "they" is not some mysterious and external instance that takes over my everyday possibilities, as it is in Heidegger, but rather an inherent tendency of the everyday to take past foundations as if they had always been there: objective and stable entities. It is the tendency to forget the double, ambiguous essence of the body, being both inside and outside, constituting and constituted.

This tendency, again, is not an experience unique to pathology; pathology only helps show it more clearly, since the negativity it presents (deficiency and finitude of the body) is radical as opposed to the "small" and almost imperceptible negativity of everyday life. One is rather led to deduce the latter from the former and understand the negativity of the everyday by examining pathological cases. Merleau-Ponty therefore adopts psychoanalytic terminology to connect the realm of pathology to the existential status of the body. He characterises the body as an "inborn complex" that leads to its *repression* as an obstacle, and which one does not find the force either to overcome or to give it up. One therefore remains blocked in "impersonal existence", which, I suggest, is equivalent to the inauthenticity described by Heidegger.[11] The easy external categories that were once fresh and personal are used as a way of bypassing the obstacle that is the body. In order to forget my unfulfilled needs, my not being whole, my situation as, so to speak, *always* lacking a hand, I must repress my bodily existence and isolate parts of my body, seeing them from now on as exterior, stable and eternal. My body itself, then, finally becomes a mere tool and a mere object, losing the movement which would connect it to my personal life.

To sum up, Merleau-Ponty's description of the loss of the limb has helped us understand the everyday as based upon negativity which tends to be ignored or repressed, thus leading to a deterioration of the movement of the everyday.[12] In order to deepen our understanding of the normal and the pathological attitudes towards the negativity of the body, I shall now examine the central case analysed by Merleau-Ponty along many chapters of the *Phenomenology of Perception*—that is, the case of the brain-damaged Schneider.

PATHOLOGY AND THE LOSS OF REFLECTION

Schneider was a German solider who had suffered a brain injury in the First World War. His peculiar and multiple symptoms made a number of physiologists study his case, particularly his personal doctor, Kurt Goldstein.[13] Merleau-Ponty examines this case and proposes a re-interpretation of it, aiming to find the common existential denominator of Schneider's apparently unrelated symptoms, which affected his intellectual, emotional, motor, visual and sexual life.

At first sight, the symptom Merleau-Ponty chooses to focus on seems to be minor: Schneider is incapable, especially when his eyes are shut, of conducting movements outside a concrete everyday situation. For instance, when he is asked to make a military salute, he engages his entire body in the situation; he stands up straight and assumes a demeanor of respect and obedience, as if his commander were really there. In order to conduct an isolated or abstract movement, Schneider thus needs to repeat the entire situation in which the movement normally takes place (PhP, 106–7/119–20). This harmless symptom actually reveals in the eyes of Merleau-Ponty a most interesting psychological and philosophical phenomenon—namely, the state of being imprisoned in the practical world without reflection. When Schneider, his eyes shut, is told to touch a specific part of his body, he cannot do so, but when a mosquito bites him he easily and spontaneously raises his hand and skillfully swats it (PhP, 105–6/118–19). Practical and spontaneous situations are the only ones that Schneider can recognise and act upon, being deprived of the ability to detach parts from the whole, the necessary condition for reflection and theory. When his eyes are open, he can easily mask his disability,[14] but when he shuts them he cannot recognise, detach and reflect upon the objects, such that he must be totally immersed in the situation in order to act: "I experience movements as a result of the situation, as the sequence of events themselves; my movements and I, we are, so to speak, merely a link in the unfolding of the whole, and I am scarcely aware of any voluntary initiative. . . . Everything works by itself" (PhP, 107/120). This description reminds us of Dasein's everyday world; yet it is a world consisting of only ready-to-hand entities which can never be transformed or reflected upon. This everyday world moves as if by itself, so although it looks harmonious, it is soon revealed to be an oppressive prison.

I claimed above that reflection is not necessarily an intellectual activity, but can also be immersed in everyday life. Immersed reflection remains simultaneously distant from and close to the world, the body and oneself; it has the capacity to detach a specific element from the totality of experience, not in order to freeze it, but, on the contrary, to create something new upon it. Immersed reflection thus permits one to be absorbed in the situation, on the one hand, but able to slightly transform it, on the other. This is the reason why Schneider's loss of reflection goes hand in hand with his inability to re-create the existing stock of objects and categories, for nothing new can be detached from the opaque mass of reality, and the only available objects are those which have already been founded before the mutilation. All Schneider can do now is mechanically repeat them. In this respect Schneider is not very different from the person suffering from a phantom limb, both being imprisoned in the past, unable in their present life to see any promise of the new.

Merleau-Ponty calls the capacity to renew the past and the present *projection*, an existential term borrowed from Heidegger and Sartre. Projection means throwing yourself from the past towards the future. More precisely, it is the ability to take one's past deeds and find in them the basis for future ones, a process which, when authentic, Heidegger calls *repetition* (*Wiederholung*). This repetition, as we have seen, does much more than simply repeat, since it also re-appropriates and re-creates the past in the light of the present and the future. Now, Merleau-Ponty claims that this repetitive process is nothing but the "movement of existence", a movement that I have tried to delineate through the term *foundation*. It is a movement in which you take what you have founded so far in order to found something new upon it, thus endlessly enriching and renewing your everyday life.

Why do I prefer the word *foundation* over *existence*?[15] One of the reasons for this is that *foundation* accentuates the ambiguity of the movement—that is, it has a double structure as a dynamic action (verb) which comes from and goes back to a rather static entity (noun). Similarly, I propose to use the term *reflection* rather than *projection* because the former underlines the *circular* character of the movement: my past life is reflected upon the present environment and possibilities, which are simultaneously reflected by it in a two-way movement. Projection, however, is a unidirectional beam, from the past to the future through the present, but it lacks the backward movement which would make it circular. Projection seems to keep the past intact (unless we speak of a double-projection), while reflection necessarily acts upon the past and changes it. It passes through a double mirror which stands between past foundation(s) and present circumstances, both poles acting upon each other. As a result, any reflection that I make transforms both the subject and the object, the past and the present, such that I never fully grasp myself without mediation. The best I can attain is my *reflected* self, [16] the image of the past created by the present, or the image of the present reflected through the past. I am always separated from myself by an invisible yet persistent screen, which actually defines me as a subject.

If we go back to Schneider and the person suffering from a phantom limb, we may say that both are imprisoned in what they have already acquired, and they cannot open themselves up to new projects, situations and significations. Both realise only one aspect of the ambiguity of the body—the constituted or founded pole—and are unable to activate their constituting or founding capacity. In other words, they use their past foundations as static entities, and they cannot reactivate them through a dynamic activity of foundation. As a result, the movement of foundation/reflection is slowed down in the case of the person suffering from a phantom limb, and it is almost completely halted in the case of Schneider. Whereas the former may still retrieve his or her capacity of foundation/reflection by accepting the mutilation, Schneider is irreversibly deprived of this function, and he thus serves as an extreme example of its loss.

What may Schneider's radical loss of reflection teach us positively about the role of reflection in the everyday? Earlier we saw that dance, sex, drugs and football are situations in which the ontological ambiguity of the body is fully realised and the mutual belongingness of the body and the world, of subject and object, comes to the fore. I asked whether something new is founded during such full experiences— whether something is reflected on and integrated into the everyday. We may now find a surprising answer to these questions by examining Schneider's sex life. If sex is presumably merely a "full" and self-enclosed experience that does not involve reflection at all, we would expect Schneider, who lacks the capacity of reflection, to have a normal or even enhanced sex life, free from unnecessary disturbing thoughts. Schneider, we might assume, would be able to get in touch with his "animal" or "instinctual" part and would spontaneously realise his desires. Yet, curiously, it is rather the opposite which turns out to be true:

> Obscene pictures, conversations on sexual topics, and the perception of a body fail to arouse any desire in him. The patient hardly ever kisses, and the kiss has no value of sexual stimulation for him. . . . In the sexual act intromission is never spontaneous. If his partner reaches orgasm first and moves away, the half-fulfilled desire vanishes. Things happen at each moment as if the subject did not know what to do. (PhP, 157/179)

Schneider's passivity and lack of interest in sex is not only psychological, since he also rarely has nocturnal emissions (PhP, 157/179), which are supposed to stem from a physiological mechanism. It is therefore the entire field of sexuality which is blocked for him.[17] Sexuality, for the human being, is revealed to be based upon something wider than a pure animal impulse. It involves imagination, virtuality and recognition of otherness. Schneider's lack of interest in sex shows how all these actually involve some form of reflection. In reflection one takes the given world and self, and, upon them, imagines something new, thus combining immersion and transcendence. Without this process I cannot make love, nor can I dance or play football.[18] All of these situations require an attunement to the current environment (a partner, music, the field, the ball), connecting some of its elements to each other and to the self, and transforming something in them. This transformation is not necessarily active, as the case of hallucinatory drugs shows, when I just need to let the hallucination penetrate me and make me float over the different possibilities and variations of the given world which remain hidden in everyday perception. But in most cases we find a combination of passivity and activity—letting myself be absorbed in the situation while being active enough to respond, when I make love, to the gestures of my partner and myself, thus creating a new act of lovemaking.

I thus suggest that every bodily gesture involves some degree of reflection. Although reflection may be purely intellectual, most of the time it is embodied and takes place within the everyday, even if one does not notice it playing a major role. A further illustration of this idea is given in another set of symptoms from which Schneider suffers: he has no ability or will to make new friends; he never spontaneously whistles or sings to himself; he does not have any opinion regarding politics, religion or other abstract matters (PhP, 159–60/182). All these attest once again to a lack of reflection and show how vast its influence upon practically every aspect of human life is. From a physical inability to locate a detached part of the body we finally arrive at a "mental" inability to reflect upon an abstract theme such as politics, and both cases are due to a lack of reflection as the ability to detach and reconnect elements in the world.

If this is so, what did Schneider's everyday life look like? The surprising answer is that it was apparently quite normal. Every day he went to a wallet factory where he was employed as a simple worker, and despite his various symptoms, his production rate was only a quarter less than the normal (PhP, 105/118). As long as he was not asked to go beyond his everyday mechanical routine, he mastered the situation almost perfectly, and yet it is reported that he had the feeling that his life was not his, as if everything came from the outside and happened independently of himself. In other words, he had the same feeling we found in Houellebecq's protagonists.

To conclude, I suggest that pathology has something important to tell us here about normal everyday life. In the introduction, I distinguished between a plastic everyday life and a mechanical everyday, the first consisting of a repetition that changes something in what it repeats, and the second consisting of a repetition that iterates exactly the same thing in a clockwork movement. I claimed that modernity is characterised by a difficulty to maintain a plastic movement of the everyday, since the foundation upon which an action or an event takes place does not manage to find the right form of repetition. Now, it seems that Schneider is nothing but a very extreme case of this problem, and as such his behavior is not completely strange to us. We, too, find it very difficult to innovate our everyday routine; we, too, find ourselves repeating time and again the same movement; we, too, are afraid of shutting our eyes and remaining in the dark, striving to control the world with our eyes wide open, choosing between ready-made objects instead of creating new ones. The difference between Schneider and us lies rather in the *degree* of stagnation, as well as in the ability to act upon it, an ability which is closely connected to the function of reflection.

THE LANGUAGE OF EVERYDAY FOUNDATION

Although Merleau-Ponty hints at a link between the patient suffering from a phantom limb, Schneider, and finally everyday "normal" perception, he still maintains a clear distinction between "normality" and "pathology". The "normal" person, rather than sharing something with Schneider or other patients, is presented as opposed to them: "For the normal person, the subject's intentions are immediately reflected in the perceptual field: they polarize it, put their stamp on it, or finally, effortlessly give birth there to a wave of significations. For the patient, the perceptual field has lost this plasticity" (PhP, 133/151). Reflection and plasticity are the share of the normal person alone, who consequently possesses a full, vital and effortless perception: "The normal person's projects polarize the world, causing a thousand signs to appear there, as if by magic, that guide action, as signs in a museum guide the visitor" (PhP, 115/129). But is it true that the "normal" always succeeds in maintaining this magic? Do we constantly give fresh sense to our everyday actions?[19]

Merleau-Ponty tends to present the normal movement of existence (foundation/reflection) as fully efficient, but he must admit time and again that it is actually deficient. This is particularly striking in the case of language. Thus, the normal person is supposed to spontaneously create his or her own linguistic categories (PhP, 130/148), but it soon appears that this creativity is more an ideal than an everyday reality: "We live in a world where speech is already *instituted*. We possess in ourselves ready-made significations for all these banal words [*paroles*]. They only give rise in us to second-order thoughts, which are in turn translated into other words that require no genuine effort of expression from us, and that will demand no effort of comprehension from our listeners" (PhP, 189/213).

The global movement of the everyday thus has an inherent tendency to slow down. Whatever is founded soon takes the appearance of something stable that does not necessitate a further foundation, but as a result it becomes to a certain degree external and objective. In Merleau-Ponty's words, "There is always a depersonalization at the heart of consciousness" (PhP, 139/158). In order to appropriate one's own foundations and make them personal, one needs to constantly re-found them—that is, to repeat the movement of the everyday and prevent it from becoming mechanical and external. As we have already seen with Heidegger, a foundation that is not picked up time and again becomes alienated from its founder. Within myself I find a foreign body that is nonetheless familiar, something I know well but that does not belong to me. Whereas this foreign body remains abstract in Heidegger, in Merleau-Ponty it really is a question of my concrete everyday body. The body is something into which I was born and which I did not choose: it is me and it is not me, and throughout my whole life I strive to appropriate and re-appropriate it.

Merleau-Ponty affirms that there is a constant struggle between personal and bodily existence: "Most of the time personal existence represses the organism without being able either to go beyond it or to renounce itself" (PhP, 86/97). We saw earlier why the body, representing deficiency and finitude, tends to be repressed. Instead of the laborious work of the foundation of the everyday, I pick an apparently solid and static foundation—for example, the objective body—attaining an illusion of a solid basis, but the price is alienation: alienation from my body, from my language and from my entire perceptive field.

Both Heidegger and Merleau-Ponty propose ways to escape the suffocating yet comfortable realm of what Heidegger call the "they" and Merleau-Ponty refers to as impersonal or instituted existence. But whereas Heidegger sees Dasein as based upon nothingness and radical negativity, Merleau-Ponty locates the basis of existence in the body, which is not a pure nothingness, but rather an ambiguous and fragile foundation. As a consequence, in order to get rid of "external" categories, I no longer need to annihilate my everyday world through anxiety, as was the case in Heidegger, but rather to re-attach myself to my body as the ambiguous vehicle of the movement of existence/foundation. But how exactly is one to do this?

I have examined earlier the experiences of dance, sex, drugs and football as possible ways to reconnect to the body and appropriate it, fully living the ontological ambiguity. The problem with these experiences is that the immersed reflection which they articulate is not linguistic. This is why Merleau-Ponty constantly seeks other cases in which the ontological ambiguity is more clear. Whereas pathology stands for an extreme case of lack of reflection, such that the ambiguity is seen as *frozen*, Merleau-Ponty identifies several figures that possess an *enhanced* capacity of reflection/foundation. These are the *baby* uttering its first word, the *lover* revealing his or her feelings, the *writer*, the *artist* and, of course, the *philosopher* (PhP, 530n7, 203/208n5, 229). All these use what Merleau-Ponty calls "speaking speech", in contrast to the everyday and common "spoken speech". They exploit the full potential of language and in this way overcome the tendency to remain only at its static and constituted pole. [20]

But what role does the body play in the life of these figures? How do they combine the two apparently distinct realms of body and language? On the one hand, language goes well beyond the body: it enables me to bypass my physical situation and arrive at the realm of words, which can invent imaginary times, places and creatures having nothing to do with the limited and weak body of their author. On the other hand, language has exactly the same structure as the body: I am born into it, I do not choose it, and yet through it I constitute my world. When I speak, I use ready-made words, and yet I pronounce them in utterances that could only be mine. I am thus touched by language and am touching it at one and the same time, moving between its constituted and constituting poles. Touching and touched, founding and founded—this is the double and ambiguous structure of both the body and language. Is it a mere coincidence?

This very difficult question is one of the mysteries of human existence. It is certain, however, that through language I acquire an objectivity that would not be possible otherwise, in a purely bodily existence. Language enables stable—sometimes all too stable—categories, and this is why it is characterised by Husserl as a *seduction* of which one should be wary,[21] in order to avoid the objectivist attitude. In the same way, Heidegger introduces the "they" that supplies general and ready-made categories, reassuring Dasein and allowing it to forget its negativity. Language consists of ready-made words that may flatten the richness of their origin and hide their movement in time and the inability to fully grasp the object they point to. But this process of stabilisation offered by language is not something to condemn or exorcise, since it equally allows one to bypass the purely corporal situation, to create new objects, new combinations, new connections between the body and the world. Foundation and reflection would therefore not be possible without language. The question is thus not how to attain a purely pre-objective realm, devoid of language or reflection, but rather how not to remain in a purely objectified one.[22]

It is here that the body may give answers to the questions raised by language. Indeed, every language and every culture has its own way of treating the body. Expressions, gestures, garments, fashion—all these radically change the relation of women, men and children to their own bodies and to the bodies of others. When I dance, make love, take drugs or play football, I tend to forget all that. I get absorbed in a corporal situation, supposedly free from the limits of language. These situations are often highly enjoyable, but they may be only a temporary escape from language. Can I learn from them new ways to relate the body to language? Can they help me retrieve my personal existence in the everyday world?

The role of these immersed experiences in Merleau-Ponty is analogous, I would suggest, to the role of anxiety in Heidegger. Both make the inauthentic or external categories disappear in favor of an authentic, yet mute, experience. But as much as it was unclear in Heidegger how to return from anxiety to the everyday, it is difficult to understand how to extract something from dance, sex, drugs and football and introduce it into everyday gestures. The "extraordinary" experience they represent seems to exclude the "ordinary" experience of everyday life, and we finally return to the same very modern opposition we were attempting to overcome.

REFLECTION, RETROACTION AND EVERYDAY TEMPORALITY

Modern French society has evolved through a series of revolutions— 1789, 1830, 1848, 1871, 1968—and these dates all signal crucial moments between which long periods of rigidity and repression often reigned. It is thus no coincidence that Merleau-Ponty compares the burst of a new artistic form to a political revolution.[23] He says that in both cases a new institution is achieved by discovering the contingent and arbitrary elements in the old one and taking action to replace it. This process, however, is endless by its definition. The new soon grows old, since it, too, is contingent, responding to precarious circumstances. It thus gives a false appearance of necessity which can be discovered as such only through another revolution, which would eventually create new apparently permanent categories, and so on indefinitely.

Now, does this model apply to everyday life? Do I need to constantly revolutionise it, or can I achieve a mode of silent renewal? In the last chapter of *Phenomenology of Perception*, which is entitled "Freedom", Merleau-Ponty presents revolution as a rather involuntary process (PhP, 467–73/514–20). It is a mysterious movement in which parts of the old foundation are substituted by new ones, fitter for the present situation, until these, too, deteriorate and eventually, through a new revolution, give way to new foundations. In the last pages of his book, Merleau-Ponty moves from political revolution to a personal revolution, and he calls on each one of us to gain freedom and transcend his or her present situation precisely by assuming it in the first place: "It is by being what I am at present, without any restrictions and without holding anything back, that I have a chance at progressing. . . . We need have no fear that our choices or our actions restrain our freedom, since choice and action alone can free us from our anchors" (PhP, 482–83/529–30). But is this enough? It seems that in order to realise this I need reflection, and yet not *any* reflection. Let us look at this difficult, yet crucial, passage: "Just as reflection borrows its desire for absolute adequation from the perception that makes something appear . . . so too does freedom become mired in the contradictions of commitment and does not notice that it would not be freedom without the roots that it thrusts into the world" (PhP, 483/530).

Merleau-Ponty draws here a direct line between reflection and freedom, but he does so through an opposition between "bad" reflection and freedom and "good" or true ones. Both reflection and freedom have a tendency to transgress their limits, and so to deteriorate and lose their vitality. Reflection goes awry when it fails to recognise its necessary distance from its object, a distance that makes reflection be not an exact representation but rather a creative process. Similarly, freedom loses its strength when it ignores its multiple and ambiguous bases in the world—it is always "imprisoned" in some old foundations which can never be fully transcended. In each of these cases, it is the negation of partiality and distance which makes reflection and freedom lose their plasticity and become trapped in an impossible ideal of absolute adequation or harmony. It is not possible to be free without also acknowledging that freedom is a continuous work of engagement/disengagement. And this work is equivalent to the work of reflection understood as immersed—that is, a part of the action rather than a purely theoretical procedure.

For Merleau-Ponty, phenomenology should serve as such an engaged and practical reflection, yet in a way that would make reflection "radical" (PhP, lxxxiv–lxxxv/xxii–xxiii). In the very last lines of *Phenomenology of Perception*, he even confers on this philosophical/radical reflection the task of teaching us to "see the world anew" by "destroying itself as an isolated philosophy" (PhP, 483/530), but the condition for its radicality is that reflection remains "conscious of its own dependence on an unreflected life that is its initial, constant and final situation" (PhP, lxxviii/xvi). Rather than an objective representation, phenomenology should be a self-conscious process in which the unreflected is revealed but also created.[24] To a large extent, this might be thought to evoke Heidegger's description of the circular movement

between the ready-to-hand and the present-at-hand: an everyday process of immersed reflection that permits a *vision* of tools in order to
better *use* them. Radical reflection consists of this circular movement
but adds to it self-awareness as a guarantee for the freedom of the act:
not because radical reflection can do whatever it wishes, but rather
because it stands as a dam against the everyday tendency to naïvely
accept ready-made categories. Radical reflection is thus both immersed
and aware of its immersion.[25] However, is radical reflection a part of
the everyday or merely a philosophical and artificial procedure?

In his posthumous work *The Visible and the Invisible*, Merleau-
Ponty returns to his discussion on reflection and gives us a hint at its
temporal structure: "What is given is not a massive and opaque world,
or a universe of adequate thought; it is a reflection which turns back
over the density of the world in order to clarify it, but which, coming
second (*après coup*), reflects back to it only its own light".[26] Reflection
is characterised here through a temporal gap between itself and its
object, since it comes "second", or, more precisely, *après coup*. I will
discuss this term at length in the next chapter through an analysis of its
Freudian origin in *Nachträglichkeit*, normally translated as "deferred
action", "belatedness" or "afterwardsness".[27] However, for reasons that
will become clear later, I shall use the term *deferred retroaction*, pointing to a two-way temporal mode in which the past determines the
present as much as the present determines the past. In reflection as
deferred retroaction, the past is simultaneously the source and the target
of the action, changing through reflection itself. Indeed, reflection is
often immersed, but its immersion is of a very particular kind, since it
does not completely coincide with the object: it reveals it not as it
originally was, but in the transformed mode which is, as I will show
later, the only way to gain access to it in the first place. In fact, any
reflection involves a certain amount of deferred retroaction, and the
persistent question is how often such a circular reflection takes place in
everyday life.

The chapter in *Phenomenology of Perception* entitled "Temporality" surprisingly reveals that the entire structure of time is based upon
deferred retroaction, although Merleau-Ponty does not explicitly mention this term.[28] He rather prefers the Husserlian notions of *retention*
and *protention*—that is, the prolongations of the "now" into the past
and future,[29] and Heidegger's concept of *ekstase*—that is, time as a
self-transcendence, opening up to other times. These three terms indi-
cate a concept of time that no longer moves one way, from the past to

the future, but both from the future into the past and from the past into the future (PhP, 437/481). When I act in the present, I maintain the past (through retention) and anticipate the future (through protention). It is only from the perspective of *objective* time, the time of the clock, that there is a chronological succession, whereas in what Merleau-Ponty calls "primordial time" the past is equally a future which no longer is, and the future is a past which is not yet.

"Time is not a line, but rather a network of intentionalities", affirms Merleau-Ponty, referring to Husserl's scheme of time, in which every moment contains infinite "profiles" (*Abschattungen*), which are "past moments" (retentions) and "future moments" (protentions) (PhP, 440/484).[30] However, this intentional network must have a "zero point" from which it is experienced and which is my current "now". Time is thus based upon the presence of the "now", but this presence is intimately linked to the absence or non-being of the past and the future, which are given only as profiles. Time is not a stable being, but rather a becoming: it is necessarily incomplete and constantly escapes, and yet every one of its moments contains all the others and acts upon them.

This combination of presence and absence makes the structure of time similar to that of the body, and Merleau-Ponty compares the passing of a moment to a corporal gesture (PhP, 442, 444–45/487, 489). However, in the same way that the objective body came to negate and repress the primordial body and its deficiency, so objective perception ignores the necessary absence that constitutes time: "The objective world is too full for there to be time" (PhP, 434/478). Like the body, time is finally split into a primordial figure that is "true" and an objective or objectified figure that Merleau-Ponty qualifies as "false". Like the body, the objective figure of time tends to characterise the everyday, whereas its primordial figure characterises radical reflection or other creative acts that *transcend* the everyday.

What is the place, then, of radical reflection and deferred retroaction in the everyday? Is there a way to move, within the everyday, from objective to primordial time? These questions are crucial for the understanding not only of the everyday but also of the possibility to integrate in it such immersed experiences as dance, sex, drugs and football. Although they contain a certain degree of embodied reflection, these experiences seem to be too full and overwhelming to permit linkage to other moments and parts of life. But if deferred retroaction—as a mode of reflection—stands at the centre of time, then these full moments, too, can be injected with some *retroactive* presence/absence and eventually integrated into the everyday through a certain mode of repetition. In the following chapters I will elaborate on the role and possibility of deferred retroaction in the everyday in general, and in the modern everyday in particular. But before this happens, let me conclude these two phenomenological chapters with a few words on phenomenology and modernity.

THE PHENOMENOLOGY OF THE EVERYDAY AND THE QUESTION OF MODERNITY

Phenomenology of Perception was published in 1945, which partly explains why its unquestionable hero is Antoine de Saint-Exupéry, the famous author of *The Little Prince*, who was killed as a war-pilot during the Second World War. Merleau-Ponty cites willingly Saint-Exupéry's *Flight to Arras* to illustrate the rich and full perception a war-pilot needs to adopt in his missions. He even closes the *Phenomenology of Perception* with a declaration that "it is precisely here that we must remain silent, for only the hero fully lives his relation with men and with the world, and it is hardly fitting for another to speak in his name" (PhP, 483/530). The philosopher should thus clear the stage for the hero. However, Merleau-Ponty seems to forget that a war-pilot is, justly, a pilot of *war*, and that in moments of peace, when the sublime efforts taken in pursuit of a noble end are no longer necessary, the body tends again towards an everyday oblivion.

To better understand the everyday, we must see it not as the ordinary, which is symmetrically opposed to the extraordinary and full, but rather as a positive phenomenon in its own right. We have encountered some everyday mechanisms in all three phenomenologists discussed above: first a theoretical suspension in Husserl, then an everyday suspension as immersed reflection in Heidegger, and finally embodied reflection and deferred retroaction in Merleau-Ponty. We likewise saw that it is always a certain negativity within the everyday that may lead to a foundation of new meanings, actions and projects, re-appropriating the everyday and renewing its movement of foundation. However, this negativity tends to be ignored or repressed in the everyday by adopting objective categories—that is, by repeating the same old meanings without seeing the need to renew them. This everyday tendency makes all three phenomenologists finally abandon the everyday in favor of a sphere of authenticity or full experience, a sphere in relation to which the everyday can be nothing but an inauthentic shadow: the stubborn ordinary which comes at the end of the extraordinary.

In order to remain within the everyday and understand not only its basic mechanisms but also their transformation in modernity, I propose to adopt for the rest of the book a different, complementary methodological approach. The thought of Freud and Benjamin will allow us to better comprehend the negativity that stands at the basis of the everyday, and also to see how the place of negativity has changed in modernity. Whereas until now negativity was articulated through such figures as deficiency, lack, finitude or distance—that is, the realm of the *too little*—I will now aim to show that modernity is equally characterised as an era that proposes *too much*. These two are in fact inter-dependent elements, as we have already seen with what Durkheim called the "malady of infiniteness": when there is too much choice, one feels deprived of all the unchosen possibilities.

In the next chapter I will follow Freud's theory of trauma to show that trauma consists of a penetration of dangerous energies into what Freud calls the "psychic apparatus". The everyday will be discovered not only as a sphere of integration of stimuli but also as a mechanism of defense against them, with deferral and repetition as its basic tools. These notions will allow us, thereafter, to explicitly move, in the two closing chapters of the book, to an analysis of the shocks of modernity and the possibility of integrating them into the everyday through deferral and repetition.

NOTES

1. Maurice Merleau-Ponty, *Phenomenology of Perception*, trans. Donald A. Landes (London and New York: Routledge, 2012), 95. See also the former translation: *Phenomenology of Perception*, trans. Colin Smith (London: Routledge, 2002), 106. Henceforth abbreviated PhP followed by the page numbers of the Landes translation and the Smith translation. I use here as a rule the Landes translation, except places where I found the old translation more accurate. See also Edmund Husserl, *Cartesian Meditations*, trans. D. Cairns (The Hague: Martinus Nijhoff, 1960); Edmund Husserl, *Ideas Pertaining to a Pure Phenomenology and to a Phenomenological Philosophy. Second Book: Studies in the Phenomenology of Constitution*, trans. R. Rojcewicz and A. Schuwer (Dordrecht: Kluwer, 1989), 152–53.

2. Simone de Beauvoir, *Memoirs of a Dutiful Daughter*, trans. James Kirkup (New York: Penguin Books, 1963), 246. Merleau-Ponty is presented by Beauvoir under the cover name "Jean Pradelle".

3. For an insightful analysis of illness as a variant of the phenomenological reduction, see Havi Carel, *Illness* (Stockfield: Acumen, 2008). For a deconstructive perspective on illness, see Jean-Luc Nancy, "The Intruder", in *Corpus*, trans. R. A. Rand (New York: Fordham University Press, 2008), 161–73.

4. See Maurice Merleau-Ponty, "Eye and Mind", trans. Carleton Dallery, in *The Primacy of Perception*, ed. James E. Edie (Evanston, IL: Northwestern University Press, 1964), 159–90; Maurice Merleau-Ponty, *The Visible and the Invisible*, trans. Alphonso Lingis (Evanston, IL: Northwestern University Press, 1968). For a classical analysis of Merleau-Ponty's notion of the Flesh, see M. C. Dillon, *Merleau-Ponty's Ontology* (Bloomington: Indiana University Press, 1988).

5. Merleau-Ponty, *The Visible and the Invisible*, 146.

6. See Merleau-Ponty's analysis of sexuality (PhP, 156–178/178–201), drugs (PhP, 237–38, 294, 356/265–66, 328, 397), and football (Maurice Merleau-Ponty, *The Structure of Behavior*, trans. Alden L. Fisher [Boston: Beacon Press, 1963], 168).

7. There are, of course, several major differences between Merleau-Ponty's early and later works. For a discussion of these, see Eran Dorfman, *Réapprendre à voir le monde: Merleau-Ponty face au miroir lacanian* (Dordrecht: Springer, 2007), 261–85; Lawrence Hass, *Merleau-Ponty's Philosophy* (Bloomington: Indiana University Press, 2008), 74–99, 124–45; Renaud Barbaras, *The Being of the Phenomenon: Merleau-Ponty's Ontology*, trans. Ted Toadvine and Leonard Lawlor (Bloomington: Indiana University Press, 2004), 3–18, 147–73.

8. Maurice Merleau-Ponty, "The Primacy of Perception and Its Philosophical Consequences", trans. James M. Edie, in *The Primacy of Perception*, 16. Translation modified.

9. In a previous work I examined this project of "learning to see the world anew" and suggested to complement it with Lacanian theory. See Dorfman, *Réapprendre à voir le monde*.

10. Heidegger himself evoked Sartre's critique on him and interpreted it as a misunderstanding of his ontology (Martin Heidegger, *Zollikon Seminars: Protocols–Conversations–Letters*, trans. Franz K. Mayr and Richard R. Askay [Evanston, IL: Northwestern University Press, 2001], 231). See also Kevin A. Aho, *Heidegger's Neglect of the Body* (Albany: State University of New York Press, 2009); Michel Haar, *The Song of the Earth: Heidegger and the Grounds of the History of Being*, trans. R. Lilly (Bloomington: Indiana University Press, 1993), 34–35; David Farrell Krell, *Daimon Life: Heidegger and Life-Philosophy* (Bloomington: Indiana University Press, 1992), 52; Didier Franck, "Being and the Living", in *Who Comes after the Subject?*, ed. E. Cadava, P. Connor and J.-L. Nancy (London: Routledge, 1991), 144–46. For interesting Heideggerian answers to these critiques, see David R. Cerbone, "Heidegger and Dasein's 'Bodily Nature': What Is the Hidden Problematic?", *International Journal of Philosophical Studies* 8, no. 2 (2000): 209–30; Richard R. Askay, "Heidegger, the Body, and the French Philosophers", *Continental Philosophy Review* 32 (1999), 29–35.

11. Merleau-Ponty distinguishes, though not systematically, between the "pre-personal" and the "impersonal" aspect of the body. He tends to present the first as that from which one emerges (the pre-objective) and the latter as that into which one falls (the objective).

12. Indeed, there is today an effective purely physiological therapy to the the phenomenon of the phantom limb, which consists in mirroring the healthy limb as to "confuse" the brain and make it understand the new body-scheme. However, it is striking to note how close the physiological descriptions of this process are to Merleau-Ponty's stress on the need to accept the loss. This is, for instance, how V. S. Ramachandran explains the success of the therapy: "A simple mirror box had exorcised a phantom. How? . . . When faced with such a welter of conflicting sensory inputs . . . the brain just gives up and says, in effect, 'To hell with it; there is no arm'. The brain resorts to denial" (V. S. Ramachandran, *The Tell-Tale Brain: Unlocking the Mystery of Human Nature* [London: Windmill Books, 2012], 34).

13. For the original case studies upon which Merleau-Ponty relied (now available online), see Adhémar Gelb and Kurt Goldstein, "Psychologische Analysen hirnpatholo-

gischer Falle auf Grund von Untersuchungen Hirnverletzer", *Zeitschrift für die gesamte Neurologie und Psychiatrie* 41 (1918): 1–142; Kurt Goldstein, "Über die Abhängigkeit der Bewegungen von optischen Vorgängen", *Monatsschrift für Psychiatrie und Neurologie* 54 (1923): 141–94. Goldstein and Gelb have been criticised in the following years for having relied on this single case who seemed to some "more like the platonic idea of a brain-injured patient than a patient himself" (H.-L. Teuber, "Kurt Goldstein's Role in the Development of Neuropsychology", *Neuropsychologia* 4 [1966]: 306). See also Georg Goldenberg, "Goldstein and Gelb's Case Schn.: A Classic Case in Neuropsychology?", in *Classic Cases in Neuropsychology*, ed. C. Code, C. W. Wallesch, Y. Joanette and A. R. Lecours (Hove: Psychology Press, 2003), 2:281–300. For a methodological critique of Merleau-Ponty's treatment of the case, see Thomas Baldwin, "Merleau-Ponty's Phenomenological Critique of Natural Science", *Royal Institute of Philosophy Supplement* 72 (2013): 203–6.

14. In fact, Schneider also had numerous sight problems such that, for instance, he needed to touch and manipulate objects in order to recognise what they were. There is thus a strong interdependence between seeing and touching, as discussed by Gelb and Goldstein.

15. In the 1950s, Merleau-Ponty himself preferred to use the term "institution" (borrowed from Husserl's *Stiftung*), which is closer to "foundation" (*Fundierung*). See Maurice Merleau-Ponty, *Institution and Passivity: Course Notes from the Collège de France (1954–1955)*, trans. Leonard Lawlor and Heath Massey (Evanston, IL: Northwestern University Press, 2010).

16. Merleau-Ponty, throughout *Phenomenology of Perception*, tries to offer an alternative to Sartre's *Being and Nothingness* with its rigid and exclusive poles of the reflective and the unreflected (see, for instance, Jean-Paul Sartre, *Being and Nothingness*, trans. Hazel Barnes [New York: Simon & Schuster, 1956], 39). As we saw above, for Merleau-Ponty the unreflected is necessarily conditioned by reflection, so the two have no independent existence. It is probably Jacques Lacan who took this idea in the most radical form, claiming in his "Mirror Stage" essay that the reflected form of the subject is the starting point of the world of vision as we know it. See Jacques Lacan, "The Mirror Stage as Formative of the Function of the I as Revealed in Psychoanalytic Experience", in *Écrits: A Selection*, trans. Alan Sheridan (London: Tavistock, 1977), 1–7.

17. Judith Butler severely criticises Merleau-Ponty's analysis of Schneider's sexuality, claiming that it is based upon a heterosexual ideology of the male as supposedly active, dominant and objectifying the female body. I totally agree with Butler that Merleau-Ponty tends to set a "normal" ideal upon which he considers pathology, but I believe that rather than dismissing or deconstructing Merleau-Ponty, we should take his analyses of pathology as an integral part of normality. In this way we may arrive at a better understanding both of socially constructed ideals of the body and the empirical inability to achieve them, which leads to their transgression. The case of Schneider may describe a man who finds himself not "manly" enough, but the problem is that, exactly as the amputated patient, he is not able to benefit from his loss to change his ideas of sexuality. See Judith Butler, "Sexual Ideology and Phenomenological Description: A Feminist Critique of Merleau-Ponty's *Phenomenology of Perception*", in *The Thinking Muse*, ed. J. Allen and Iris M. Young (Bloomington: Indiana University Press, 1989), 85–100.

18. The opposite case of Schneider is that of Chuck Knoblauch, the baseball player who, due to an unexplained pathology, started to reflect upon his throwing the ball and consequently hit the crowd instead of the first base. This case has been debated by Hubert Dreyfus and John McDowell, the former deducing that reflection is not involved in coping skills, and any introduction of it would only disturb them (Hubert L. Dreyfus, "The Return of the Myth of the Mental", *Inquiry* 50, no. 4 [2007], 354). McDowell,

94 *Chapter 2*

however, sees this case as proving that "when mindedness gets detached from immersion in activity, it can be the enemy of embodied coping" (John McDowell, *The Engaged Intellect* [Cambridge, MA: Harvard University Press, 2009], 325). I tend to agree with McDowell here, putting the emphasis not on one of the poles (immersion/reflection), but rather on their relationship.

19. In a radio broadcast from 1948, Merleau-Ponty claims himself that normality is only an ideal: "In the case of children, primitive people, the sick, or more so still, animals, the world which they occupy—insofar as we can reconstruct it from the way they behave—is certainly not a coherent system. By contrast, that of the healthy, civilised, adult human being strives for such coherence. Yet the crucial point here is that he does not attain this coherence: it remains an idea, or limit, which he never actually manages to reach. It follows that the 'normal' person must remain open to these abnormalities of which he is never entirely exempt himself; he must take the trouble to understand them. He is invited to look at himself without indulgence, to rediscover within himself the whole host of fantasies, dreams, patterns of magical behaviour and obscure phenomena which remain all-powerful in shaping both his private and public life and his relationships with other people" (Maurice Merleau-Ponty, *The World of Perception*, trans. Olivier Davis [London and New York: Routledge, 2004], 72–73). It is remarkable to note, however, that in the eyes of Merleau-Ponty, abnormality only inspires fantasy and magic and never rigidity and disenchantment.

20. See Thomas Baldwin, "Speaking and Spoken Speech", in *Reading Merleau-Ponty: On Phenomenology of Perception*, ed. Thomas Baldwin (London and New York: Routledge, 2007), 87–103.

21. Edmund Husserl, "The Origin of Geometry", in Maurice Merleau-Ponty, *Husserl at the Limits of Phenomenology*, ed. and trans. Leonard Lawlor and Bettina Bergo (Evanston, IL: Northwestern University Press, 2002), 100.

22. See Emmanuel Alloa, *La Résistance du sensible: Merleau-Ponty critique de la transparence* (Paris: Éditions Kimé, 2008), 45–68; Françoise Dastur, *Chair et langage: Essais sur Merleau-Ponty* (Paris: Encre Marine, 2002).

23. PhP, 471/517. See also Maurice Merleau-Ponty, *The Prose of the World*, trans. John O'Neill (Evanston, IL: Northwestern University Press, 1973), 71.

24. "Reflection does not work backward along a pathway already traveled in the opposite direction by constitution, and the natural reference of the matter to the world leads us to a new conception of intentionality" (PhP, 253/283).

25. On this theme, see Eran Dorfman, "Freedom, Perception and Radical Reflection", in *Reading Merleau-Ponty: On Phenomenology of Perception*, ed. Thomas Baldwin (London and New York: Routledge, 2007), 139–51.

26. Merleau-Ponty, *The Visible and the Invisible*, 35.

27. Merleau-Ponty was probably aware of the Freudian notion, since it was frequently discussed by his friend Jacques Lacan on many occasions during the 1950s. See, for example, Jacques Lacan, *The Seminar of Jacques Lacan, Book I: Freud's Papers on Technique, 1953–1954*, trans. John Forrester (New York and London: Norton, 1988), 191, 217.

28. For a similar line of thought, see Mauro Carbone, *The Thinking of the Sensible: Merleau-Ponty's A-philosophy* (Evanston, IL: Northwestern University Press, 2004), esp. 1–13; Mauro Carbone, *An Unprecedented Deformation: Marcel Proust and the Sensible Ideas*, trans. Niall Keane (Albany: State University of New York Press, 2010), 23–32.

29. For a highly original analysis of temporality in Husserl with relation to Freudian *Nachträglichkeit*, see Nicholas Smith, *Towards a Phenomenology of Repression: A Husserlian Reply to the Freudian Challenge* (Stockholm: Stockholm University, 2010), 176–98.

30. See Edmund Husserl, *On the Phenomenology of the Consciousness of Internal Time (1893–1917)*, trans. John Barnett Brough (Dordrecht: Kluwer, 1991), 238. Derrida famously criticised Husserl's ideal of presence; yet Merleau-Ponty insists upon the necessary absence in every presumed presence, which is probably the reason why Derrida almost never refers to the work of Merleau-Ponty, being both too close and too remote from his own theory of absence as *différance*. See Jacques Derrida, *Voice and Phenomenon*, trans. Leonard Lawlor (Evanston, IL: Northwestern University Press, 2011).

Chapter Three

Trauma, Deferral and Repetition in Freud

Freud is primarily known today for his discovery of the unconscious and his exploration of human sexuality. Such terms as the id, ego, superego, Oedipus complex, castration anxiety, slips of the tongue, repression—all these notions have become common figures of speech in Western culture. However, Freud's theory has been rejected, at least in its initial form, by most scientists and academic psychologists, who consider it devoid of rigorous empirical validity.

Why do I propose, then, to see Freud as a theorist of the modern everyday? Even if one rejects Freudian theory as dated or invalid, one cannot deny that it is still practically used on a daily basis by millions of people who have integrated its vocabulary into their everyday language. Psychoanalysis seems to have managed to capture and incarnate something crucial about the modern condition. Is it something about sexuality? Early childhood? The unconscious? I suggest that it is rather its notion of the psychic apparatus as a defensive mechanism in a hostile yet seductive everyday environment.

As we saw in the introduction with Simmel, the modern city has been conceived at the turn of the twentieth century as the site of intensified nervous stimulation. Indeed, the city never constituted an active and explicit role in Freud's theory, since he aimed to give a universal account of the human being as such, but it has nevertheless always stood in the background of his writings: the bourgeois women and men of Vienna served as the raw material upon which the adventures of the unconscious and sexuality took place. I therefore propose to shift the accent from the foreground of Freud's theory to that which lies beneath it—that is, to the psychic apparatus insofar as it tries to adapt itself to a rapidly changing everyday environment. It is an environment that offers both too much and too little, a paradoxical combination that will be investigated in this chapter.

When thinking about Freud and the everyday, one would expect an analysis of Freud's work from 1901, *The Psychopathology of Everyday Life* (SE 6:1–279). Freud's book describes and explores a variety of "pathological" mechanisms that are actually common in everyday life, such as the forgetting of names, slips of the tongue, errors, bungled actions and superstitions. In all of these, pathology stems from an unconscious and repressed content that often has something to do with sexuality. However, this idea has, since Freud's time, become so common that only few would hesitate to admit that they "repress" sexual or other fantasies. It seems that sexuality has become much less of a taboo than it was, but perhaps, as Foucault famously claims, it has never really been one in the first place. [1]

In what follows I will show that repression is closely connected to trauma, and although Freud has initially located these two in the field of sexuality, the mechanisms he elaborates actually pertain to an everyday reality that has become too overwhelming. Sexuality is only one of the instances that play a role in a traumatic everyday reality, and I will therefore focus on the global structure in which is it presented—namely, the psychic apparatus. I will begin with Freud's early model of the apparatus and then show how he changed it after the First World War, moving from a concept of a unique sexual trauma to a vision of the modern everyday as generally shocking.

THE FIRST MODEL OF THE PSYCHIC APPARATUS

The psychic apparatus is conceived of as a receptive mechanism, and it was first theorised by Freud in various letters and manuscripts he sent to his Berlin friend Wilhelm Fliess in the 1890s. The most elaborate model is presented in a long manuscript from 1895, posthumously published under the title *Project for a Scientific Psychology*. In this text Freud describes the process through which the psychic apparatus handles external stimuli. The language of the model is indeed extremely technical and juxtaposes neurological and psychological terms, but the principles it suggests are highly relevant to the mechanisms of everyday foundation I am trying to develop here. It is thus worthwhile becoming acquainted with this model despite its obscurity, as it will serve us in various forms in the remainder of the book.

The basic activity that takes place in the psychic apparatus is the movement from perception to reaction. When a stimulus enters the apparatus from the sense organs,[2] it is first consciously perceived through *primary perception*. It then passes through different unconscious layers of neurons, until it finally arrives at the internal end of the apparatus, where it becomes conscious again and provokes a *motor* reaction in order to discharge the stimulus (SE 1:312–17). For example, I hear a noise coming from behind me; I then process and understand it as someone calling my name, and finally I respond by turning to see who is calling me.

The distinction between primary perception and motor reaction lies in the fact that in every given moment we receive a huge amount of stimuli that we cannot completely absorb if our organism is to maintain normal functioning. We therefore need to select the right stimuli to react to; although we are vaguely conscious of many stimuli in our primary perception, we can concentrate upon, process and finally react to only very few of them. I hear, for instance, many noises in my environment, but I need to react only to the most relevant ones which concern me.

The sense organs at the external end of the apparatus not only absorb stimuli but also serve as *screens* against quantity (energy) and as *sieves* for the qualitative characteristics of the stimulus. Their main function is to absorb and pass the appropriate quality (what is perceived)[3] and to block much of the quantity (how much is perceived). In this way, only a manageable amount of sampled stimuli would finally arrive at the neurons at the internal end of the apparatus, which are highly sensitive (SE 1:313). These neurons therefore need to be protected such that the psychic apparatus is not simply a receptive mechanism, but equally a mechanism of defense, and the entire apparatus is engaged in the work of screening. Freud describes the vast domain between the two poles of the apparatus—the sense organs at the external end and elaborate consciousness at the internal end—as a differentiated complex of neurons equipped with *contact barriers* through which stimuli must pass in order to penetrate consciousness in a safe form.

Yet the stimuli do something more than simply pass through the contact barriers of the neurons: in fact, every such passage influences and changes the barriers. This alteration, according to Freud, is a form of *registration* (*Umschrift*), which retains the passage of particular stimuli together with different associations of other stimuli, according to the context and circumstances of the passage. This allows a constant fine-tuning and differentiation of the psychic neurons, the apparatus constantly shaping and reshaping itself to adapt to external reality. So the next time a particular stimulus enters the apparatus, its passage is conditioned and facilitated by its previous registrations (SE 1:300). The contact barriers thus have *memory*—or rather, they *are* memory, defined as a dynamic set of filters which register every stimulus passing through them and adjust themselves to it in order to facilitate or inhibit the passage of similar stimuli in the future. [4]

Freud thus gives us an original scheme of perception, memory and consciousness, whose most peculiar characteristic is that only stimuli which do *not* smoothly reach the internal end of the apparatus are recorded as memory traces. [5] Otherwise, when the perception is too easily generated, it "does not persist for long and disappears towards the motor side; nor, since it is allowed to pass through, does it leave any memory behind it" (SE 1:313). A too banal perception does not leave an impression and fades away unnoticed. The condition for the creation of memory is thus the encounter of *obstacles* in the passage towards consciousness.

With Freud's model of the psychic apparatus we can now better understand the scheme of the everyday as elaborated in the previous chapters. I have presented the integration of actions and events into one's everyday life as being facilitated by minor suspensions and immersed reflection. Suspension takes place only when something does *not* behave as expected, and it is precisely the *abnormality* of things that leads to a certain detachment and reflection, yet one that is immersed in and regains the global movement of the everyday. Now, for Freud, this suspension and reflection are carried out by giving the stimuli proper "names" and memories. This enables the discharge of the stimuli through certain reactions. [6] The proper "name" would permit a smooth perception of the stimulus the next time it appears, and the more this perception is repeated, the more it becomes a habit and recedes to the background.

Freud does not actually speak of names, but rather of *Vorstellung*, translated as "idea" by James Strachey, but a more accurate translation would be *representation*—that is, the registration of stimulus that persists when the stimulus is no longer there. The aim of Freud's method is therefore to give proper language to representations in order to facilitate their processing and make them conscious. The problem is that representations somehow tend to get "stuck" within the apparatus with no adequate name, and in what follows I will try to explain how that can actually happen.

LOST IN (NON)TRANSLATION: THE ORIGIN OF DEFERRED RETROACTION

In a letter to Fliess dated 6 December 1896, Freud describes the trajectory of every stimulus as consisting of three consecutive registrations in three successive layers (see figure 4). These registrations point to a gradual movement of the stimulus from a sensual or visual representation to a more conceptual one. The stimulus thus follows its path and receives various forms of representation until it eventually arrives at the inner conscious pole of the apparatus in an adequate linguistic form whose energy is easy to discharge with an appropriate reaction. However, in order for this movement to take place, a *translation* of the stimulus's representation is needed at the boundary of each layer, so that the language of the former layer can be understood, processed and registered in the language of the present layer. It is precisely this translation which often fails, and Freud names this failure *repression*, adding that "the motive for it is always a release of unpleasure which would be generated by a translation" (SE 1:235).

Repression is conceptualised here as a pathological incident which halts the normal work of screening before it is completed—that is, before the stimulus either fades away in the process or fully arrives at

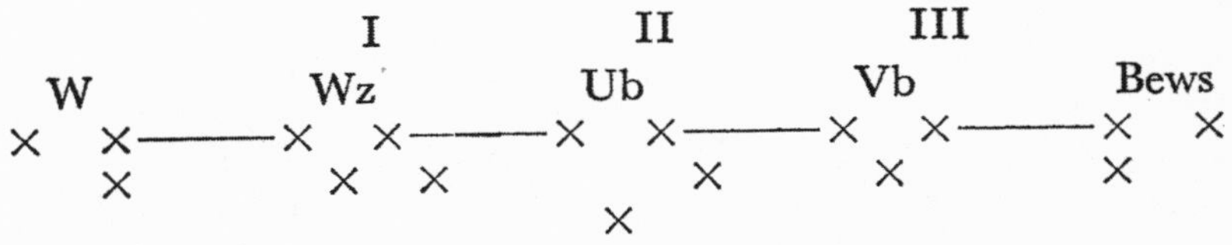

Figure 4. Freud's Schema of the Apparatus's Various Registrations (SE 1:234)

consciousness and is discharged. Repression is thus an *extraordinary* mechanism of defense that builds a shield around the stimulus and prevents its further passage. The stimulus, or rather its representation, remains stuck somewhere amidst the apparatus in its relatively primitive, speechless and unconscious form, since it is too dangerous to allow it to arrive at consciousness, which is, let us recall, extremely fragile.

What kind of a stimulus or event may fail to be translated, causing such a dramatic reaction? Freud claims that there is only one specific family of events which leads to repression: the sexual. He conceives the different registrations in the apparatus as relating to different sexual and psychological phases in early life, the first taking place at one year and a half and the last at fourteen (SE 1:236). An event that occurs in very early life may be perceived and elaborated only up to a limited degree according to the present stage of the child's development. With every phase, new possibilities of understanding and translation become available, and the representation of the stimulus becomes increasingly verbal and conceptual, relating to a larger context of thoughts and perceptions.

This is true not only for fresh perceptions in childhood but also for memories of past events. Memories are not just static entities, but rather consist of registrations that may be *awakened* by fresh events. The fresh event would partly repeat the old event, relaunching something like (and yet distinct from) a process of perception. However, memories of early childhood have a further complexity, because the time passed involves both a cognitive development of the child and a sexual development. Thus, an event that did not have a clear sexual meaning at the age of three may receive one at the age of twelve, which makes its memory much more than a mere reminiscence. In Freud's words, such a memory is "behaving as though it were some current event", since, for sexual events, "the magnitudes of the excitations which these release increase of themselves with time (with sexual development)" (SE 1:236).

What Freud means here is that early perceptions and experiences, such as suffering an instance of sexual abuse, but also, more simply, seeing one's parents make love, enter the apparatus, pass through some contact barriers and are then stored as speechless and obscure memories. They are not yet translatable into clear concepts, since these do not exist at this stage. So, on the one hand, the stimuli are too strong to naturally fade away, but, on the other hand, only a small portion of their meaning can arrive at elaborate consciousness and be discharged.[7] The event is not yet properly repressed, but rather serves as a Trojan horse, admitted to the apparatus and waiting for the right time to burst out, when the sexual development of the child permits it to do so.

Yet, contrary to what happened in Troy, the event does not just wait, as if in a period of incubation, for the right moment to burst forth. Rather, a new event should act upon and *repeat* the old one, retroactively leading to its repression. There are thus two events involved in this process: a first that could not be fully perceived, and a second that makes the child live or re-live it retroactively. Freud names this double-phase mechanism *Nachträglichkeit*, literally "after-carrying", which I translated in the previous chapter as *deferred retroaction*.

As Jean Laplanche emphasises, this mechanism works in both temporal directions: from the past to the present and from the present to the past.[8] No English translation fully and adequately expresses this two-way movement. The term *belatedness* does not stress the movement from the future to the past. The term *retroaction* does not mention the halt and suspension involved in *Nachträglichkeit*. Lastly, the term *deferral*[9] or *deferred action* mentions only the movement from the past to the present but not the opposite direction. For these reasons, I propose the somewhat awkward expression *deferred retroaction*, with which one can capture the full range of the original term.

In his letters to Fliess from that period, Freud laboriously tries to understand the double-phase mechanism of deferred retroaction (SE 1:220–32). Repression, he says, must have unpleasure as its origin, but the crucial point seems to lie in the highly energetic character of the original event combined with the impossibility of fully understanding and discharging it. It is only in the second phase that the original event would actually provoke unpleasure and anxiety, as shown by the various cases presented in *Studies on Hysteria*,[10] as well as the case of Emma described in the *Project*.

Let us briefly look at the latter case. The twelve-year-old Emma was at a shop, when suddenly the laughter of two shop assistants provoked anxiety in her. This happened, according to Freud, since the scene repeated some elements of a sexual assault of which she had been victim at the age of eight. This retrospective anxiety led her to flee from the shop and avoid any similar situations in the future; instead of facing the original traumatic scene of the sexual assault, she presented agora-phobic symptoms and could not go shopping alone. According to Freud, it is only when the *original* event becomes conscious and re-

ceives a name that it can become a normal memory and stop overload-
ing the apparatus from within. Only then would the energy of the
original stimulus be fully discharged and the symptoms disappear (SE
2:17).[11]

The aim of the therapy at that stage in Freud's thought was therefore
to *name* what would otherwise be a repressed event. But Freud soon
discovered that naming the event was not enough: the event had to be
repeated and worked through during the analysis itself. This famously
forced him to give up hypnosis in favor of what would become the
psychoanalytic treatment, but also, I would claim, to doubt the very
existence of the original traumatic scene, since it can be attained only
through repetition. In what follows, I will show that with repetition as a
fundamental mechanism of defense, Freud moved from a concept of
trauma as resting on *specific repressed sexual events* to a much more
general notion of modern everyday life as structured around *repetitious
responses to unspecific shocks*.

BEYOND THE PLEASURE PRINCIPLE (I): TRAUMA AND REPETITION

Around 1897 Freud made a discovery that transformed his entire understanding of psychic activity: he came to the realisation that his patients'
reports of past sexual events were fictitious. They did not reveal what
had happened in reality, but rather what they unconsciously desired:
their fantasies (SE 1:259–60, SE 20:34).[12]

The object of repression was consequently no longer a sexual *event*,
but rather a sexual *wish*, which led Freud in 1905 to develop a systematic theory of the drives in his *Three Essays on the Theory of Sexuality*
(SE 7:7–122). This theory shifted the accent from the external reality to
the internal drives, which flood the apparatus from within while still
relating to representations of external objects, in a constant interplay
between the inside and the outside, fantasy and reality.[13]

What happens to repetition and deferred retroaction when instead of
sexual events there are fantasies and desires? In the case of the *Wolf
Man* (1914/1918) Freud is still convinced of the existence of a "primal
scene"—that is, a primordial traumatic event which is deferred and
retroacted in later life. However, he admits that the exact content of the
primal scene cannot be known for sure (SE 17:57). Repetition—per-
formed through the mechanism of deferred retroaction—appears to in-

creasingly overshadow its presumed sexual origin, culminating in the discovery in 1914 of the *compulsion to repeat*.

Freud's key text on the compulsion to repeat is *Beyond the Pleasure Principle* from 1920. It was therefore only after World War I and its unprecedented horrors that he came to explicitly admit, albeit quite reluctantly, that his theory of sexuality should be complemented by a theory of repetition as a both conservative and destructive force.[14] This avowal was to complicate things greatly for the founder of psychoanalysis, but at the same time it helped him broaden the scope of his theory and adjust it to its time: the age of *shock*.

Indeed, one of the remarkable side effects of the Great War was the large number of shell-shocked soldiers. The shell-shocked, instead of repressing their shock or trauma, tended to repeat it in nightmares, obsessive thoughts or even real acts of repetition, reproducing the scene time and again.[15] Moreover, the trauma of the shell-shocked did not seem to be sexual, and Freud was thus forced to broaden his concept of trauma and relate it back to its original sense as a (mental) *wound*. The wound is produced in situations of sudden *danger* for which one is not prepared and which one eventually survived. Freud thus wondered why trauma victims, apparently against their conscious efforts to distance themselves from the painful event, return to it repeatedly. He suspected there is something in repetition that is related to trauma and goes beyond the pleasure principle, and he thus looked for other cases of repetition to better understand its functioning.

The next case of repetition he found was in children's games. Freud describes one particular game, which would later be known as the *fort-da* game. The one-and-a-half-year-old boy who invented the game was Freud's grandson Ernst. He took great pleasure in throwing his toys towards corners or hidden places in his room, shouting "o-o-o-o", which Freud interpreted as the German word *fort*—that is, *gone*. But the game was sometimes composed of two parts: the child would repeatedly take a wooden reel with a piece of string tied around it, throw it towards his cot surrounded by curtains until it disappeared, cry "o-o-o-o", and then pull on the string until the reel reappeared, at which time he would emit a joyful "*da*" ("there") (SE 18:14–15).

Freud saw in the child's *fort-da* game an attempt to compensate for the painful event of the mother's daily departure by translating it into joyful play. But, he asked, how is such a game compatible with the pleasure principle? Could repetition itself be a source of pleasure, independently of its object? The answer seems to be positive, at least in the case of children, since their games generally tend to repeat "everything that has made a great impression on them in real life", even if the repeated experience was originally unpleasant (SE 18:16–17). But what about adults? What is their attitude towards repetition?

Rather than analysing the role of repetition in adult "normal" and everyday life, Freud next turned to hysterical patients, who all share "fixations to the experience which started the illness" (SE 18:13). In order to address the repetition of the patients, it is the role of the *analyst* to make the patient "re-experience some portion of his forgotten life" (SE 18:19).[16] The therapeutic session thus becomes an arena in which the patients repeat "unwanted situations and painful emotions" (SE 18:21). But Freud does not mention whether these situations are necessarily traumatic or sexual. The important thing for him is that there is a repetition of an unpleasant event, a repetition that finally leads him "to assume that there really does exist in the mind a compulsion to repeat which overrides the pleasure principle" (SE 18:22).

BEYOND THE PLEASURE PRINCIPLE (II): THE SECOND MODEL OF THE PSYCHIC APPARATUS

With this hypothesis of the compulsion to repeat, Freud presents a new model of the psychic apparatus, aiming to fully explore the role which repetition plays in it. The psychic apparatus is now depicted as a living vesicle floating in the dangerous external world. The cortex of the vesicle serves as a protective shield against stimuli, and yet it simultaneously receives the relevant information for its survival, a mission accomplished through the work of sampling and screening of data (SE 18:27), as we already saw in the old model.

At first sight, this model seems to resemble the old model of the psychic apparatus as it is presented in the Fliess correspondence from 1895 to 1896.[17] However, Freud introduces now a crucial innovation regarding the role of trauma. We saw earlier that certain stimuli that enter the apparatus during childhood are only later repressed through an event which repeats and retroacts them. Accordingly, these stimuli were necessarily of a sexual character, since only sexuality gradually develops in the child and may lead to the double-phase mechanism of deferred retroaction.[18] Twenty-five years later, Freud no longer speaks of a *double-phase* mechanism, nor even exclusively of sexual events in childhood. It is now a question of the adult who finds him- or herself in a hostile everyday environment. Like Simmel's theory, what counts now is not the quality of stimuli, but their quantity. Every perception and every event carries with it a certain amount of energy, and if this energy passes a certain threshold, it *immediately* causes trauma. In Freud's words, trauma occurs due to "excitations from outside which are powerful enough to break through the protective shield", causing "a breach in an otherwise efficacious barrier against stimuli" (SE 18:29).

How can such a breach be created? Trauma is caused by a surprise or a lack of preparation. The stimulus enters the apparatus through an unprotected zone, but here the military metaphor ends, since it is still not too late to fill in the gap and prevent the intrusive energy from going further. The apparatus now invests *internal* energy around the psychic wound and *repeats* the traumatic event in prepared and controlled conditions. Through this simulation or reproduction, the apparatus gains mastery over the energy which has entered it, and gradually, with every repetition, tames its effects.

The nightmares that follow the trauma, for example, "are endeavoring to master the stimulus retrospectively, by developing the anxiety whose omission was the cause of the traumatic neurosis" (SE 18:32). These dreams do not aim to fulfill a wish, but rather reveal a function more primitive than the pleasure principle, a function which does not contradict it but is indifferent to and independent of it. The pleasure principle "is for the moment put out of action" (SE 18:29), since there is "another task, which must be accomplished before the dominance of the pleasure principle can even begin" (SE 18:32).

What exactly is the urgent task of the apparatus that is achieved by way of repetition? Freud calls it *binding* (*Bindung*), the work of which was actually already described under the name of the contact barriers in the old model of the psychic apparatus. Let us recall that the double task of the contact barriers is to reduce the energetic quantity of the stimulus and arrange or translate its quality into a more conceptual representation. Through this double work, the energy is bound and tamed, so that the stimulus arrives at consciousness in a safe form, arranged in clear representations which are easy to manipulate. Without the gradual work of binding, the energy would remain free—that is, wild, mobile and, above all, not firmly attached to specific representations.

The energy of a stimulus is thus free at first, only to become gradually bound through the contact barriers. But when a stimulus is too strong, the normal work of binding cannot take place, and the apparatus enters an *emergency* state. In the old model Freud called this state "a failure of translation", which was another name for *deferred* repression. But in *Beyond the Pleasure Principle* there is no mention of deferral at all. As a result, there are three major differences between the old and the new models of the psychic apparatus and the ways in which they treat trauma:

1. *Cause*: the cause of trauma in the old model is a stimulus with sexual quality which could not be understood at the time of its occurrence and was later repeated through a second event, causing unpleasure and retroactive trauma. The cause of trauma in the new model, conversely, is not a particular quality of the stimulus, but its quantity—that is, a powerful energetic penetration into the apparatus.
2. *Time*: trauma in the old model takes place in a double phase mechanism. The stimulus enters the apparatus rather peacefully and is repressed and retroactively felt as traumatic only at a later period of development. In the new model, however, the trauma is felt as such immediately after the penetration of the stimulus. It remains isolated from the subject's life, but it is not unknown to him or her.
3. *Effect*: the trauma in the old model results in a deferred battle of energies between the stimulus and the ego, the former pushing in and the latter trying to push back and quarantine the stimulus, until a compromise is arrived at whereby the original representation is displaced and replaced with a substitute, around which a *symptom* is formed (e.g., Emma's agoraphobia). In the new model of trauma, conversely, the binding is achieved through a more or less *exact* repetition without any displacement. The traumatised person repeats mechanically what happened to him or her without significantly changing the details of the original event. The only thing that may vary is the quantity (strength) of the repetition, not its quality (content).

How are we to understand these changes in Freud's model of the psychic apparatus and trauma? At first sight, they seem only to restitute his original belief in the existence of a unique primal scene, only that this primal scene is immediately repeated. For instance, the shell-shocked soldiers suffer from a trauma in a battle they keep repeating. However, there is a further crucial difference between the old and the new model, which does not allow us to locate such specific trauma. Freud affirms that the origin of trauma is not only the *external* world but also the apparatus itself, or more exactly its drives, which are "the representatives of all the forces originating in the interior of the body and transmitted to the mental apparatus" (SE 18:34). Hunger, thirst, love and hate, desire, hostility, pain and anxiety are all sources of stimulation that provoke free energy to bind. But while the apparatus has a protective shield against external excitations, it does not have any such shield against internal excitations. These are indeed "more commensurate with the system's method of working" (SE 18:29), so it is easier to control them, but if they fail to be bound, they provoke "a disturbance analogous to a traumatic neurosis" (SE 18:34–35).

This new traumatic element may seem at first quite insignificant, but it actually changes the entire picture of the psychic apparatus: far from being a rare accident, *the failed process of binding becomes a constitutive part of adult life.* If the drives themselves may cause trauma, then trauma becomes a constant threat without a definite place and time, and with no distinct boundaries between the outside and the inside, the event and its repetition. In other words, *everyday life becomes (post)traumatic or shocking.* This claim is further supported by the two closing sections of *Beyond the Pleasure Principle*, in which Freud introduces his famous hypothesis of the death drive. I do not intend to defend here this hypothesis, but rather to connect it to the question of trauma, showing that the death drive points not only to the crucial role which trauma plays in everyday life but also to the inability to distinguish clearly between everyday repetition and its presumed traumatic origin.

Freud's argument goes as follows: from the dominance of the compulsion to repeat he deduces "an urge inherent in organic life to restore an earlier state of things" (SE 18:36). This "organic compulsion to repeat" (SE 18:37), combined with the fact that "inanimate things existed before living ones", implies that the organic wants to return to a previous inorganic state. In other words, "the aim of all life is death" (SE 18:38), and "the pleasure principle seems actually to serve the death instincts" (SE 18:63).

We arrive here at the ultimate domain or limit which is situated beyond and before the pleasure principle. But is the death drive a necessary conclusion from the presence of the compulsion to repeat? Following many commentators on Freud,[19] I would be content with a more minimalistic hypothesis, for if life was created "by the action of a force of whose nature we can form no conception" (SE 18:38), and if this very creation is conceived as a traumatic primordial event, it follows that *life stems from and is a reaction to trauma.* This trauma is not a part of life itself, but is rather at its threshold. It is an opaque, prehistoric event, a mythological "primal scene" whose effects we can see only through the compulsion to repeat.

But how is the compulsion to repeat set in motion in the first place? In order for that to happen, a new agency had to be created—namely, the *drives* or instincts: "The tension which then arose in what had hitherto been an inanimate substance endeavoured to cancel itself out. In this way the first instinct came into being: the instinct to return to the inanimate state" (SE 18:38). The birth of drives is thus a response to the traumatic appearance of life, trying to undo the trauma by way of the repetition compulsion.[20]

However, there are two groups of drives, according to Freud: the death drives, wishing to return to the inanimate state *immediately*, and the life drives, wishing to *defer* this return: "It is as though the life of the organism moved with a vacillating rhythm. One group of instincts rushes forward so as to reach the final aim of life as swiftly as possible; but when a particular stage in the advance has been reached, the other group jerks back to a certain point to make a fresh start [*nochmals zu machen*] and so prolong the journey" (SE 18:40–41).

The deferral which at first seemed to disappear in *Beyond the Pleasure Principle* thus finally reappears, yet in a twisted version, relating to a mythological scene that can never be retrieved in life.[21] Even if the drives originate in a primordial trauma, they soon acquire an independent existence, flooding the apparatus independently of their presumed source. They endlessly perpetuate the trauma and repeat it until they achieve their final goal in death. Thus we may see how everyday life becomes inherently traumatic or shocking, and before I draw some conclusions from this finding, I wish to briefly examine another version of the primordial trauma which includes two further important repetitive forces—namely, *anxiety* and *symptom.*

ANXIETY, SYMPTOM AND THE AUTOMATON

In his 1926 text *Inhibitions, Symptoms and Anxiety*, Freud returns to the question of the primordial trauma in a different form. Here, he no longer locates trauma in the appearance of life in general, but rather in the concrete appearance of the baby at *birth*.[22] This allows him to stress another factor that takes place in trauma—namely, *anxiety*.[23]

Together with the drives, anxiety is a highly important notion for our discussion of the everyday, since it ties together the "too much" with the "too little". According to Freud, the anxiety of the outside is internally reproduced by the drives in situations of lack: the drives overflow the apparatus when a need is felt, thus leading to a feeling of anxiety in situations such as hunger or thirst, castration anxiety, and finally the anxiety of losing the loved object (SE 20:130).[24] All these are traumatic moments in which a threatening lack, deficiency or mutilation are felt through an overflow of the drives.

But is every anxiety justified? Can we not live a peaceful everyday life? Freud's answer seems to be negative, since for him anxiety takes place not only in cases of *actual* trauma but also in cases of *potential* trauma. In the latter, anxiety is not a passive and automatic reaction to a real trauma, but rather an active *alarm signal* against an incoming trauma that is to be parried:

> The signal announces: "I am expecting a situation of helplessness to set in", or: "The present situation reminds me of one of the traumatic experiences I have had before. Therefore I will anticipate the trauma and behave as though it had already come, while there is time to turn it aside". Anxiety is therefore on the one hand an expectation of a trauma, and on the other a repetition of it in a mitigated form. (SE 20:166)

This is the paradox of trauma: in order to avoid it, one must repeat and reproduce it through anxiety. Trauma is inescapable, and the best one can do is to turn the passive situation into an active one, as in the case of little Hans, who, in order to escape the anxiety caused by his father, actively developed a phobia of horses. Anxiety can thus take different shapes and objects, and the process through which one moves from one anxiety to another Freud calls *displacement*.

Whereas in *Beyond the Pleasure Principle* it seemed that the repetition of a trauma is more or less its *exact* reproduction, Freud now reintroduces displacement as one of the major effects of trauma. He says that, after a process of several displacements, the original anxiety is replaced by an active anxiety (alarm signal) produced by the *symptom* (SE 20:167). The symptom is a simulation of anxiety that presents a major advantage—namely, it can be avoided through inhibition. For instance, Emma can avoid her anxiety by not going to shop anymore, and Hans can avoid any sight of horses by remaining at home. But it is evident that the result for Emma and Hans is an everyday life that is constantly guided by trauma. Indeed, once the symptom has set in, there seems to be no way back. As Freud puts it, the symptom "will run its course under an automatic influence—or, as I should prefer to say, under the influence of the compulsion to repeat" (SE 20:153).

The symptom, which has been carefully chosen in order to avoid further traumas, soon becomes itself a source of anxiety that repeats and perpetuates the trauma. The symptom is an exterior entity that has been internalised, becoming what Freud characterises as a *foreign body*.[25] It is a reaction to trauma at the same time that it is a repetition of it. It stems from a signal which is no longer distinguishable from the danger it was supposed to thwart, a peculiar alarm system that continues to disturb the residents of a house years after the burglars have been imprisoned. Freud's distinction between actual and potential trauma thus collapses, and anxiety is discovered as an inherent mechanism in the compulsion to repeat: a *Zwang*—that is, an automaton.

The procedure of *Inhibitions, Symptoms and Anxiety* is therefore very similar to that of *Beyond the Pleasure Principle*: both texts start with a concrete traumatic event that necessitates an immediate response with no deferral, and end with a series of displacements which defer their presumed origin so much that they finally acquire an independent force in the compulsion to repeat or the symptom. Indeed, Freud does not give up his attempt to track a presumed origin, but it seems that there is either no deferral at all between the first event and its repetition or too much of it.[26] Consequently, the original notion of deferred retroaction, as developed in Freud's early writings, loses its influence upon life.

To return to the theme of the everyday: whereas the first model of the psychic apparatus seemed to show us a possibility of integrating an extraordinary event into everyday life through its deferred retroaction,[27] the later model depicts the everyday as ruled by numerous repetitions and shocks whose origin is no longer known. To better understand the different possibilities of deferred retroaction and their place in both everyday and extraordinary situations, I propose to examine two literary works by Marguerite Duras, an author who is often associated with the theme of trauma and repetition. I shall first present *Hiroshima mon amour* and through it discuss Cathy Caruth's interpretation of Freud, and then move to *The Ravishing of Lol Stein* to show the implications of trauma in everyday life.

DURAS: EXTRAORDINARY VERSUS
EVERYDAY REPETITION

"You see, Nevers is the city in the world, and even the thing in the world, I dream about most often at night. And at the same time it's the thing I think about the least",[28] says the heroine of Alain Resnais's 1959 film *Hiroshima mon amour*, with a screenplay by Duras. Nevers, the heroine's birthplace, is the traumatic place in which she lost, at the end of World War II, her German lover, shot during the Liberation by the French resistance. After a year of mourning that involved disgrace, psychotic rage, depression and isolation, she is forced by her parents to leave Nevers, to which she will probably never return, but by which she is haunted in her nights. Only twelve years later, in another traumatic place—namely, Hiroshima—and with another traumatised person, a Japanese man, can she consciously and deliberately retrieve her traumatic memory. At the end of a very long night, during which she not only tells the Japanese man her story but actually repeats and retroacts it by identifying her new lover with her lost German lover, she finally receives from him her name, and the "therapeutic session" that the film constitutes ends with an act of baptism: "Your name is Nevers. Ne-vers in France".[29] One cannot escape one's traumatic past—or rather, one is defined by it.

The film thus shows how a traumatic event is repressed although it is available to consciousness.[30] It is repressed to the extent that it is not adequately repeated and discharged: it should be repeated not only in dreams but also in reality, and—crucially—with the mediation of another person. This person, who serves as an object of transference, would permit *deferred retroaction* of the original scene, enabling the elaboration, translation and finally the discharge of the original event. We thus see here a possibility of a *therapeutic* deferred retroaction: a retroaction that integrates rather than parries or quarantines the trauma.

As Freud states, repression does not necessarily involve forgetting,[31] but rather the inaccessibly of a certain memory to the present affective life—that is, its isolation from other events and associations such that it remains intact, frozen in time. Repression thus involves the meeting point of the past and the present, as Freud wrote already in 1896: "Pathological defense [repression] only occurs against a memory-trace from an earlier phase which has not yet been translated" (SE 1:235). To translate the memory-trace, it must first be retroacted—that is to say, repeated through another event which would revive and integrate it in the present.

One could thus say that the French woman, through a process of "therapeutic" repetition of her experience of loss, managed to translate what had happened to her, thereby (re-)experiencing and overcoming her trauma. However, it is important to note that the deferred retroaction she was involved in fits only to the old model of the psychic apparatus—that is, a deferral of a concrete and well-defined event which awaits its retroaction in a later period. But what about the much more complicated deferral introduced in the new model, in which no real traumatic event can be located?

In her 1996 book *Unclaimed Experience*, Cathy Caruth analyses *Hiroshima mon amour*, using it to articulate her own theory of trauma as deferred experience, summarised as follows: "The experience of trauma, the fact of latency, would thus seem to consist, not in the forgetting of a reality that can hence never be fully known, but in an inherent latency within the experience itself".[32] Trauma is not a definable event, but rather "a possibility always there but never certain" (115). To illustrate this idea, Caruth examines Freud's three introductions to his 1939 text *Moses and Monotheism* and claims that Freud's own personal trauma in the time of writing them did not consist in the *invasion* of Austria by Nazi Germany, but rather in his *leaving* Vienna. Trauma "is borne by an act of departure" (21–22), a claim that is equally illustrated by the *fort-da* game, stemming from the mother's daily leaving (65–67).

Hiroshima mon amour, Caruth continues, also presents a trauma based upon departure, this time of the German lover who died in the French woman's arms. However, the event of departure is hardly clear: the heroine could not recognise when precisely death took place during that night, nor even the spatial difference between his dying body and hers. Caruth meticulously analyses the various displacements, exchanges and crossings within and between the two traumas: that of Nevers and that of Hiroshima. But despite all the uncertainties she finds in the trauma of departure, her basic hypothesis remains that a concrete trauma *did* take place, and the question that consequently interests her is how to "properly" evoke, testify and verbalise it despite its overwhelming (yet uncertain) character.

This last point is crucial to the understanding of Caruth's ambitious project, which is not only to explain what trauma is but also to resolve the postmodern crisis of reference—that is, the uncertainty of a presumed origin. On the one hand, Caruth allows a relatively stable reference—a traumatic event of departure—but on the other hand, using both deconstructive and Lacanian terminology, she characterises this experience as a *missed* encounter, deferring it to an indefinite moment of departure. This suggestion would seem at first glance to fit Freud's theory of deferred retroaction, but, as Ruth Leys shows, Caruth considers the belatedness (deferral) of the traumatic experience to be an "incubation period" that does not change or influence the original event.[33] In other words, Caruth does not fully recognise the primacy of repetition upon the repeated and consequently does not seriously deal with questions such as these: In what ways can one displace and repeat the "primal scene"?[34] What outlets may these repetitions have? By not addressing these questions, the everyday risks becoming once more separated from an allegedly constitutive traumatic event in a past life that one can never attain, a mystified extraordinary realm that overshadows the ordinary, non-traumatic everyday life. Indeed, how comfortable it would be if all the dullness of our everyday life were to be attributed to some extraordinary traumatic event!

However, I do not wish to say that concrete traumas never occur. A helpful distinction in this context would be Dominick LaCapra's elaboration of two kinds of trauma, the first structural and the second historical.[35] The structural trauma is universal and abstract, concerning the traumatic structure of human life as such, whereas the historical trauma refers to a concrete event, such as sexual abuse, a car accident or the experience of genocide. Stated in other terms, structural trauma is the one appearing at the end of *Beyond the Pleasure Principle* (the creation of life as traumatic), whereas historical trauma is depicted in the old model of the psychic apparatus as well as in the beginning of *Beyond* (the shell-shocked soldiers). Caruth's theory seems to slip between these two traumas, since it implies, on the one hand, that all of us have suffered from trauma, but, on the other hand, this trauma is located in an archaic event of departure—for instance, Moses leading the Hebrew people to leave Egypt—which can somehow be transmitted between generations.

Indefinite as it may be, the traumatic structure of modern experience is supposed by Caruth to be based upon a primordial event, a suggestion that was already made by Freud and which is difficult to uphold. The challenge of the present book is to delineate the traumatic aspect of modern everyday life, without locating the traumas in extraordinary

events, on the one hand, and without negating the existence of historical traumas, on the other hand.

In order to exemplify the ordinary aspect of trauma, let us turn to a
second example, taken from Duras's 1964 novel *The Ravishing of Lol
Stein*.[36] Lol is a young and attractive woman engaged to the handsome
and rich Michael Richardson. The two seem to make a perfect couple,
but one evening when they attend a ball, a mysterious older woman
enters (or rather, *penetrates*) the scene and attracts the attention of the
young fiancé. Michael and Lol dance one more time, their last time,
after which Michael turns to the woman and dances with her—again
and again, all night long. What is Lol's reaction to this betrayal? Curiously, she does not try to talk to Michael or do something to stop the
couple and break their burgeoning intimacy. Instead, she remains quiet
and passively watches them from a distance, standing at the back of the
dancing hall, with her best friend Tatiana at her side, holding her hand
and caressing it. After hours of rigid passivity, dawn finally breaks, the
orchestra ceases to play, the ball ends and the new couple makes its
way towards the exit. Only then does Lol open her mouth, yelling that
they must stay and continue to dance, for the morning has not yet come.
She wants to perpetuate the night. She wants to prolong and repeat the
scene. The two, however, do not even seem to hear her screams and
calmly walk away, upon which Lol finally collapses, sinking into a
long period of illness.

Similar to the heroine of *Hiroshima mon amour*, Lol slowly recov-
ers from her traumatic loss. She, too, leaves her hometown, gets married and has children. But she has not entirely recovered. Years later,
Lol and her family move back to her hometown, where she soon no-
tices a man who reminds her of Michael Richardson: an opportunity to
repeat. She follows him and discovers that he is the lover of Tatiana,
the childhood friend who held and caressed her hand during the night
of the ball. Lol falls in love with this man, but, curiously, she does not
want to make love with him, but to watch him make love with Tatiana.
She needs her lover to dance with another woman; she needs to watch
him, from a safe distance, "betray" and "abandon" her. She thus asks
him to continue his meetings with Tatiana in a hotel where she can
watch them from the rye field behind it. After several such voyeuristic
experiences, Lol asks her "lover" to accompany her to the dance hall
where the primal scene took place. They take a train, arrive at the dance
hall, but, disappointingly, nothing happens, and Lol does not even recognise the place. The wish to repeat the scene once and for all, as in

Hiroshima mon amour, collapses, and Lol must find a new solution to the problem. She thus abandons herself to her lover, letting him make love to her for the first time, but this awkward experience does not give her much pleasure. There seems to be no way out of Lol's illness, and the novel ends upon her return from the trip, when she finds herself lying again in the rye field, the only place where she can find satisfaction, watching her loved object from a distance, both present and absent, present *as* absent: *fort-da*.

It is tempting to evaluate the repetition of the *Hiroshima* heroine as plastic or therapeutic and that of Lol as mechanical or destructive. After all, the former seems to have been cured of her fixation through the name—the translation—she received, whereas Lol has only sunk even more deeply into her untranslatable neurosis, or even psychosis.[37] The heroine of *Hiroshima* has actively revived her past, permitting herself to re-experience loss, and freeing herself to feel love again. Lol, however, has remained largely passive, finding her satisfaction only in the desire of the other which she must watch from a safe and voyeuristic distance. She compulsively repeats her loss, but this repetition does not seem to have any therapeutic effect on her. Like Freud's patient Emma, who would not go out to shop alone, as every shopping experience represented her past trauma, Lol perpetuates her traumatic experience by finding substitutes for it which are nonetheless mechanical.

However, I would suggest that it is precisely the *non*-therapeutic value of Lol's repetition—that is, its persistent, compulsive character—which makes it closer to the repetition of modern everyday life as "post-traumatic" or shocking in general ("structural trauma"),[38] whereas the repetition of the French woman in *Hiroshima mon amour* refers to a concrete moment in time, indefinite and remote as it may be ("historical trauma"). Indeed, the *Hiroshima* repetition is much more appealing, corresponding to our fantasies of salvation through an extraordinary event. Yet we rarely travel to exotic places in order to reproduce the traumas of our past, and we rarely ever recover from them. Rather, it is mostly in our everyday lives that we find ourselves, consciously or not, repeating things—small and big, trivial and significant. We repeat things, but this repetition does not seem to have any meaning for us, since meaning is attributed only to the new and not to the repetitious. Is there a hidden meaning to everyday repetition? Does it relate to a primal scene of a traumatic character? Indeed, Lol is a limit case, since she seems to have suffered not only from a structural trauma but also from an historical trauma—namely, being abandoned during the ball.

However, this primal traumatic scene soon turns out to be less primal than it seemed at first sight:

> Tatiana did not believe that Lol Stein's insanity could be traced back solely to that ball, she traced its origins back further, further in Lol's life, back to her youth, she saw it as stemming from somewhere else. In school, she says, there was something lacking in Lol, she was already then strangely incomplete, she had lived her early years as though she were waiting for something she might, but never did, become. In school, she was a marvel of gentleness and indifference, she changed friends with abandon, she never made the least effort to combat boredom, nor had she ever been known to shed a sentimental schoolgirl's tear. [39]

Lol's early years are described here in a manner that would curiously fit Houellebecq's heroes: a feeling of boredom mixed with a vague impression of lack, a lack which does not stem from concrete unfulfilled needs, but rather from the inability to locate any need in the first place. The result is an everyday which is both boring and unsatisfying, thus leading to the hope of salvation in an external "big" event—for example, a passionate love affair. However, this love affair, too, would never be enough. It is only when it is *over*, drawn to an end in a traumatic scene, that the indefinite lack can become definite, or, in Lol's extreme case, the boredom can turn into madness. [40]

The primal scene is thus an effect of the trauma no less than it is its cause. As such it exemplifies, much more than the *Hiroshima* trauma, Freud's notion of deferred retroaction, for even if the primal scene repeats an earlier traumatic loss, the latter cannot be located outside the event that has retroactively caused it. The primal scene thus declares itself to be "the" event: an external and well-defined trauma which Lol can only passively follow, watching her own destruction with a negative *jouissance*—that is, an absence which is so total that it is no longer distinguishable from presence.

The end of Duras's novel may be regarded as a mechanical repetition of the primal scene, but at the last minute something halts this movement: "Lol had arrived there ahead of us. She was asleep in the field of rye, worn out, worn out by our trip" (181). Lol wanted to repeat the scene, but she fell asleep due to the tiredness caused by the trip to the dance hall—that is, the trip of repetition. Perhaps, after this trip, she understood that the primal scene, the night of the ball, was not important in itself, but was necessary, rather, to create her own mythology of the lost object of love. Lol is thus tired of repeating the scene and shuts her eyes, refusing to watch it again, to reproduce the extraordinary traumatic event which supposedly stands at the basis of her illness. The problem is that she does not know any other form of repetition, and the novel ends with this *aporia*, which equally characterises modern every-day life, repeating something whose origin no longer explains or re-solves the repetition.

Does any introduction of deferral necessarily lead to an endless repetition with no possibility of retrieving a traumatic origin that would end the repetition?[41] It would be tempting to use my analysis to decon-struct Freud and show, for instance, that he looks for presence but repeatedly ends up with absence, deferring the presence of the traumat-ic experience for an indefinite period. Indeed, deferred retroaction can be considered as a Derridean *différance*:[42] a difference that defers it-self, a persistent inability to trace back a stable origin. However, Derri-da's conceptualisation follows the same scheme of two extreme poles that nourish and complement each other: an automatic repetition, on the one hand, and an indefinite deferral, on the other hand—a combination that stands at the basis of many postmodern theories. My aim in this book is different and consists of understanding the possibility of an everyday repetition that would *not* end up as an automatic symptom. Lol may be an extreme example of the modern or postmodern subject, but I believe that there are other forms of everyday repetition that are yet to be discovered. Such a possibility is attributed in Freud to a figure I wish now to further investigate—namely, the child.

CHILDHOOD, TRAUMA AND REPETITION

I examined earlier the different repetitions mentioned in *Beyond the Pleasure Principle*: the repetition of a "real" traumatic event, the repe-tition of children's games and the repetition of neurotic patients. The only repetition which is not discussed by Freud, save for anecdotal remarks regarding fatal repetitions, is that of "normal" adults in their everyday lives. It is our task to fill the gap and try to deduce, from the repetition of neurotics and children, what the precise function of the "adult" repetition is.

Children's games, as we saw, are based upon a repetition which is not quite automatic, but rather consists of various displacements (e.g., replacing the mother with a wooden reel or replacing the doctor with a

playmate). But at the same time children also practice exact and mechanical repetitions (e.g., when they listen to the same story time and
again, angrily noticing any deviation from it). These two repetitions
seem to complement each other: a playful, displaced and slightly deferred repetition, on the one hand, and a fetishistic, exact and rather
immediate repetition, on the other hand. In his 1927 paper "Fetishism",
Freud links this notion to traumatic experience, saying that "it is as
though the last impression before the uncanny and traumatic one is
retained as a fetish" (SE 21:155).[43] The wooden reel of the *fort-da*
game can serve as an example of such a fetish, incarnating the last
impression before the mother disappeared—and yet this game is not
fetishistic in the way this term is used regarding the adult, since the
child cheerfully makes the reel not only appear but also *disappear*,
playing on the movement from absence to presence and vice versa.

Children thus have a higher capacity to play with absence and disturbance, which they reproduce in their games in various forms. This
capacity is further enforced by the fact that, for them, "repetition, the
re-experiencing of something identical, is clearly in itself a source of
pleasure" (SE 18:36). For the adult, however, it is much more difficult
to engage in a play of repetition, since it is conceived as a source of
boredom and annoyance. The adult rather looks for *novelty* as "the
condition of enjoyment" (SE 18:35).

But why should enjoyment come only out of novelty? And how
does the child nonetheless manage to extract pleasure from repetition?
In order to answer this, I suggest to historicise Freud's distinction between the child and the adult in relation to repetition, and connect it
with the question of the modern everyday. My claim is that the child
serves as a *pre-modern* figure: for him or her, the categories of "everyday" and "event", the "ordinary" and the "extraordinary", do not yet
exist in a binary way, since the presumed "everyday" consists of constant novelties, which need to be repeated and processed again and
again. As the 1895 model of the psychic apparatus shows, every passage of stimulus alters the facilitation of the contact barriers, so that
even if the stimulus passes through exactly the same paths as it did
previously, it would still be experienced differently while retroactively
shaping the memory traces. For the adult, however, the stimuli are
experienced through well-defined linguistic categories which facilitate
their passage to consciousness. The nuances between different recur-
rences of similar stimuli are thus blurred, so that all, say, cubes look
very similar, whereas for the child every cube is individually perceived

and the differences between them are registered precisely in order to eventually locate and elaborate the stable element of experience, in what might be considered a free variation on the method elaborated by Husserl.

The infantile everyday life thus consists of countless "tiny" events which necessitate countless "tiny" repetitions. But the interesting thing is that in 1926 Freud conceives of these infantile events, at least by way of analogy, as *traumatic*: "The ego, which experienced the trauma passively, now repeats it actively in a weakened version, in the hope of being able itself to direct its course. It is certain that children behave in this fashion towards every distressing impression they receive, by reproducing it in their play" (SE 20:167).

It seems that the degree of novelty of the event determines how and when it shall be repeated. Whereas in the early theory of deferred retroaction the child needed to passively wait for a subsequent sexual phase in order to repeat the trauma,[44] now he or she can *actively* repeat it in the game, since the trauma is not necessarily sexual. In other words, Freud applies here the shift from a sexual to a more quantitative model of trauma. The question remains, however, whether the mechanism of deferred retroaction still has a place in trauma in general, or only in sexual traumas with their two different phases.

The condition for deferred retroaction, let us recall, is a second event that makes the memory of the first one behave as if it were a fresh event. Deferred retroaction can thus cause a trauma in the first place, but it can also bind and "heal" it, as we saw in the example of *Hiroshima mon amour*. Now, can we not say that the playful repetition in children's games is a form of such deferred retroaction? The game could be regarded as precisely the second event that permits the child to relive the original scene and repeat its content until it is discharged. Moreover it is a mechanism which is unconsciously and actively used by the child in a way that is similar to and yet distinct from the work of the symptom. Although Freud hardly mentions deferred retroaction following the publication in 1918 of the *Wolf Man*,[45] it is interesting to note that the term reappears at the beginning of *Inhibitions, Symptoms and Anxiety*: "Many women are openly afraid of the sexual function. We class this anxiety under hysteria, just as we do the defensive symptom of disgust which, arising originally as a deferred reaction [*nachträgliche Reaktion*] to the experiencing of a passive sexual act, appears later whenever the idea of such an act is presented" (SE 20:88).

Disgust is an active reaction to a passive situation, and, as with any symptom, it involves a displacement of the original traumatic helplessness, which could not be experienced as such, onto a clearer emotion which serves as an alarm signal. But if we admit that the symptom is created through deferred retroaction, and if children's games can be compared to the creation of a symptom, it follows that children's games involve deferred retroaction as well, despite the relatively short interval between the original event and its repetition in the game. The traumatic event can thus be actively simulated through repetition both by the child (game) and by the adult (symptom), and the difference between the two lies rather in the result of the retroaction: whereas the game soon gives way to other games and other repetitions, the symptom tends to become a stubborn automaton and a constant cause of anxiety.

Is the symptom to be treated as a failed game, a game that has been frozen? If we return to the lack of clear boundaries in the child between the everyday and the event, we might say that the child must face a multiplicity of "traumas" to be handled and repeated, so that the everyday itself becomes a continuous repetition of numerous trauma-like events.[46] Infantile everyday life is so eventful as to be necessarily traumatic, but not in the way adults use the term. Children's "traumas" are constantly deferred and displaced, whereas adult trauma, such as the car accident at the beginning of *Beyond*, is well defined and isolated, therefore leading to an exact form of repetition.

It is this "confusion of tongues"[47] between the child and the adult which leads to the contradictions and entanglements in Freud's changing conception of trauma, starting with a definable trauma and ending up eventually with a trauma which is impossible to track. As we saw, this change occurs not only within the development of Freud's theory but also within single texts such as *Beyond* and *Inhibitions*. In both cases Freud starts by presupposing a definite trauma and ends with a repetition that overshadows its origin. The origin is either mechanically repeated or endlessly deferred, and the question is whether it is possible to avoid this deadlock of an either/or situation.

It is in this terrain *between* not deferring at all and indefinitely deferring that children's games are to be located: deferring, displacing, retroacting—all these are intertwined in the repetitive games which are plural and overlap each other. The aim of the games is to bind the tiny traumas of everyday life, traumas that cannot be located outside their repetition. It is only when a trauma crosses a certain threshold, such as in the case of sexual abuse, that the game cannot help anymore and that a longer mechanism of deferred retroaction should take place—a mechanism which can be seen only much later, through the work of the symptom.

If we recall Simmel's picture of modern everyday life characterised by infinite shocks, we may ask if the modern adult is not supposed to handle a situation which once only the child knew—that is, constant novelty. Can adults as well have access to the mechanism of deferred retroaction to address the modern condition? To tackle this question, the next two chapters will endeavour to further situate deferred retroaction in the modern everyday, by drawing on Walter Benjamin's vision of modernity as the shocking age of mechanical reproduction.

NOTES

1. Michel Foucault, *The History of Sexuality*, vol. 1, *An Introduction*, trans. Robert Hurley (New York: Random House, 1978), 53.

2. Freud also speaks of internal or endogenous stimuli, which will eventually become the drives. See also "Editor's Introduction to the *Project for a Scientific Psychology*" (SE 1:291). I will return to this point later.

3. Freud develops here a theory of quality as *periods*—that is, different temporalities of the stimuli (SE 1:307–10). However, contrary to his conception of quantity, this qualitative aspect of his theory is soon abandoned.

4. See Werner Bohleber, "Remembrance, Trauma and Collective Memory: The Battle for Memory in Psychoanalysis", *International Journal of Psychoanalysis* 88 (2007): 329–52.

5. For an interesting review of the relationship of Freud to the neuroscience of his time, as well as his anticipation of Donald Hebb's model from 1949 of synaptic plasticity, see Diego Centonze et al., "The Project for a Scientific Psychology (1895): A Freudian Anticipation of LTP-memory Connection Theory", *Brain Research Reviews* 46, no. 3 (2004): 310–14.

6. According to Freud this reaction is "motor", but he often simply refers to the movement of *thought*.

7. Freud says that it is only at the age of fourteen that one fully acquires elaborated consciousness (SE 1:236–37).

8. Jean Laplanche, *Problématiques VI: L'après coup* (Paris: Presses Universitaires de France, 2006), 29–32. He further explained his position in an interesting interview with Cathy Caruth from 1994. See Cathy Caruth, "An Interview with Jean Laplanche", *Postmodern Culture* 11, no. 2 (2001).

9. The verb "to defer" is derived from the Latin "dis" (away from) and "ferre" (carry), literally meaning "carry apart", which is quite close to the German term. The Latin verb combined—as the French *différer*—the meanings of both "defer" and "differ", which shows, as Derrida has argued, that every deferral already introduces a difference, and this difference changes the origin from the outset in both temporal directions. See Jacques Derrida, "Différance", in *Margins of Philosophy*, trans. Alan Bass (Chicago: University of Chicago Press, 1982), 1–27. For a lucid discussion of *Nachträglichkeit* as translation, see Andrew Benjamin, "Translating Origins: Psychoanalysis and Philosophy", in *Discourse, Subjectivity, Ideology*, ed. Lawrence Venuti (London and New York: Routledge, 1992), 18–41.

10. SE 2:19–181. For an excellent analysis of the mechanisms involved in hysteria, see Monique David-Ménard, *Hysteria from Freud to Lacan: Body and Language in Psychoanalysis*, trans. Catherine Porter (Ithaca, NY, and London: Cornell University Press, 1989).

11. See Laplanche's analysis of the case of Emma in *Problématiques VI*, 47–55.

12. For an evaluation of this shift and its consequences for Freud's theory of trauma, see M. Baranger, W. Baranger and J. M. Mom, "The Infantile Psychic Trauma from Us to Freud: Pure Trauma, Retroactivity and Reconstruction", *International Journal of Psychoanalysis* 69 (1988): 113–28. I do not intend to discuss here the polemic launched by Jeffery Masson in 1984 with regard to the seduction theory. My opinion will rather become evident from what follows. See Jeffrey Moussaieff Masson, *The Assault on Truth: Freud's Suppression of the Seduction Theory* (New York: Farrar, Straus & Giroux, 1984).

13. Ruth Leys discusses this shift (in her *Trauma: A Genealogy* [Chicago: University of Chicago Press, 2000], 20–21), and illustrates its significance with a quotation from Freud's text from 1899 on "Screen Memories" (SE 3:322): "It may indeed be questioned whether we have any memories at all from our childhood: memories relating to our childhood may be all that we possess. Our childhood memories show us our earliest years not as they were but as they appeared at the later periods when the memories were aroused". See also, among other discussions, Philippe Van Haute and Tomas Geyskens, *From Death Instinct to Attachment Theory* (New York: Other Press, 2007), 8–10; N. C. Marucco, "Between Memory and Destiny: Repetition", *International Journal of Psychoanalysis* 88 (2007): 309–28; Jean Laplanche and J.-B. Pontalis, "Fantasy and the Origin of Sexuality", *International Journal of Psychoanalysis* 49 (1968): 1–17; Jean Laplanche, *New Foundations for Psychoanalysis*, trans. D. Macey (Oxford: Blackwell, 1989).

14. This, I admit, is an over-simplified claim, since as Laplanche, amongst others, has shown, sexuality in Freud is always in a conflict with other forces: at the beginning self-preservation and later the death drive. See Jean Laplanche, *Life and Death in Psychoanalysis*, trans. J. Mehlman (Baltimore: Johns Hopkins University Press, 1985), 25–29.

15. This is illustrated by some unforgettable scenes in *The Deer Hunter*. See Van Haute and Geyskens, *From Death Instinct to Attachment Theory*, 16.

16. Freud actually reiterates here his findings from *Remembering, Repeating, and Working-Through* (SE 12:145–56), the first of his works to invoke the compulsion to repeat.

17. Indeed, Freud now posits a single perception-consciousness system rather than two separate systems. This, however, does not yet have significant consequences, since the apparatus maintains the same topography extending between two poles, external and internal. As before, stimuli enter the apparatus through the sense organs, go through an unconscious processing and finally, if they manage to pass through all the filters, appear in elaborated consciousness and bring about a motor reaction of discharge. I will return to this point in the next chapter.

18. As we saw in the case of the Wolf Man, Freud retained in the middle period of his theory his model of a double-phase repression and deferred retroaction with slight changes in terminology, supposing the existence of a "primal repression" that is later followed by "repression proper" or "after-pressure". See *Repression*, SE 14:148.

19. See in particular Laplanche's analysis, which shows how Freud moved from a conception of the pleasure principle as aiming at an *equilibrium* of energy to a conception of the pleasure principle as aiming to *diminish* all psychic energy. See Laplanche, *Life and Death in Psychoanalysis*, 106–24. On the speculative character of *Beyond the Pleasure Principle*, see Jacques Derrida, *The Post Card: From Socrates to Freud and Beyond*, trans. Alan Bass (Chicago: University of Chicago Press, 1987), 409.

20. It is important to note that the drives do not try to repeat the trauma itself (namely, the appearance of life), but rather what preceded it (namely, the inanimate state of death). In other words, they do not aim at simply repeating (*wiederholen*) but rather restoring (*wiederherstellen*) a previous state.

21. The deferral of the life drives does not refer, however, to a trauma caused by high tension, but rather to a trauma of *separation*. Freud draws on Plato's *Symposium* and the myth of Eros as a force wishing to return to archaic whole from which one has been separated (SE 18:58). The primordial trauma is thus double: trauma caused by *too much* energy (death drives, immediacy) and trauma caused by *lack* and separation (life drives, deferral).

22. The notion of *birth trauma* consists of the same two traumatic elements we found in the primordial trauma depicted in *Beyond the Pleasure Principle*—namely, (1) the high tension involved in birth and (2) the brutal separation of the baby from the mother.

23. As will be immediately clear, this anxiety has an object, and as such it is very different from the anxiety presented by Heidegger.

24. In his introduction to *Inhibitions, Symptoms and Anxiety*, James Strachey gives a brief summary of the dangers leading to trauma during life: "birth, loss of the mother as an object, loss of the penis, loss of the object's love, loss of the super-ego's love" (SE 20:82).

25. Already in 1893 Breuer and Freud wrote in their *Preliminary Communication*, "But the causal relation between the determining psychical trauma and the hysterical phenomenon is not of a kind implying that the trauma merely acts like an *agent provocateur* in releasing the symptom, which thereafter leads an independent existence. We must presume rather that the psychical trauma—or more precisely the memory of the trauma—acts like a foreign body which long after its entry must continue to be regarded as an agent that is still at work" (SE 2:6). The symptom thus always carries with it the traces of the original trauma, and in 1895 Freud adds the nuance that the memory does not remain completely exterior to its surrounding layers, so that "the pathogenic organization does not behave like a foreign body, but far more like an infiltrate" (SE 2:290).

26. Freud tries to develop in *Inhibitions* and other texts the idea of "primal repression", a traumatic archaic event that would stand at the beginning of the causal chain. See above, note 18.

27. Indeed, this integration is depicted by Freud as a traumatic *failure* of translation, but this failure can be repaired by the analyst who gives a name to the primal scene and thus makes the patient discharge it. "Successful" deferred retroaction is thus effected in the analysis itself.

28. Marguerite Duras, *Hiroshima mon amour*, trans. Richard Seaver (New York: Grove Press, 1961), 37.

29. Duras, *Hiroshima mon amour*, 83.

30. Christopher Bollas has tried to explain this phenomenon by his notion of the *unthought known*. See his *The Shadow of the Object: Psychoanalysis of the Unthought Known* (New York: Columbia University Press, 1987).

31. See, for example, *Remembering, Repeating and Working-Through*, SE 12: 148–49.

32. Cathy Caruth, *Unclaimed Experience: Trauma, Narrative and History* (Baltimore: Johns Hopkins University Press, 1996), 12.

33. Leys, *Trauma*, 270–72.

34. This question is largely dealt with, albeit in a slightly different context, by Ned Lukacher in his *Primal Scenes: Literature, Philosophy, Psychoanalysis* (Ithaca, NY: Cornell University Press, 1986).

35. Dominick LaCapra, *Writing History, Writing Trauma* (Baltimore: Johns Hopkins University Press, 2001), 76–85.

36. Marguerite Duras, *The Ravishing of Lol Stein*, trans. Richard Seaver (New York: Grove Press, 1966).

37. See Jacques Lacan, "Homage to Marguerite Duras", in *Writing and Psychoanalysis: A Reader*, ed. John Lechte (London and Sydney: Arnold, 1996), 136–42. Lacan puts the emphasis, however, on the *containing* function of the narrator, Jacques Hold.

38. I thus claim that structural trauma is historical as well, since it changes during modernity. I will return to this point later.

39. Duras, *The Ravishing*, 71.

40. This is why Lol faces her trauma only when the ball ends. Caruth would see it as another proof that trauma is the result of departure, but I would claim that it is only upon departure that one can (and must) confront the consequences of the invading energies. To answer Caruth, it is only when Freud left Vienna that he was able to fully understand the implications of the Nazi invasion.

41. To use Leys's terms, is there a way out of the dilemma between mimetic (repetitive, yet non-representational) and anti-mimetic (referential and representational) trauma? Leys declares that each of these two paradigms eventually collapses and leads to the other (Leys, *Trauma*, 298–307). The question which I would like to raise is whether the everyday itself, post-traumatic as it may be, is equally trapped in this dilemma, or rather whether, precisely as an everyday repetition which does not pretend to allude to a particular trauma, it permits a different dialectic.

42. Indeed, Derrida discusses *Nachträglichkeit* as *différance* in "Freud and the Scene of Writing", in *Writing and Difference*, trans. Alan Bass (Chicago: University of Chicago Press, 1978), 196–231.

43. On the temporal dimension and memory in fetishism, see Alan Bass, "The Problem of 'Concreteness'", *Psychoanalytic Quarterly* 66 (1997): 642–82. See also Elissa Marder, *Dead Time: Temporal Disorders in the Wake of Modernity (Baudelaire and Flaubert)* (Stanford, CA: Stanford University Press, 2001), 116–30.

44. "The traumas of childhood operate in a deferred fashion (*nachträglich*) as though they were fresh experiences. But they do so unconsciously" (*Further Remarks on the Neuro-Psychoses of Defence*, SE 3:167).

45. See Laplanche, *Problématiques VI*; Christine Kirchhoff, *Das psychoanalytische Konzept der "Nachträglichkeit": Zeit, Bedeutung und die Anfänge des Psychischen* (Gießen: Psychosozial, 2009); Friedrich-Wilhelm Eickhoff, "On Nachträglichkeit: The Modernity of an Old Concept", *International Journal of Psychoanalysis* 87, no. 6 (2006): 1453–69.

46. I do not refer here to the notion of "cumulative trauma", since this would again presuppose isolated events from which the subsequent symptoms stem. See Tutté, who asks, "So, when we speak of trauma, are we thinking of one or many traumas?" (J. C. Tutté, "The Concept of Psychical Trauma: A Bridge in Interdisciplinary Space", *International Journal of Psychoanalysis* 85, no. 4 [2004]: 903). Tutté proposes to adopt M. Khan's idea of "cumulative trauma" from 1963, but this seems to imply that infantile trauma is avoidable, contrary to my suggestion.

47. See Sándor Ferenczi, "Confusion of the Tongues between the Adults and the Child—(The Language of Tenderness and of Passion)", *International Journal of Psychoanalysis* 30 (1947): 225–30. For Ferenczi, however, this confusion of tongues is the origin of infantile trauma, whereas my argument is that this confusion of tongues is equally what obfuscates the differences between infantile and adult traumas. See also Philippe Van Haute and Tomas Geyskens, *The Confusion of Tongues: The Primacy of Sexuality in Freud, Ferenczi and Laplanche* (New York: Other Press, 2004).

Chapter Four

The Shock of Modernity

Throughout this book we have encountered several instances of "crisis": the crisis of European sciences and culture in Husserl, the crisis of fallen Being in Heidegger, the crisis of objectified body in Merleau-Ponty and the crisis of stimuli integration in Freud. Each of these thinkers can be shown to have located the crisis in a particular domain, and yet I have argued that for all of them the everyday plays a crucial role. The everyday serves as a locus of deferral and repetition whereby its function is to elaborate and integrate that which somehow transcends the everyday—that is, shocks.

Anything that repeats itself for a long enough period of time is entitled to the adjective "everyday": an "everyday shirt", for instance, is a shirt that I might wear every day—that is, in normal and ordinary circumstances. It is generally relatively cheap and does not draw much attention. This shirt is appropriate in most circumstances, and yet it is not a garment that I wear with particular pride: there is something in the attribute "everyday" that makes me feel it is not very special and, consequently, neither am I. The everyday shirt is ubiquitous, too widely produced and reproduced; it satisfies my basic needs but won't help me stand out or feel extraordinary.

What, then, is the relationship between the everyday, repetition and mass production? And how do these affect my self-identity? In the previous chapter I examined Freud's conceptualisation of trauma and argued that he gradually replaces it with the notion of shock. Both trauma and shock are characterised by an event that is too overwhelm-

127

ing to be fully experienced when it takes place. However, whereas trauma refers to a unique and primordial event,[1] shock is much less definable in place and time. The result, I argued, is a vision of the modern everyday as consisting of infinite imperceptible shocks which cannot be located outside their stubborn and automatic repetition in the symptom. This is why we often hear that our culture is based upon shocks,[2] but we are hard pressed to find specific shocks in everyday life itself. Shock allegedly belongs to the realm of the extraordinary, but it is actually the task of the ordinary—that is, of the everyday—to process and integrate it into life, such that the two are intimately linked despite their apparent modern opposition.

In this chapter, drawing mainly on Walter Benjamin and Freud, I will further investigate the modern everyday as a constant response to repetitive shocks. I will also examine what Benjamin describes as "the decline of the aura", and I will argue that this decline is intrinsically linked to changes in the mechanism of deferred retroaction (*Nachträglichkeit*). Indeed, Benjamin never mentions this mechanism, and he was probably not acquainted with it. Nevertheless, I will claim that this notion motivates his writings precisely through its absence. By modifying Freud's notion of deferred retroaction and adapting it to modern reality, I will plead for the possibility of another form of aura, *the aura of the habitual*, that I will explore and elucidate in the following chapter.

SHUTTING OUT EXPERIENCE

In some of his texts from the 1930s, Benjamin states that experience in modernity has undergone a process of *destruction*, and he attributes this destruction to the horrors of the Great War. Indeed, as we have already seen in Freud, World War I, as a global and bloody catastrophe, was a formative moment for numerous European intellectuals. However, the war was not the only significant event at the time, for it took place alongside vast technological innovations that were to announce a thorough transformation of Western society, for better or worse. It is this transformation, together with the destructive effects of the war, that stands at the basis of twentieth-century thought and still has great relevance with regard to contemporary reality.

A hint of this transformation can be found in Paul Valéry's 1928 declaration: "For the last twenty years neither matter nor space nor time has been what it was from time immemorial. We must expect great innovations to transform the entire technique of the arts, thereby affecting artistic invention itself and perhaps even bringing about an amazing change in our very notion of art".[3] Benjamin chose this statement as an epigraph to the third version of his essay "The Work of Art in the Age of Its Technological Reproducibility", the various versions of which were written between 1935 and 1939. But what about the earlier declaration of the destruction of experience? Has Benjamin become an optimist, or does his strategy consist precisely in oscillating between pessimism and optimism? It is the latter option that I shall promote here, arguing that Benjamin's style is quite similar to Merleau-Ponty's. Indeed, both thinkers point to the *duality* of experience, a duality that necessitates an ambiguous manner of writing, able to exemplify but also to overcome the two poles between which experience moves.

Whereas Merleau-Ponty focused on the objective-subjective duality in order to arrive at a primordial experience, Benjamin's vocabulary, as we will see, is more complex. On the one hand, he views the spatio-temporal changes brought about by technology not so much as leading to the destruction of experience, but as an opportunity for liberation from the chains of tradition. On the other hand, however, he ceaselessly points to the dangers brought about by technology, the first of which is fascism. He thus often oscillates in his texts from the 1930s between the chances and the risks of the new era, without choosing sides. Moreover, Benjamin's peculiar strategy consists of adopting an apparently descriptive point of view, yet one that does not focus on the present, but rather on the near past—that is to say, the French Second Empire (1852–1870). This, according to Benjamin (and, as we saw in the introduction, Lefebvre), is the period in which the (late) modern era begins: it is, he claims, a primal scene upon which to understand the present, starting with a key figure of that time, Charles Baudelaire, whom Benjamin considers the precursor of modernity.

Between 1927 and 1929 and from 1934 until his tragic death in 1940, Benjamin worked on what he called the *Arcades Project* (*Passagenwerk*),[4] a colossal enterprise which attempts to grasp the origins of modernity in the everyday life of mid-nineteenth century Paris. Similar to Tönnies and Durkheim, Benjamin locates the catalyst of modernity in the collapse of intimate, small, rural and religious communities, and the rise of anonymous, industrial and secular metropolises. Benjamin claims that the city has a certain inhuman character, but, far from reproving or deploring this character, he is rather fascinated by it and the ways it has been described by nineteenth-century writers such as Baudelaire. The inhuman character of the city, he says, is related to a new figure that emerges as a result of the new mode of existence— namely, the crowd: "Fear, revulsion, and horror were the emotions which the big-city crowd aroused in those who first observed it" (SW 4:327). If we are looking for the shock of modernity, Benjamin finds the crowd to be one of its primal sources.

To see how shock shapes and transforms modern experience, I propose to follow Benjamin's delicate argumentation in the essay he wrote in 1939, "On Some Motifs in Baudelaire".[5] Judging from the title, one might expect the essay to focus on Baudelaire, but the very first lines reveal that the real figure on which the text reflects is not the French poet but his readers, and not, moreover, his *contemporary* readers, but rather his *future* ones—in other words, us. Baudelaire "would eventually find the reader his work was intended for" (SW 4:313), declares Benjamin, seeing *Les Fleurs du mal* as a projection, a work to be eventually retroacted by its future readers. Benjamin, moreover, is not very kind with the description of these readers: "Willpower and the ability to concentrate are not their strong points. What they prefer is sensual pleasure; they are familiar with the 'spleen' which kills interest and receptiveness" (SW 4:313). It is thus less a question of Baudelaire in the text as of modern experience, which is situated somewhere between Flaubert and Houellebecq, between boredom and fatigue, or between the hope for redemption and total disenchantment.[6]

According to Benjamin, Baudelaire managed to anticipate and crystalise a certain change in the structure of experience which would be globally recognised only at the end of the nineteenth and the beginning of the twentieth century. More than forty years after the publication in 1857 of *Les Fleurs du mal*, various philosophers began to debate the question of experience, endeavouring "to grasp 'true' experience, as opposed to the kind that manifests itself in the standardized, denatured life of the civilized masses" (SW 4:314). To use the vocabulary of phenomenology, the two opposite experiences they discuss would be the "authentic" (primordial) and the "inauthentic" (everyday) experience, but Benjamin, who was only superficially familiar with phenomenology, instead refers to the "philosophy of life" (*Lebensphilosophie*) of Dilthey, Jung and especially Bergson.

Bergson, in Benjamin's view, had conceptualised the spontaneous and intuitive experience of duration (*durée*) not simply as a theory of the hidden or "true" perception, but rather as a part of a virulent and cruel battle against something else: namely, the crisis of experience. Bergson thus dismisses objectified time—that is, the quantified time of the clock, which is a degenerated form of the dynamic and subjective time of spontaneous perception. However, this dismissal would constitute nothing but turning his back to the historical and material circumstances that led to objectified time in the first place. Benjamin therefore concludes that Bergson had not described real—and I would say everyday—experience, which is in crisis, but rather *poetic* experience, which comes prior to, after or above the crisis (SW 4:314–15).

Now, it is tempting to apply Benjamin's critique of Bergson to Husserl's procedure in *The Crisis of European Sciences*. As we saw in chapter 1, Husserl gives a detailed analysis of the crisis and its sources, but then his solution comes as a *deus ex machina*, a magic method that turns away from the crisis towards a purified and transcendental sphere. The same critique might be addressed to Merleau-Ponty, who aims at a primordial experience that would transcend everyday, objectified experience. Indeed, Merleau-Ponty's attitude is much more complex than this caricature, but he nevertheless shares with Bergson the search for primordial temporality in a spontaneous and lively experience. Criticising this endeavour, Benjamin notes that it can only take place elsewhere from reality, in the phantasmic and imaginary world obtained when one *shuts one's eyes* to the disturbing reality—that is, "the alienating, blinding experience of the age of large-scale industrialism" (SW 4:314).

Are we, then, to blame Bergson, Husserl and Merleau-Ponty for having remained blind to the conditions of modernity? In fact, Benjamin depicts the modern experience as blinding to the extent that one has no other choice but to shut it out, arriving thus at "a complementary experience—in the form of its spontaneous afterimage, as it were" (SW 4:314). Bergson, Husserl and Merleau-Ponty are now revealed to have described not simply idealised experience, but rather a complementary experience, an *after*image (*Nachbild*) that follows the shutting of their eyes and refers to this process of shutting. It is something on the threshold between reality and fantasy, something which comes after reality and, to a certain extent, retroacts and creates it. Indeed, the shock does not explicitly appear in Bergson,[7] Husserl or Merleau-Ponty, precisely because their philosophy is an enterprise to parry it through the creation of concepts. This retroactive limit-experience of shutting the eyes is contrasted by Benjamin with the experience of Baudelaire, who strug-

gled to keep his eyes *open*. He thus dared to watch the inverse, "undis-
torted" image of his *future* reader.

Benjamin analyses Baudelaire's shock as a two-phase encounter. In
the first encounter, Baudelaire is shocked by the overwhelming reality
of his time, and in the second he is retroactively shocked by his future
reader. More precisely, Baudelaire appeals to a future reader and antici-
pates his or her shocked and shocking face. In this way he creates
himself the second encounter that enables him to write his poems as an
anticipating retroaction: he is shocked, starts to write, imagines his
reader and, by doing so, retroacts the first shock in his writing. But then
another retroaction occurs, which is Benjamin's, or that of the present/
future reader who looks at the past through the prism of his or her
present shock. Benjamin thus offers a hint of what reading (and writing) is: a performative act of retroaction that brings the text to the
present and lets it enact what was not possible or was not fully experienced at the time. [8]

Rather than as two opposites, Benjamin presents Bergson's and
Baudelaire's attitudes as complementary strategies of defence against
shock: the first attitude involves shutting one's eyes and imagining an
idealised world, and the second aims to defy shock by keeping one's
eyes open, thus creating the required conditions for a future retroaction.
Again, Benjamin does not choose sides, but rather endeavours to seize
both the idealistic and the materialistic, imaginary and real, internal and
external poles of modernity. In this way he hopes to expose the
shocked, everyday subject, not in its paralysed or "inauthentic" form,
but rather in an in-between position; a shocked subject, yet one who
still possesses the capacity of creation, poetry and even revolution. This
subject moves between various poles and thus acquires a *third* kind of
experience that Benjamin himself never thematised. It is neither totally
objectified nor fully creative and spontaneous experience, but rather a
hybrid of the two, maintaining the possibility to use static objectifica-
tions precisely as a source of creative inspiration. In what follows I will
try to gradually expose this hidden subject of the everyday.

VOLUNTARY AND INVOLUNTARY MEMORY

So far I have tried to show what strategies Bergson and Baudelaire use
in order to deal with the shock(s) of modernity according to Benjamin.

I argued that Benjamin actually retroacts these past strategies in order to transform shock into creation. His reading of them is anything but naive, using them to elaborate the shocks of his own time. But Bergson and Baudelaire are not the only figures who deal with shock through retroactive deferral as a motor of creation. A third figure evoked by Benjamin is Marcel Proust. In a celebrated scene from *In Search of Lost Time*, Proust makes his narrator taste a madeleine pastry that suddenly causes him to recall his childhood in Combray. Prior to this moment, says the narrator, he held only *voluntary* memory of this past. Voluntary memory belongs to the realm of the conscious intellect, and is available to each one of us whenever we want. However, the scope of this memory is very narrow since it is disconnected from other memories and times, like a snapshot that shows a well-framed image but misses its historical and interpersonal context. In order to arrive at a deeper and larger memory, Proust's narrator had to wait for the encounter with the madeleine, a magic open-sesame experience which gives him sudden access to the realm of *involuntary* memory. This is a rich and boundless memory, spreading upon an indefinite temporal and spatial range of events, places and experiences, linked between them through a wide set of associations and references.

In a characteristic move, Benjamin takes from Proust these two opposed notions, voluntary and involuntary memory, and applies them to other spheres to delineate the social and mental processes that take place in modernity. He thus compares voluntary memory to newspaper items which are short, sensational and detached from each other, such that their intention is "to isolate events from the realm in which they could affect the long experience [*Erfahrung*] of the reader" (SW 4:315–16).[9] Involuntary memory, however, is compared with the old and vanishing art of storytelling, which does not "convey an event per se", but rather "embeds the event in the life of the storyteller in order to pass it on as experience to those listening" (SW 4:316).

Proust, however, is not a storyteller.[10] Similarly to Baudelaire, he is regarded by Benjamin as a limit-case, an idea he further elaborates in an essay from 1929, "On the Image of Proust", written as a part of his translation (together with Franz Hessel) of several volumes of *In Search of Lost Time*. Benjamin claims that Proust has invented a genre of his own, trying to articulate the crisis of experience in a way that would *reflect* rather than *overcome* it. Being aware of the "irresistibly growing discrepancy between literature and life" (SW 2:237), Proust chose not to focus on experience itself, but rather on the art of *remem-*

bering experience, "the Penelope work of recollection" (SW 2:238). In other words, the madeleine does not lead the narrator to the lived experience of his childhood, but rather to its *retroactive* fabrication through a *deferred* experience. Such deferred retroaction, as we saw in Freud, requires as much oblivion as it does remembrance, and this is why, according to Benjamin, Proust invested so much effort to develop the "ornaments of forgetting", the dream-like images of the night that the voluntary memory of the day were to unravel. Moreover, Proust "finally turned his days into nights", shutting out the blinding light of the outside world in favor of an artificially controlled interior illumination (SW 2:238).

In the previous chapter we began to see that the work of deferred retroaction has become highly problematic in the modern world of the adult, where urging stimuli continuously flood the apparatus and necessitate an immediate rather than a deferred response. Proust seems to have found a solution to these external obstacles by refusing present stimuli and artificially cultivating deferral. The only way to tell his story—to remember certain things by forgetting others—is to cease to experience the present. Indeed, Benjamin sees no coincidence in the fact that Proust wrote the majority of his work in a horizontal position—that is, in bed, where he "held aloft the countless pages covered with his handwriting, dedicating them to the creation of his microcosm" (SW 2:247).[11] It is on the background of this refusal to acquire any real-time experience in order to attain the (retroactive) past that we may understand Proust's famous declaration:

> Real life, life at last laid bare and illuminated—the only life in consequence which can be said to be really lived—is literature, and life thus defined is in a sense all the time immanent in ordinary men no less than in the artist. But most men do not see it because they do not seek to shed light upon it. And therefore their past is like a photographic darkroom encumbered with innumerable negatives which remain useless because the intellect has not developed them.[12]

The past is compared here to negatives that need to be developed and exposed: not in order to simply be *seen*, but in order to be *lived*, leading to what we commonly call "real life". But this process of retroaction must take place in special conditions and with a kind of light quite different from the normal light of the day, which is too blinding. Proust therefore had to construct himself a darkroom, an inner room in which he could actualise his past life and live it for a second time, which was simultaneously the first:

> Proust has brought off the monstrous feat of letting the whole world age a lifetime in an instant. But this very concentration, in which things that normally just fade and slumber are consumed in a flash [*blitzhaft*], is called rejuvenation. *A la Recherche du temps perdu* is the constant attempt to charge an entire lifetime with its utmost mental awareness [*Geistesgegenwart*]. Proust's method is actualization, not reflection. He is filled with the insight that none of us has time to live the true dramas of the life that we are destined for. This is what ages us—this and nothing else. The wrinkles and creases in our faces are the registration of the great passions, vices, insights that called on us; but we, the masters, were not home. (SW 2:244–45)

This is indeed a most beautiful description of deferred retroaction—that is, letting the shock in, waiting for the right moment and then repeating it through an abrupt shock-like perception that retroactively permits one to (re)live the original event. However, it is important to note that Proust is not interested in enabling the acceptance of shocks when they actually take place, but rather in their retroactive repetition, a repetition which he considers as infinitely more significant and "real" than the original event it repeats. He thus tries to say that in order to live, reshape and create reality, one should cease to be shocked by it and shut it off, similarly to Bergson's method. Proust becomes young again by living the great passions, vices and insights which shocked him and scarred his face at the time. His literature is made upon this rejuvenating retroaction, but this seems to imply that literature and life, creation and the everyday, retroaction and experience exclude each other.[13] Is there no way to simultaneously live and retroact, be shocked and retro-shock? Benjamin's answer, based on a citation from Jacques Rivière, is no: "'Marcel Proust died of the same inexperience [*Unerfahrenheit*] which permitted him to write his works. He died of ignorance of the world, and because he did not know how to change the conditions of his life which had begun to crush him. He died because he did not know how to make a fire or open a window.' And, to be sure, of his neurasthenic asthma" (SW 2:246).

Creation goes hand in hand with *in*experience, or, more accurately, with inexperience of the everyday, such that the everyday and "real" or "true" experience are split again. We finally return to the Husserlian procedure of phenomenological reduction, which halts experience in

order to better approach it through its creative repetition. Both Husserl
and Proust suggest that one escape the everyday in order to retroact it in
better circumstances, but my aim in this book is to investigate the
possibility of deferral and retroaction *within* the everyday, as we saw
with Heidegger and Merleau-Ponty. For that to happen, the everyday
must allow for both moments—that is, shock and deferral. In other
words, the voluntary memory of everyday life must somehow communicate with involuntary memory, allowing for a deferred margin to be
repeated and lived not outside the everyday but in it.

Is there a mode of the everyday that allows for such retroaction of
shocks? Benjamin points to ancient religious rituals which knew how
to balance the two memories and treat them as complementary rather
than contradictory: the repetition of a particular religious ceremony
would help community members access their past experiences and integrate them in the present. For instance, going to church every Sunday
gradually creates a multilayered memory that encompasses various
events (e.g., birth, marriage and death ceremonies). Every visit to the
church may thus recall another, intertwining both voluntary and involuntary memory, making the everyday into a solid (yet sufficiently plastic) structure that can integrate further events.

Modern secular life, however, gives only little room for such repetitive procedures, which are now conducted in the private sphere rather
than in public. I therefore propose to interpret Benjamin as following
the same line of thought we found in Freud, attributing the taste for
repetition only to ancient times or to children, and seeing the modern
adult as reluctant to repeat the old. Perhaps it is no coincidence that
new age techniques proposing to "reconnect" one to oneself have become increasingly popular recently. However, this reconnection often
only serves to further accentuate the split between present and past.
Such techniques promise to lead to extraordinary experiences that completely transcend the "old" everyday and allow one to "invent" oneself.
But upon "returning" to the everyday, one soon realises that the old
continues to haunt a present that does not acknowledge it.

What exactly, in modernity, makes retroaction of the past so difficult to access? It would be helpful here to compare involuntary memory to the *Freudian unconscious*. My claim is that paradoxically Freud's
discovery of the unconscious led to its decline rather than its liberation.
If Freud's enterprise has received such resonance, it is not so much
because it *freed* the unconscious but, on the contrary, because it sup-
plied ways to control, tame and overcome it.[14] Let us recall Freud's

claim that the free energies that characterise unconscious processes must be *bound* through the secondary processes of consciousness; otherwise a trauma takes place. Indeed, trauma (or shock) is unavoidable given that the drives perpetually invade the apparatus from within, but perhaps the role of ceremonial repetition in religious rituals was to facilitate the work of binding, whereas in modernity one has to do it alone or with the help of such instances as psychoanalysis.[15] In what follows, I will demonstrate that Freud was not so much the discoverer of the *unconscious* as the discoverer—or even the guardian—of *consciousness*, conceived as a mechanism of defense against internal and external shocks.

IMMEDIATE AND LONG EXPERIENCE

In *On Some Motifs in Baudelaire*, Benjamin dedicates several pages to an analysis of *Beyond the Pleasure Principle*. However, it is crucial to note a minor yet decisive mistake he commits while citing Freud: "Freud's fundamental thought, on which these remarks are based, is the assumption that 'consciousness arises at the site of (*an der Stelle*) a memory trace'" (SW 4:317). Yet Freud's original text actually says, "Consciousness arises in place of (*an Stelle*) a memory trace".[16] Thus, instead of seeing consciousness as lying *behind* the unconscious, as in Freud's original model of the psychic apparatus, Benjamin brings consciousness to the site of the memory trace itself. It seems that modern consciousness can no longer afford to passively wait for stimuli from the more frontal systems. It must move forward, but in doing so it prevents the impressions from arriving at the unconscious.

The movement forward of consciousness, as Benjamin describes it, corresponds to the gradual disappearance of fantasy and dream-like associations in favor of well-structured categories. This process was equally described by Simmel, as we saw in the introduction, but whereas Simmel attributed the "rise of the intellect" to the impossibility of distinguishing between different stimuli, Freud and Benjamin focus on the question of shock and the way it changes the structure of experience and memory. Benjamin cites Freud's affirmation that vestiges of memory are "often most powerful and most enduring when the incident which left them behind was one that never entered consciousness", and he comments that "only what has not been 'lived' ['*erlebt*'] explicitly and consciously, what has not happened to the subject as an 'immediate experience' ['*Erlebnis*'], can become a component of involuntary memory" (SW 4:317). Indeed, this inaccessibility to consciousness is the basic condition of deferred retroaction, and as such it plays a crucial role in Freud's early theory of infantile trauma. Benjamin's novelty lies in his historicisation of this condition, seeing it as a mechanism that is no longer possible in modernity: the deferred traumas of childhood must give way to the abrupt shocks of the adult, modern age. These necessitate an *immediate* response, and as a result the very structure of memory and experience changes as well.

We saw in the previous chapter how Freud gradually moves from a concept of a well-defined deferred trauma (the case of Emma) to a concept of an inaccessible and hypothetical deferred trauma (the Wolf Man), and finally, in *Beyond the Pleasure Principle*, to two apparently opposite types of trauma: either a very concrete trauma that is *immediately* repeated, as in the case of the shell-shocked soldiers, or a primordial trauma that is endlessly deferred and repeated through the work of the drives. In both cases there is either *not enough* or *too much* deferral, which amounts to the same thing—repetition becoming mechanical and rigid. We now find in Benjamin a historical interpretation of an equivalent development, modernity giving up the gradual and retroacted absorption of reality in favor of its immediate consumption that parries any shock.

In an overwhelming reality it becomes difficult to integrate shocks. One rather parries them, such that instead of getting access to what Benjamin calls "long experience" (*Erfahrung*), one remains with "immediate experience" (*Erlebnis*):[17]

> The reception of shocks is facilitated by training [*Training*] in coping with stimuli. . . . As a rule . . . this training devolves upon the wakeful consciousness, located in a part of the cortex which is "so frayed by the effect of the stimulus" that it offers the most favorable situation for the reception of stimuli. That the shock is thus cushioned, parried by consciousness, would lend the incident that occasions it the character of an immediate experience [*Erlebnis*], in the strict sense. This would sterilize the incident—incorporated directly in the registry of conscious memory—for poetic long experience [*Erfahrung*]. (SW 4:318)[18]

We see here clearly that consciousness, for Benjamin, is located at the front of the apparatus, aiming to parry any shock[19] and block its arrival at the depth of the apparatus, the home of the unconscious and long experience. Let us recall that, according to the early theory of Freud, the impression first enters the apparatus through the sense organs and arrives at primary perception. This perception is conscious but not yet elaborate, so that if the stimulus does not go further, it quickly fades away without leaving a trace. It is only when it crosses several unconscious layers of registration ("contact barriers") that the stimulus can become conscious in the common sense of the term. This is where Benjamin differs from Freud: for him, there is a sort of "conscious memory" that is located in the very front of the apparatus and consists of superficial registration of the stimulus as a way to parry it.

Benjamin thus extends the role of primary perception which, in Freud, was too vague and non-verbal to register anything whatsoever. It now receives the crucial task of taming and controlling the shock by transforming the stimulus into an immediate, yet isolated, experience that belongs to the realm of voluntary memory. In other words, the reception of shock in modernity necessarily means registering and parrying it, such that the impression never arrives at the depths of the apparatus.

If we recall the double movement of the everyday presented in the introduction, shock is equivalent to that which partially reaches beyond the global movement of the everyday and is then supposed to return to it. Every such shock is, in Benjamin's terms, an immediate experience that is yet to be integrated into long experience—that is, the global movement of the everyday. However, having been parried, the shock is indeed registered as an "extraordinary" event, but one that does not connect to long experience. This explains why the modern everyday is full of "events" or "shocks" that nevertheless leave the impression that nothing "happens". They are perceived as immediate experiences that somehow remain "outside", and the question is now, according to Benjamin, how to let them in, so as to reconnect the everyday and experience, the ordinary and the extraordinary.

As we saw, Benjamin does not consider consciousness as rising instead of (*an Stelle*) memory traces, but rather at their site (*an der Stelle*), and the distinction he makes between voluntary and involuntary memory allows him to envisage such a peculiar conscious registration that does not exist in Freud's early theory.[20] This registration corresponds to voluntary memory and is conducted by isolating a stimulus; giving it time, place and name; and thus depriving it of any further displacement, play or deferral. In this way the shocking stimulus becomes an event "to remember", and yet an event that does not call for any future retroaction. Freud's original concept of trauma thus completely disappears in Benjamin in favor of shocks that can no longer be deferred.

Are all stimuli in modernity so shocking as to create only immediate experience? For Benjamin, shock is not a rare event, but has rather become the *norm* in modernity (SW 4:318); as a result, the peculiar work of conscious registration can never actually cease:

> The greater the shock factor in particular impressions, the more vigilant consciousness has to be in screening stimuli [*Reizschutz*]; the more efficiently it does so, the less these impressions enter long experience and the more they correspond to the concept of immediate experience. Perhaps the special achievement of shock defense is the way it assigns an incident a precise point in time in consciousness, at the cost of the integrity of the incident's contents. This would be a peak achievement of the intellect; it would turn the incident into an immediate experience. Without reflection, there would be nothing but the sudden start [*Schreck*] occasionally pleasant but usually distasteful, which, according to Freud, confirms the failure of the shock defense. (SW 4:319)

The conscious registration of the incident is aimed at avoiding fright, despite the potential pleasure or joy to which the fright may lead. This peculiar frightful joy is probably possible only in well-defined and protected zones, and I can think of horror films or amusement parks as examples.[21] But other than in such particular cases, fright is avoided and the impression is isolated, first and foremost through the work of "reflection"[22] that gives name to the incident. Rather than being repressed, the incident is registered as a well-defined event, yet excluded from involuntary memory, long experience and deferred retroaction.

Benjamin thus radicalises and historicises Freud's later theory of modern everyday life as consisting of infinite shocks that must be immediately registered and parried. The difference between the two thinkers lies in their location of consciousness and its ability to register shocks. But as a matter of fact, Benjamin's procedure of moving consciousness forward is also present in Freud, especially in a text from 1925,[23] describing the psychic apparatus as a self-erasing "mystic writing-pad". In this model of the apparatus, the unconscious is placed *behind* consciousness and sends periodical feelers outwards before pulling them back. It thus seems that the distinction between the unconscious and consciousness is blurred, and that, rather than letting the stimuli enter the apparatus, it is now the apparatus itself that goes out looking for stimuli.

In another text from the same year[24] Freud attributes to the *ego* this capacity to send feelers out into the world: "The ego periodically sends out small amounts of cathexis into the perceptual system, by means of which it samples the external stimuli, and then after every such tentative advance it draws back again" (SE 19:238). The ego, the unconscious and consciousness thus now collaborate to control reality, and this is through the *repetitive* movements of the feelers with their "rapid periodic impulses" (SE 19:231). These movements outwards and inwards seem to be automatic and do not follow any clear pattern; they just repeat,[25] so it seems that shock has become a norm not only of reality but also of the functioning of the apparatus itself. The slow and passive absorption of stimuli, as it had been described in the early *Project*, is no longer possible; instead, much more active levels of perception, attention and consciousness are required. However, these are soon revealed to work in a way that recalls the *symptom*, which, as we saw in the previous chapter, starts as an attempt to gain control of the situation and ends as automatic and rigid behavior, constantly shocking the apparatus from within.

Whereas in Freud the repetition of the symptom is supposed to be the result of specific trauma, Benjamin shows that in modernity the *normal* functioning of the apparatus follows the same model. Even if consciousness moves forward, even if the ego sends feelers, the mode of the apparatus is still that of *emergency*: a repetition that desperately tries to react to and bind the external and internal stimuli, but does nothing but alienate reality by mechanically registering and parrying it.

The emergency mode of the psychic apparatus thus goes hand in hand with the decline of long experience and involuntary memory, and the rise of immediate experience and voluntary memory. This is all the more true in a society that functions upon the mode of the *extraordinary event*, in which one invests energy, time and money, but which does not necessarily communicate with everyday life. The more one prepares, say, a marriage ceremony, the more one is likely to be disappointed by the dull routine of married life thereafter. In other words, as soon as the event, exciting as it be, comes to an end, an emptiness sets in, which leads to a search for new events and adventures, and so on, compulsively, without a means to connect the different traces which have been left behind.

AURA, PRACTICE AND DRILL

Luckily, Benjamin is not content with a mere diagnosis of the crisis of modern experience, but rather aims to supply a complementary prognosis. Is there, then, a way to let the shock in through deferred retroaction and involuntary memory? A clue is given in the figure of Baudelaire, who aimed, according to Benjamin, at an "emancipation from immediate experiences" (SW 4:318). This emancipation—the move from immediate to long experience—could be achieved by Baudelaire only through a painstaking struggle with a very high price:

> Betrayed by these last allies of his, Baudelaire battled the crowd—with the impotent rage of someone fighting the rain or the wind. This is the nature of the immediate experience to which Baudelaire has given the weight of long experience. He named the price for which the sensation of modernity could be had: the disintegration of the aura in immediate shock experience [*Chockerlebnis*]. He paid dearly for consenting to this disintegration—but it is the law of his poetry. This poetry appears in the sky of the Second Empire as "a star without atmosphere". (SW 4:343, translation modified)

By letting himself be penetrated by shocks, Baudelaire managed to transform immediate experience into long experience. But did this pertain to his life or only to his poetry? Or is poetry precisely the deferred and retroactive perception of shocks? We should recall that Benjamin criticises the romantic vision of poetry as representing a superior experience that would escape the crisis of the everyday. What he looks for in poetry is precisely the attempt to make the everyday itself a theme for poetic endeavor, both in content and in form. Such a poetry of the everyday, or an everyday poetry, would incarnate the shock as a moment of modernity. It would show, on the one hand, how it is parried by immediate experience while integrating it into long experience, on the other hand.

In order to explain this paradoxical task, Benjamin must add another crucial element to his conceptual apparatus—namely, the *aura*. The aura is one of the most enigmatic notions in Benjamin's terminology, as attested by the numerous attempts at analysis and interpretation it has received in the last decades.[26] In what follows I shall examine the different definitions Benjamin gives to the aura in his writings from the 1930s, not in order to seize all its aspects and implications, but rather to understand its relation to the mechanism of deferred retroaction within and outside the everyday. My aim is to investigate the possibility of an aura that does not concern an extraordinary event but the everyday itself: the aura of the habitual. Let us begin with one of the definitions Benjamin provides of the aura in the Baudelaire essay:

> If we think of the associations [*Vorstellungen*] which, at home in the involuntary memory, seek to cluster around an object of perception, and if we call these associations the aura of that object, then the aura attaching to the object of perception corresponds precisely to the long experience which, in the case of an object of use, inscribes itself as long practice [*Übung*]. (SW 4:337)

In order to define *aura*, Benjamin uses here the word "associations" or "representations", which is the same term used by Freud to describe the content of the unconscious, for the aura is possible only through the formation of unconscious traces or, in Benjamin's terminology, involuntary memory and long experience. Indeed, these two have become rare in modernity, but we receive here a clue as to what may enable them (and the aura). It is, according to Benjamin, a certain type of practice or exercise: a long-term manual, haptic and embodied use of an object that leads to an understanding of its different parts as well as their relation to other objects.

One cannot avoid thinking here of Heidegger's and Merleau-Ponty's descriptions of how things and objects in the world are (re-)appropriated by work (Heidegger) or by the body (Merleau-Ponty), in a process I characterised as immersed or embodied reflection. But in the same way that Heidegger and Merleau-Ponty delineate an ideal world of use or embodiment only to contrast it later with a deteriorated sphere of ready-made objects, Benjamin, too, opposes the work of the skilled craftsman to the automatic movements of the worker in the assembly line. The factory worker, according to Benjamin, no longer has access to long exercise (*Übung*) but rather to drill (*Dressur*):[27] "All machine work", he cites Marx, "requires prior drilling of the workers" (SW 4:328–29).[28] Drill, contrary to practice, involves a repetitious and mechanical activity like that in *Modern Times*, the result of which is the elimination of long experience: "The unskilled worker is the one most deeply degraded by the drill of the machines. His work has been sealed off from long experience; practice counts for nothing in the factory" (SW 4:329).

The automaton is thus opposed to long experience, but Benjamin soon reveals that it characterises not only the activity of the factory

worker but also modern perception and action in general. To use Freudian terms, the psychic apparatus adjusts itself to reality and starts to
behave as an automatic machine, of which the factory worker is only an
extreme example. Benjamin traces the decline of practice up to the
invention of the match in the nineteenth century. This, he says,
"brought forth a number of innovations which have one thing in common: one abrupt movement of the hand triggers a process of many
steps" (SW 4:328). The sudden tiny shock-movement of the *hand*
which instantaneously brings light to the *eye* is the archetype of modern
technology and the shock it provokes. This stands in contrast to the old
practice that involved long manual movements, thus giving the external
stimulation enough time to find adequate motor abreaction just as in
Freud's early schema.

Modern activity is fast and necessitates immediate reaction, and as
such it rather corresponds to Freud's *later* theory. Instead of letting the
stimulus in, elaborating it in different phases and finally abreacting it
while still keeping some traces for a potential retroaction in the future,
the psychic apparatus now protects itself by adopting mechanical patterns from the outset. Similar to the self-erasing mystic writing-pad, the
apparatus no longer perceives reality as shocking, but rather adjusts
itself to it through repetitious contra-shocks that repel the stimulation,
such that it is no longer possible to tell who delivers shock to whom.[29]
Working in a factory and walking in the street, but also numerous other
everyday activities, produce shocks from within and from without,
making shock-experience and immediate experience one and the same
thing: "The immediate shock experience [*Chockerlebnis*] which the
passer-by has in the crowd corresponds to the immediate 'experiences'
of the worker at his machine" (SW 4:329).[30]

Whereas the passerby and the factory worker only reproduce the
shocks they receive from the outside, Benjamin mentions another figure that *actively* produces shocks. However, this activity is also not
very productive or even enjoyable, since this figure is the *gambler*. In
German, more than in English, *Spieler* has a double meaning of
"player" and "gambler", and Benjamin stresses this ambiguity to suggest that the gambler is he or she who no longer plays the cheerful
games of children, but rather the tedious games of modernity. Gam-
blers do not invent numerous playful ways to repeat; instead, they are
victims of an automatic repetition, playing mechanically and compulsively again and again until they no longer have anything to play with,
losing not only their money but also their experience, life and history:

> The hand movement of the worker at the machine has no connection with the preceding gesture for the very reason that it repeats that gesture exactly. Since each operation at the machine is just as screened off from the preceding operation as a *coup* in a game of chance is from the one that preceded it, the drudgery of the laborer is, in its own way, a counterpart to the drudgery of the gambler. Both types of work are equally devoid of substance. (SW 4:330)

The throw of the dice, the *coup*, lacks any connection with its past. It is not sedimented into historical layers, but rather repeatedly restarts the same process over and over again. The result is the impoverishment of (long) experience, which equals once more the external shock and the subject who is victim to it and causes shocks in return, making betting "a device for giving events the character of a shock, detaching them from the context of long experience" (SW 4:351n54). Like the psychic apparatus that sends "feelers" forwards, the gambler throws the dice, and both activities are unable to create history or (involuntary) memory. Is there a way to stop this mechanical shocking movement? If being modern, for Benjamin, means being "cheated out of one's experience" (SW 4:332), how can one make the cheater undo his or her ruses?

THE RISE AND FALL OF THE AURA:
THE TRIUMPH OF THE WILL

The first definition of the aura did not teach us what it is in the present, but rather what it *used* to be, since the various elements that condition the aura (involuntary memory, long experience and practice) are in decline. Does Benjamin try to promote and restore this vanishing aura? Many commentators have pointed to his ambivalence: on the one hand, he sees the decline of the aura as a possibility for political and cultural renewal, but, on the other hand, he deplores the loss of long experience and involuntary memory, the secret of one's own life.[31]

In "The Work of Art in the Age of Its Technological Reproducibility", written in three different versions between 1935 and 1939 (thus preceding the Baudelaire essay), Benjamin sets for himself the political task of fighting against fascism and promoting communism. He expresses his concerns regarding the fascist use of aura as a part of the cult of the leader, the people, the nation and so on. The fascist or totalitarian regime strengthens itself through a supposedly eternal presence of auratic objects to be worshipped and admired uncritically.

In order to better understand what Benjamin has in mind here, I propose to examine Lenny Riefenstahl's 1935 propaganda film, *The Triumph of the Will*. The film begins with a dazzling auratic scene with clouds surrounding an aircraft, first shown from the interior and then from the outside, flying over the beautiful old city of Nuremberg ornamented with Nazi flags. The aircraft then lands, welcomed by ecstatic cheering masses which repeat over and over again the same gestures and cries of worship and adoration, coming to a climax when, at last, the door of the aircraft opens and the leader comes out to show his auratic presence: Adolf Hitler, the Führer.[32]

The film was contemporary to Benjamin's writing of his artwork essay, which implies he knew very well that, far from simply declining, the aura was in the process of being diverted from religious to political needs.[33] In this way, the national leader could be regarded as representing the eternal being of the people, whereas Benjamin sought to contrast this picture by showing the hidden absence and ephemerality of the aura. However, does the aura necessarily refer to presence or might it also imply absence?

Before I return to the film, let me first examine the two definitions of the aura provided in the artwork essay. The first definition is negative: "What withers in the age of the technological reproducibility of the work of art is the latter's aura" (SW 4:254). The reproduced object loses its aura since it no longer has a material or "authentic" presence to refer to, being a mere reproduction without a solid origin to refer to. Benjamin thus locates the withering aspect of aura in *tradition*:

> It might be stated as a general formula that the technology of reproduction detaches the reproduced object from the sphere of tradition. By replicating the work many times over, it substitutes a mass existence for a unique existence. And in permitting the reproduction to reach the recipient in his or her own situation, it actualizes that which is reproduced. These two processes lead to a massive upheaval in the domains of objects handed down from the past—a shattering of tradition which is the reverse side of the present crisis and renewal of humanity. (SW 4:254; italics in original)

This notion of tradition may help us connect this definition to the definition of the aura given in the Baudelaire essay. The associations that "cluster around an object of perception" and lead to its aura are now understood as *tradition*, which is, I would suggest, a social and political form of involuntary memory. When something is massively reproduced it cannot become a part of tradition due to two processes mentioned by Benjamin: the first is the disappearance of the *unique* origin, especially in photography,[34] such that there are no longer authority and authenticity to constitute tradition. The second process is the *actualisation* of the reproduced object in time and in space, so that it no longer remains in the past, but rather belongs to the present life of its spectators whenever they wish. In this way, again, the temporal hierarchy of the origin, which is necessary to tradition, no longer exists, and the reproduced object therefore belongs to the realm of a superficial present and ceases to contribute to the gradual sedimentation of meaning and history.

It would be tempting to consider the decline of tradition and the rise of superficial present as signs of decay, but Benjamin develops here a different idea, since, for him, the "liquidation of the value of tradition" is not a regrettable process, but rather corresponds to and reinforces "the mass movements of our day". In other words, the decline of aura and tradition opens up the rise of revolutionary forces, whose "most powerful agent" is the film (SW 4:254).[35]

What makes film revolutionary according to Benjamin? On the one hand, it is a work with no origin; on the other hand, its destination is the masses who watch it whenever they want, gaining access to unprecedented scenes and images. This combination of lack of origin together with an easy access to different times and places leads to a radical transformation of various spatio-temporal categories and to a dramatic decrease in the force of tradition, which loses its authoritative origin. While watching the filmed stories of the Bible, for instance, the spectators may see them as realistic plots, such that they no longer maintain their majestical sovereignty of an inaccessible past. The stories rather become contemporary with their spectators and blur the distinctions between past and present, origin and reproduction. In this way, according to Benjamin, the masses are able to see the origins of tradition with a critical eye and thus to give the tradition up in favor of a new and different reality.

However, if we return to *The Triumph of the Will*, we note that, contrary to Benjamin's claim, the film uses the technique of reproduction precisely in order to *enhance* tradition and aura. So technological reproduction does not necessarily weaken tradition and may actually help manipulate and adapt it to the needs of the governing power, as attested by the efforts and money that the Nazi regime spent on propaganda films. Moreover, technological reproduction presents a triple advantage for fascism: (1) it enables a rapid distribution of images; (2) it creates a forceful emotional tie between the people and their leader; (3) it implements in the life of the spectators an instant tradition, turning, for example, the young Nazi movement into a venerable and traditional party whose roots go far back to the very birth of Germany.

This last point is demonstrated in the prologue of the film, when, accompanied by a dramatic musical score by Herbert Windt,[36] the opening titles, running very slowly, are presented title after title in large decorated letters:

> *On 5 September 1934*
> *20 years after the outbreak of the World War*
> *16 years after the beginning of German suffering*
> *19 months after the beginning of the German rebirth*
> *Adolf Hitler flew again to Nuremberg to review the columns of his*
>   *faithful followers*

The imaginary chronological history of the Third Reich is thus conveyed through detailed numbers and dates, preparing the ground for the auratic object, Adolf Hitler, who can now *re*appear, flying to Nuremberg *again*. This repetition, though, is quite manipulative, since the "again" (*wiederum*) intentionally conflates two levels: on the explicit level, the filmed event repeats the former rallies, for it is the sixth Nazi Party Congress and the fourth to be held in Nuremberg, but on the implicit level, the event retroacts something which goes much earlier in history, coming full circle back to a mysterious origin—a primordial birth which had occurred years before the *re*birth of the German Nation which only retroacts it.

Deferred retroaction is thus used by the film to prepare the ground for a fascist and superficial aura. Moreover, we can clearly see here how deferred retroaction connects the realms of voluntary and involuntary memory, through a mixture of various dates and events which are either precise and clear or mythical and indistinctive ("German suffering" and "German rebirth"). All these events appear after a mysterious mention of a date in the first title ("On 5 September 1934") and before the revelation of what happened that day ("Adolf Hitler flew again"), so that the voluntary memory (an exact day to remember) literally wraps the involuntary memory, at the same time that it is wrapped by the small word "again". In this way involuntary memory (tradition) is not simply evoked but simultaneously instigated and reinforced through a deferred retroaction which juxtaposes "objective" events (the

Nazi rally, the World War) with mythical and "subjective" events (suffering and rebirth).

We may recall Benjamin's affirmation that the ancient religious rituals knew how to balance voluntary and involuntary memory, whereas modern life accentuates the first and neglects the second. However, with Riefenstahl we see a modern movement that appropriates tradition precisely through a sophisticated use of reproduction as part of ritual.[37] Moreover, the formal element of reproduction in the film is accompanied in Riefenstahl by a reproduction of its content. Thus, when Hitler gets out of the aircraft and starts his short journey from the airport to the hotel, he is driven between two columns of masses, the same masses seen previously from above as small ants, serving as a part of their leader's aura. The physical clouds surrounding Hitler are equivalent to the human clouds which do not have any individual identity. Consequently, the Nazi movement acquires an allure which is both organic (an entire, healthy body) and mechanical (automatic and repetitive movements of all the "organs"). "Mass reproduction is especially favored by the reproduction of the masses" (SW 4:282n47), writes Benjamin, but the result of both reproductions is not necessarily the decline of aura (and deferred retroaction), as he argues,[38] but also the enhancement of a fascist and superficial aura and retroaction.

TOWARDS AN EVERYDAY DEFERRED RETROACTION

The aura is closely linked to the mechanism of deferred retroaction, and the question is how to make a use of these two in a way that would lead to an integrated everyday life—yet an integration that is not superficial or fascist. Let us, then, examine Benjamin's famous next definition of *aura*, given first in 1931 and then reproduced in all three versions of the artwork essay.[39] This definition does not concern historical or cultural objects, but rather what Benjamin calls "natural objects": "We define the aura of the latter as the unique apparition of a distance, however near it may be. To follow with the eye—while resting on a summer afternoon—a mountain range on the horizon or a branch that casts its shadow on the beholder is to breathe the aura of those mountains, of that branch" (SW 4:255).

This aura thus necessitates an isolated meditative contemplation of nature,[40] characteristic of nineteenth-century romanticism which prescribed a retreat from the crowd as a means to achieve unity with nature. The problem is that this meditative situation is itself conditioned by cultural circumstances, which are no longer possible in the modern everyday and in a society based upon constant availability. Benjamin thus introduces the "natural" aura only in order to mention two modern cultural forces that ward it off: "the desire of the present-day masses to 'get closer' to things spatially and humanly, and their equally passionate concern to overcome each thing's uniqueness by assimilating it as a reproduction" (SW 4:255).

The two conditions of the aura of natural objects are (1) uniqueness and (2) balance between distance and proximity.[41] These conditions are subjected to changing cultural forces, which bring the aura of *both* natural and cultural objects to decline. Indeed, we hardly ever find ourselves lying lazily in a field,[42] and even if we did, we would probably feel the urge to capture this sensation, if not with our cameras, then at least in our minds through a snapshot-like voluntary memory. Letting oneself be penetrated by reality is the condition for aura, but this penetration, I argue, has become either too dangerous or simply undesirable. Reality carries with it the threat of a shock which must be avoided and parried through its registration—that is, its transformation into a repetitious reproduction which is easy to control.

To better understand the relationship between shock and the aura, I propose to briefly examine how the two above-mentioned conditions of the aura are affected by shock. The first condition of the aura is uniqueness: something which occurs only once. When an event or an object has no precedent and is *totally* new, it is inevitably perceived as shocking and therefore must be somehow repeated and practiced in order to be comprehended. But although every object I perceive was once new, it is obvious that not every object becomes auratic.[43] Something about the newness and uniqueness of the thing must *persist* despite (or rather *through*) its repetition, leading to the gradual appearance of its aura. The aura thus results from a shock that has somehow managed to enter the apparatus and be repeated while still never fully abreacted.

This situation is further articulated in the second condition of the aura: the uniqueness of the object is not enough for the creation of the aura and should be characterised by a distance as well, no matter how near it may be. But how is shock related to distance? The totally new stimulus that has penetrated the psychic apparatus cannot fully arrive at consciousness. Something in it must remain inaccessible, in the depths of the unconscious. But once again, this is not sufficient to create an aura, since the stimulus must get closer to consciousness while still remaining at a distance. In Freud, the only way to achieve this peculiar combination is through the mechanism of deferred retroaction, which plays a crucial role in the creation of aura. According to Freud's early theory, the original shocking event is deferred and can be accessed only later on through its retroaction. This retroaction makes it reappear as close, but, on the other hand, it (re)introduces distance in time and space, since, rather than simply repeating the original event, it retroacts it in the light of the present. No matter how alive the repeated event or the object may be, it still carries with it the mark of difference from the original event.

Differently put, although every object was once new and shocking, only those that had *not* been elaborated immediately, only those that were first deferred and then retroacted through a second event, are those which would provoke an experience of aura. This experience was achieved, for instance, by Proust, who had "great familiarity with the problem of the aura": present sensations (taste of the madeleine, balancing between two uneven tiles, the sound of a spoon knocking a plate, etc.) suddenly evoked in him past events or times (childhood in Combray, journey to Venice, holidays in Balbec) and gave them weight and force they did not seem to originally possess. Something in the narrator's childhood, but also in events during his adult life,[44] remained in their primitive and unelaborate state, partly blocked from consciousness, and it is precisely this inaccessibility which permitted Proust to attain the experience of aura.

The experience of aura itself, then, necessitates and involves a certain form of repetition, which affects, I claim, the uniqueness of the auratic object. This point is illustrated by Benjamin's description of the mountain and the branch: although—and because—one has already seen many mountains and branches beforehand, something in their here and now, their present perception, suddenly crosses the threshold needed for aura, combining uniqueness and repetition, distance and nearness, strangeness and familiarity. This exceptional moment does not stand in a simple contrast to the former encounters with the mountain or the branch, but is rather achieved *through* these encounters, in a manner that cannot be fully known in advance or controlled.

I thus propose that an object may become auratic through deferred retroaction with the following three phases: (1) first encounter with the object; (2) repetitive practice and habituation; (3) an auratic encounter with the object. In the early theory of Freud, as we saw, deferred retroaction has a different structure, consisting of (1) a traumatic event;

(2) a period of latency; and (3) a similar event which provokes repetitive symptoms around a displaced object. It is the second phase which is different in the two schemes, since whereas the period of latency in Freud seems to be quite idle, keeping the original object or event inactive and static, this period, or at least a part of it,[45] now consists of an active practice in some elements of the first encounter, to be fully revealed in the third phase.

Indeed, we saw that the more Freud advances in his theory, the more significant the role he attributes to repetition becomes. Repetition now tends to come *immediately* after a traumatic event, as in the case of the shell-shocked soldiers. I have suggested, however, that deferred retroaction may take place not only through a long lapse of time after the original event but also through a much shorter interval, as in the case of the *fort-da* game, and in children's games in general.[46] With Benjamin we now find an explanation for this more or less immediate retroaction that becomes a phase of practice *before* the advent of another retroaction, much later, which gives the practiced object or activity an auratic allure. In the next chapter I will claim that this "aura of the habitual" may both resolve the tension between the different directions in Benjamin and offer important insights as to how to overcome the modern opposition between the everyday and experience.

NOTES

1. I refer here to "historical trauma", and I propose that "structural trauma" belongs more to the domain of shock.

2. See, for example, Douglas Rushkoff, *Present Shock: When Everything Happens Now* (New York: Current, 2013).

3. Paul Valéry, "The Conquest of Ubiquity", in *Aesthetics*, trans. Ralph Manheim (New York: Pantheon Books, 1964), 225. Quoted by Walter Benjamin in "The Work of Art in the Age of Its Technological Reproducibility. Third Version", in *Selected Writings*, 4 vols., ed. Howard Eiland, Michael W. Jennings and Gary Smith (Cambridge, MA: Harvard University Press, 2003), 4: 251. All references from the Harvard University Press edition of Benjamin's *Selected Writings* will be abbreviated henceforth as SW followed by the volume and page number. In several places I have modified the translation.

4. Walter Benjamin, *The Arcades Project*, ed. Rolf Tiedemann, trans. Howard Eiland and Kevin McLaughlin (Cambridge, MA: Belknap Press, 1999). Henceforth abbreviated AP.

5. SW 4:313–55. For an excellent analysis of this essay, see Andrew Benjamin, "Tradition and Experience: Walter Benjamin's 'On Some Motifs in Baudelaire'", in *The Problems of Modernity: Adorno and Benjamin*, ed. Andrew Benjamin (London: Routledge, 1989), 122–40.

6. Baudelaire was born in the same year as Flaubert and published *Les Fleurs du mal* a year after *Madame Bovary*. Both authors were thereafter persecuted for immorality; Flaubert was acquitted, Baudelaire convicted.

7. As a matter of fact, shock does appear several times in Bergson's *Matter and Memory*. I do not pretend to give here a satisfying account of Bergson's philosophy, but rather to see it through the angle of Benjamin's own theory of modern experience. See Henri Bergson, *Matter and Memory*, trans. Nancy Margaret Paul and W. Scott Palmer (New York: Zone Books, 1991), 50, 119, 171, 199. See also Deleuze's fascinating analysis of Bergson in the context of cinema, which conveys the complexity of Bergson's theory: Gilles Deleuze, *Cinema 1: The Movement-Image*, trans. Hugh Tomlinson and Barbara Habberjam (Minneapolis: University of Minnesota Press, 1986); Gilles Deleuze, *Cinema 2: The Time-Image*, trans. Hugh Tomlinson and Robert Galeta (Minneapolis: University of Minnesota Press, 1989). Discussing Bergson and Deleuze, however, even in the context of cinema, would take me too far from my aim here, which is to understand the everyday. In this sense I tend to agree with Benjamin that Bergson (as well as Deleuze) aims to overcome the everyday rather than to linger in it.

8. Elissa Marder pushes this idea further and suggests, following Lyotard, that Baudelaire (and Flaubert) be re-written as "a temporal technique that enables us to counter the temporal disorders of modernity" (Marder, *Dead Time: Temporal Disorders in the Wake of Modernity [Baudelaire and Flaubert]* [Stanford, CA: Stanford University Press, 2001], 12).

9. Blanchot gives the same example and connects it to the contemporary status of the everyday: "The everyday is without event; in the newspaper this absence of event becomes the drama of the news item. In the everyday everything is everyday; in the newspaper everything is strange, sublime, abominable" (Maurice Blanchot, "Everyday Speech", in *The Infinite Conversation*, trans. S. Hanson [Minneapolis and London: University of Minnesota Press, 1993], 243). I will later argue that long experience (*Erfahrung*) refers in Benjamin to the global movement of the everyday.

10. In his 1936 essay, "The Storyteller: Observations on the Works of Nikolai Leskov", Benjamin opposes the story to the novel, seeing the latter as a modern articulation of the crisis of experience. Contrary to a story, a novel does not relate the author's personal experience to the experience of the readers: "The novelist has secluded himself. The birthplace of the novel is the individual in his isolation, the individual who can no longer speak his concerns in exemplary fashion, who himself lacks counsel and can give none" (SW 3:146).

11. Incidentally, Benjamin also had a habit of writing while lying down on his sofa. See his letter to Gerhard (Gershom) Scholem from 20 December 1931: "I now write only while lying down. I have a sofa inherited from my predecessor. It lends itself most wonderfully as a place to work because of its qualities—it is quite useless for sleeping" (*The Correspondence of Walter Benjamin 1910–1940*, ed. Gershom Scholem and Theodor W. Adorno, trans. Manfred R. Jacobson and Evelyn M. Jacobson [Chicago: University of Chicago Press, 1994], 387).

12. Marcel Proust, *Time Regained*, trans. Andreas Mayor and Terence Kilmartin (New York: Modern Library, 2003), 298–99.

13. Eli Friedlander argues that Proust managed to show that "the striking and the boring are two sides of the same texture of life" (Eli Friedlander, *Walter Benjamin: A Philosophical Portrait* [Cambridge, MA: Harvard University Press, 2012], 99). I entirely accept this claim, but I wonder if this interdependency between the ordinary and the extraordinary can be understood in the *present* or only *retroactively*, with regard to *past* everyday circumstances.

14. More than any other movement, surrealism explored the unconscious through free association and displacement, aiming to free one's mind and access one's hidden life and ideas. However, rather than "healing" the subject, André Breton wished to free

it from everyday constraints, blurring the limits between consciousness and the unconscious (Breton, *Manifestoes of Surrealism*, trans. Richard Seaver and Helen R.
Lane [Ann Arbor: University of Michigan Press, 1969], 10). In an essay Benjamin dedicated
to surrealism in 1929, he characterises it not as a *theory*, but rather as an *experience* of
"profane illumination" that can be provoked through intoxication (SW 2:208–9). Finally, Freud himself, in a letter he wrote in reply to Breton on 26 December 1932, con-
fessed that he was "not in the position to explain what Surrealism is or what it is after"
(F. B. Davis, "Three Letters from Sigmund Freud to André Breton", *Journal of the
American Psychoanalytic Association* 1, no. 21 [1973]: 131). We may thus conclude
that Freud's enterprise and the surrealists' project were almost contradictory, the first
trying to better *control* the unconscious and the second to *set it free*.

15. See Freud's paper from 1909, "Obsessive Actions and Religious Ceremonies",
SE 9:115–27.

16. See SE 18:25. I modified both translations. Strachey's translation of Freud says,
"Consciousness arises instead of a memory trace", whereas the *Selected Writings* tried
to bypass the problem by saying, "Emerging consciousness takes the place of a memory
trace". See on this topic Sigrid Weigel, *Body- and Image-Space: Re-Reading Walter
Benjamin*, trans. Georgina Paul (London and New York: Routledge, 1996), 107. Weigel
notes that the German *an Stelle* has the same ambiguous meaning as the English *in place
of* that can be understood as both "instead of" and "in the site of".

17. It is impossible to properly translate into English the difference between *Erfahrung* and *Erlebnis*, which are both referred to as "experience".

18. Translation modified. The original English translation of the last sentence is very
misleading: "If it were incorporated directly in the registry of conscious memory, it
would sterilize this incident for poetic experience". The reader thus gets the impression
of an alternative: *either* to parry the shock *or* to incorporate it directly, whereas, for
Benjamin, it is precisely *through* the registration/incorporation that one parries the
shock. The German original says, "Es würde diesen Vorfall (unmittelbar der Registratur
der bewußten Erinnerung ihn einverleibend) für die dichterische Erfahrung sterilisieren"
(Walter Benjamin, *Gesammelte Schriften*, Band I [Frankfurt am Main: Suhrkamp,
1991], 614). The "Es" at the beginning of the phrase ("This would . . .") refers to the
sentence before and not to shock, which is masculine in German. For an example of this
misunderstanding, see Mark Hansen, *Embodying Technesis: Technology beyond Writing* (Ann Arbor: University of Michigan Press, 2000), 244–45.

19. I follow here a line of thought developed by Susan Buck-Morss, who locates in
modernity the need for "anaesthetics" as an elaborate defence technics. See Susan Buck-
Morss, "Aesthetics and Anaesthetics: Walter Benjamin's Artwork Essay Reconsidered",
October 62 (Autumn 1992): 3–41.

20. Freud's *Project* was published posthumously in 1950, and obviously could not be
read by Benjamin. On Benjamin's reading of Freud, see Weigel, *Body- and Image-
Space*, esp. 106–7. See also Sarah Ley Roff, "Benjamin and Psychoanalysis", in *The
Cambridge Companion to Walter Benjamin*, ed. David Ferris (Cambridge: Cambridge
University Press, 2004), 115–33.

21. See Benjamin's analysis of world exhibitions in AP 17–18, as well as his charac-
terisation of "Lunaparks" as "a prefiguration of sanatoria" (SW 1:487).

22. This reflection, as will become clear below, has nothing to do with the immersed
or embodied reflection we found in Heidegger and Merleau-Ponty.

23. See *A Note upon the "Mystic Writing-Pad"*, SE 19:227–32.

24. See *Negation*, SE 19:235–39.

25. This movement is described by Derrida in "Freud and the Scene of Writing", in
Writing and Difference, trans. Alan Bass (Chicago: University of Chicago Press, 1978),
esp. 223–29.

26. See in particular Andrew Benjamin, "The Decline of Art: Benjamin's Aura", *Oxford Art Journal* 9, no. 2 (1986): 30–35; Miriam Bratu Hansen, *Cinema and Experience* (Berkeley: University of California Press, 2012), 104–31.

27. The English translation of Benjamin's *Selected Writings* uses here the word "training", but I prefer the old translation of "drill" (*Illuminations*, trans. Harry Zohn [New York: Shocken Books, 1968], 176), since it avoids a possible confusion with a third term used by Benjamin—namely, *Training*, which is more neutral. Training is in particular presented by Benjamin in the context of coping with shocks as an attempt to gradually get used to them. Training takes place, for instance, in the cinema, whereas drill is a mechanical repetition which is more a *surrender* to the shock than a real confrontation with it.

28. This citation from *Capital* is typically altered by Benjamin, who appropriates and adjusts it to his theory, replacing the original term *Anlernung* (inculcation) with the more oppressive *Dressur* (drill). See Karl Marx, *Capital: A Critique of Political Economy*, vol. 1, trans. Ben Fowkes (London: Penguin Books, 1976), 546. This translation says, "All work at a machine requires the worker to be taught from childhood upwards".

29. "Moving through this traffic involves the individual in a series of shocks and collisions. At dangerous intersections, nervous impulses flow through him in rapid succession, like the energy from a battery" (SW 4:328).

30. This may also be a reply to Maurice Samuels, who has criticised the extensive use in recent years of trauma theory inspired by Benjamin. He asks sarcastically how it could be that, given their constant traumas, the inhabitants of Paris managed to so actively rebuild their capital during the Second Empire (Maurice Samuels, "2000: Trauma on the Boulevard", *Romanic Review* 101, no. 1/2 [2010]: 115–122). The answer is, of course, that they were not traumatised but shocked, which means precisely that they *parried* the shocks. If one wishes to phenomenologically look for shock, it is rather in the complaints of boredom and emptiness, so recurrent in the literature of that period, that it is to be found.

31. See, among others, Marleen Stoessel, *Aura: Das vergessene Menschliche: Zur Sprache und Erfahrung bei Walter Benjamin* (Munich and Vienna: Carl Henser Verlag, 1983); Hansen, *Cinema and Experience*, 104–31; Carolin Duttlinger, "Imaginary Encounters: Walter Benjamin and the Aura of Photography", *Poetics Today* 29, no. 1 (2008): 79–101.

32. See Susan Buck-Morss's short analysis of this auratic image in *The Dialectics of Seeing: Walter Benjamin and the Arcades Project* (Cambridge, MA: MIT Press, 1991), 245, as well as her "Aesthetics and Anaesthetics", 38. See also on this theme Soren Pold, "An Aesthetic Criticism of the Media: The Configurations of Art, Media and Politics in Walter Benjamin's Materialistic Aesthetics", *Parallax* 5, no. 3 (1999): 22–35.

33. This does not mean that the old religious rituals were not political, but rather that they were not conceived in the abrupt way the fascist regimes were.

34. Benjamin chooses to focus on photography as the art which has no unique material origin. However, it is doubtful if the technology of reproduction implies a loss of origin in other domains. What can be said, for instance, of the millions of reproductions of the *Mona Lisa*? Don't they rather magnify the aura of their origin in the Louvre?

35. Rosalind Krauss justly remarks that mass movements may be fascist and reactionary as well. See Krauss, *The Optical Unconscious* (Cambridge, MA: MIT Press, 1993), 179.

36. On the role of music in *The Triumph of the Will*, see Stefan Strötgen, "'I compose the Party Rally . . .': The Role of Music in Leni Riefenstahl's *Triumph of the Will*", trans. Anita Ip, *Music & Politics* 2, no. 1 (2008): 1–14.

37. This is why Adorno criticised Benjamin's revolutionary expectations from films. See his letter to Benjamin from 18 March 1936 in Adorno et al., *Aesthetics and Politics*, ed. Frederic Jameson, trans. Harry Zohn (London and New York: Verso, 2007), 120–27.

38. "The stripping of the veil from the object, the destruction of the aura, is the signature of a perception whose 'sense for sameness in the world' has so increased that, by means of reproduction, it extracts sameness even from what is unique" (SW 4:255–56). However, it is precisely this presumed link between equality and loss of aura which is refuted by *The Triumph of the Will*: the crowd is the same, but the Führer is unique.

39. See "Little History of Photography", in SW 2:518–19. The "unique apparition of a distance" reappears in the Baudelaire essay, SW 4:338.

40. See Benjamin's interesting remarks on yoga in "One-Way Street", SW 1:466, as well as on ecstatic trance, SW 1:486–87.

41. On Klages's idea of distance and nearness and its influence on Benjamin, see Hansen, *Cinema and Experience*, 122–27.

42. It is interesting to return here to Lol Stein and recall the rye field behind the hotel, in which she lay down to watch her lover betray her from a distance. She thus reinforced his aura, at least until the end of the novel, when she falls asleep.

43. Although the aura is generally defined as characterising perception, Benjamin tends to attribute it to concrete objects as well. The aura is thus created at the meeting point between perception and objects.

44. As Roland Barthes mentions, it is not clear how old the narrator is and who he actually might be (Roland Barthes, "The Death of the Author", in *Image–Music–Text*, ed. and trans. Stephen Heath [New York: Hill & Wang, 1977], 144). Since Proust's entire novel is written as a part of deferred retroaction, assigning an exact time (and thus age) to the depicted event would be impossible.

45. As I will later show, Benjamin's retroaction consists of an "idle" latency as well, but only *after* an initial practice of the object.

46. This is why Benjamin could retroact his own childhood in various occasions. See in particular "Berlin Childhood around 1900", in SW 3:344–413.

Chapter Five

The Aura of the Habitual

The aura of the habitual appears only once in Benjamin, in his *Arcades Project*, and it is attributed to "childhood, memory and dream".[1] Indeed, whereas memory and dream have been diverted in modernity, as we saw in the previous chapter, the child seems to remain a privileged, "incorruptible" character. At the end of chapter 3, I presented the child as a "pre-modern" figure that is still able to playfully elaborate shocks, and this through a certain use of deferred retroaction. In this chapter I will analyse such use of deferred retroaction through Benjamin's notion of "room for play". I will ask what room for play is possible in adult everyday life, and I will conclude the chapter with a discussion of a striking example of this possibility that I find in Cindy Sherman's artistic work.

A ROOM FOR PLAY

In the previous chapter I confronted Benjamin's optimistic vision of film with the fascist manipulation of film as it is exemplified by *The Triumph of the Will*. The propaganda film re-introduces the aura into what is supposed to resist it—namely, the film—and this through a superficial use of deferred retroaction. The question I wish to elaborate on now is whether another use of deferred retroaction may permit a different aura, and if so where we are to locate it.

Miriam Hansen proposes that in film there is an *interplay* between art, technology and the masses.[2] She turns to the second version of the artwork essay from 1935 and finds in it two types of technologies: a first that "existed only in fusion with ritual" (SW 3:107) and a second, modern technology, which is secular and promotes provisionality, constant transformations and, most importantly, *play*. The role of cinema, to summarise Hansen's interpretation, is to teach us the playful use of this second technology.

When I watch a film I can practice the new possibilities of perception brought by the second technology: "The function of film is to train human beings in the apperceptions and reactions needed to deal with a vast apparatus whose role in their lives is expanding almost daily" (SW 3:108). Although a film such as *Modern Times* may look at first dark-humoured or pessimistic, it actually aims to make its spectators become used to the new technological era, overcoming their anxiety of machines in order to start playing with them. Seen from this perspective, the hero of *Modern Times* does not wish to sabotage the machines so much as to make *fun* of them; he wants to destroy only their overwhelming and alienating aspect, such that instead of being a source of slavery they might become the arena of play: "Because this technology aims at liberating human beings from drudgery, the individual suddenly sees his scope for play, his field of action [*Spielraum*], immeasurably expanded" (SW 3:124n10).

What is the relationship between this new scope for play and the aura? For Benjamin, play excludes the aura, since the latter belongs only to the old art of semblance (*Schein*): "What is lost in the withering of semblance and the decay of the aura in works of art is matched by a huge gain in the scope for play [*Spiel-Raum*]. This space for play is widest in film" (SW 3:127n22). But does the new scope for play exclude *all* forms of aura? Hansen claims that Benjamin actually fights against the aura as a part of "a desperate experiment", whose real goal is to save the aura *obliquely*. Employing a sophisticated strategy, Benjamin would actually wish "to place the aura under erasure, to mark it as constitutively belated and irreversibly moribund", while simultaneously transferring some of its element into other terms, which Hansen locates in the "mimetic faculty" and the "optical unconscious".[3] I fully adhere to Hansen's line of thought, and on this basis I shall now try to further develop what she merely sketches—namely, the belated and oblique character of "the aura of the habitual" and the role of play in it.

LOST-AND-FOUND AURA

In a section of the early text *One-Way Street* (written between 1923 and 1926), entitled "Lost-and-Found Office" (*Fundbüro*), Benjamin describes what seems to be two opposite groups of objects:

> *Articles lost.*—What makes the very first glimpse of a village, a town, in the landscape so incomparable and irretrievable is the rigorous connection between foreground [*Nähe*] and distance. Habit has not yet done its work. As soon as we begin to find our bearings, the landscape vanishes at a stroke, like the façade of a house as we enter it. It has not yet gained preponderance through a constant exploration that has become habit. Once we begin to find our way about, that earliest picture can never be restored.
>
> *Articles found.*—The blue distance which never gives way to foreground or dissolves at our approach . . . is the painted distance of a backdrop. It is what gives stage sets their incomparable character. (SW 1:468)

This is indeed a very peculiar lost-and-found office, in which what is found is not necessarily what has been lost. So what is it? I would suggest that it is nothing but the aura, which disappears (is "lost") in everyday life, goes through a transformation, and reappears (is "found") as theatre decor.[4] To a large extent this oblique description of the aura foresees Benjamin's later declarations of its decline, while slightly twisting them, since the aura is not only something lost but also something found, yet only through an optic *illusion*—the unique "blue distance".[5]

However, the picture is in fact even more complicated, since the aura is found in both the second compartment and the first,[6] through, I argue, the mechanism of deferred retroaction. What Benjamin describes as initially lost is not yet the aura but only the first impression of an object—namely, its "façade". This impression is too new and shocking to become auratic: "Habit has not yet done its work". It must first be practiced, repeated and "lost" in order to later return and bring with it the aura. The notion of deferred retroaction that I locate in Benjamin is, as we have begun to see, slightly different from the one presented by Freud; the (temporary) loss of the impression is not the consequence of trauma and repression, but quite the opposite. It is due to an everyday *practice* of the object that its first impression gets lost:

one enters the house and therefore loses the sight of its façade. But when and how does this sight return?

If we recall the scheme of deferred retroaction I presented in the previous chapter, we may note that the lost-articles compartment presents the two first phases of Benjamin's mechanism: (1) first encounter with the object, and (2) repetitive practice and habituation. Phase 3—namely, the auratic encounter with the object—does not seem to belong to this compartment. However, the two phases prepare the necessary conditions for the third phase: the everyday repetitive use of the object familiarises one with what at first seemed extraordinary, thus leading to a dialectic between the extraordinary and the ordinary, the event and the everyday, distance and proximity—a dialectic that is the very definition of the aura. This second phase of habituation does not immediately bring one closer to the first impression, nor does it simply create a distance from it. It rather integrates the impression into one's global movement of the everyday *as lost*—and thus as potentially auratic in the future.

Slow habituation, for Benjamin (but also for Heidegger and Merleau-Ponty), stands in contrast to immediate vision, and getting used to something means losing sight of it: "As soon as we begin to find our bearings, the landscape vanishes at a stroke". The visual is the condition for aura, as indicates its literal meaning of "halo". But when I get used to an object, my relationship with it ceases to be visual and becomes tactile and embodied: I use, manipulate and touch it rather than stare at it. The sight of the thing somehow disappears in favor of an everyday practice, but this practice, rather than excluding the future aura of the thing, is already a part of the process of deferred retroaction. If I remain solely with the visual image of the object without further elaborating it, I may have access only to a voluntary memory of it— that is, something similar to a beautiful postcard or snapshot which I have photographed, registered and therefore parried. However, if I see a beautiful façade and then *get inside* its depths and make it a part of my everyday, I may eventually experience its aura through its retroaction.

An example of such auratic deferred retroaction could be Proust's experience of the madeleine, which brought him back to Combray and Combray back to him. This experience, let us recall, goes as follows: the taste of the madeleine suddenly evokes the childhood habit of tasting a madeleine after immersing it in a cup of tea during the narrator's Sunday visits to his aunt. It is thus not a single event that is retroacted, but a series of repetitive events—a *practice*—which then brings with it other series of events that took place in Combray. To describe these, Proust uses the past tense of the imperfect (*imparfait*) that expresses habits and regularities rather than singular events. He recounts how the entire town of Combray slowly rises up from the madeleine like a theatre décor, and it is only upon this auratic background that his story can start (again).[7] Yet even then, when singular events in Combray are recounted, they all seem to relate to very trivial details—so much so that one of Proust's contemporary critics was scandalised by the number of pages written about a childhood in which nothing extraordinary happened.[8] However, it is precisely the apparently *ordinary* aspect of Proust's childhood which permitted him to integrate it into his life and years later to retroact it through what *suddenly* becomes an extraordinary event (e.g., tasting the madeleine). The extraordinary is perceived in an isolated form only by the adult, whereas for the child the everyday consists of the ordinary practice of extraordinary events—that is, of a continual integration of events into the global movement of the everyday by their repetition.

A second example could be Citizen Kane's last word before his death—namely, "Rosebud": a mysterious reference that is sought for the entire film in order to try to discover the hero's supposed life secret. It is only at the very end of the film that the spectators find what Rosebud actually was: a simple sled with which Kane used to play as a child. This everyday toy has become auratic in the eyes of Kane, implying a mechanism of deferred retroaction that takes place upon Kane's approaching death: a total absence or loss (radical negativity) that retroacts a lost everyday object ("small" negativity).[9]

Both these examples show an everyday practice during childhood that is retroacted in adult age and consequently receives an aura. But can the aura result also from adult practice? The decline of the (adult) aura declared by Benjamin seems to stem from the modern inability to get inside a visual object ("façade") and dwell in it. Differently put, modernity is so anxious to get hold of things and control them that it cannot accept giving up its gaze, losing a thing to win it back retroactively. Indeed, the first impression we have from things necessarily gets lost due to the passing of time, but it is only through accepting this loss and integrating it into our lives through various practices that the thing's later retroaction may be enabled. If, on the other hand, we attempt to seize the impression through its registration, we may only gain access to a mechanical repetition (or voluntary memory) that cannot provoke retroaction.

Moreover, we see here clearly how the two dimensions of shock are united: the "too little" (absence, deficiency and finitude described by phenomenology) and the "too much" (the overwhelming reality described by Freud and Benjamin). The first impression is too new and, as such, perceived as dangerous, but the threat lies not only in letting it *in* (danger of "too much") but also in letting it *go* (danger of "too little"). Both aspects are avoided through registration of the impression. It is thus held inside, yet as a foreign body that is not yet integrated into the everyday.

This is why it is so difficult to get inside the first compartment ("Articles lost") and one is rather tempted to turn to the second ("Articles found"). In it one finds ready-made objects, but also a ready-made aura: objects and aura that do not belong to the everyday and do not necessitate any practice or work. They are rather artificially produced beforehand, such that the spectators can easily and immediately get hold of them, while still attaining the auratic balance between distance and nearness. This kind of aura belongs, according to Benjamin, to the world of *theatre*, literally meaning in Greek "place for viewing". It involves a visual dimension without an everyday practice or habituation. It borrows from the ancient rituals some aspects, such as the collective and spectacular character of the ceremony, but it disconnects the event from the spectators' global movement of the everyday, rendering the theatre show something that has nothing to say about one's life: a pure spectacle.

The split between the "lost" and the "found" compartments thus corresponds not only to two different types of aura but also to the modern split between the "everyday" (long experience, tactile habituation) and "experience" (immediate experience, spectacle). In order to overcome this split, in order for the aura of the habitual to take place, one must not cling to the striking event that stands at the origin ("façade"), but rather dare to get inside and practice it. In other words, one needs to repeat the event and make it a part of the everyday, so that only *retroactively* it may be reconstituted as auratic. The "found" aura in the second compartment is, however, entirely different. It is constituted outside the everyday in a sterile and well-defined location, being produced through external arrangements that realise for the spectators the otherwise tedious task of balancing between distance and nearness.

There is no deferral or retroaction in it, but rather immediacy and uniqueness of the auratic event—namely, the theatre show.

SHOCK AND HABITUATION

Is there a way to get inside the first compartment in an age that prefers the immediate reproduction of the visual upon the long practice of the haptic? In the artwork essay Benjamin further develops the distinction between visual and tactile, showing how in order to get used to something, one needs to gradually touch it and be touched by it, just as Merleau-Ponty describes it. However, this process may in fact involve visual perception as well, provided that it takes place through *distraction (Zerstreuung)*. Such distraction is a common practice of everyday experience, as exemplified by one's attitude towards buildings in an urban environment: most of the time one does not directly look at them, and yet they are an integral part of our environment. Whether we want to or not, when living in a city, we distractedly encounter numerous buildings which we get used to, combining thus the visual and the tactile aspects of perception and integrating them into our lives (SW 4:268).

The façade from the lost-articles compartment, which we encountered in a different context, may now be considered in the light of architectural distraction. Whereas we saw earlier the impossibility to combine the visual (façade) and the tactile (dwelling), Benjamin now mentions another kind of practice and use: no longer habituation from the *inside* (dwelling), but rather from the *outside* (passing by),[10] in what he calls "reception through distraction". Even if I am careful not to get inside a house and just stare at its façade and register it, my daily and repetitive encounters with it eventually make me distractedly let it in. In other words, rather than getting inside the house, I can simply let the house get into me.

The importance of this reception through distraction, according to Benjamin, lies in its ability to make one practice and repeat images in an age that is not inclined to repeat, thus arriving at a new balance between the visual and the tactile. Moreover, it is not only while moving in the city that I may attain this visual/tactile practice, but also while in the *cinema*: "The distracting element in film is also primarily tactile, being based on successive changes of scene and focus which have a percussive effect on the spectator" (SW 3:119).[11]

Whereas one can easily understand why the experience of seeing a house, dwelling in it or making it dwell in me involves a mixture of the visual and the tactile, it is perhaps more difficult to realise wherein exactly the tactile dimension of film lies, since, as in a dream, the only part of the body that really moves when a person is watching a film is his or her eyes. However, it is precisely the liberation from the need to move in the protective and dark environment of a cinema that enables the "percussive effect" of the film. In addition, no matter how shocking the film is, one knows that it is only a mechanical reproduction with well-defined and predictable limits. One can thus reflect on various everyday situations and elements without the pressure to immediately react to them. In other words, the possibility of immersed or embodied reflection that we found in Heidegger and Merleau-Ponty is opened up in film due to this combination of distraction and habituation, whereas in the everyday one is busy surviving in the face of "increased threat to life" (SW 4:281n42).[12]

However, what is so shocking about film? This point is never really explained by Benjamin. In order to elucidate it, let us recall that a shock is not only an impression that is too overwhelming to be absorbed but also simply everything that is more or less new. In other words, shock is not a unique event, as in Freud's early theory of trauma, but rather defines the structure of modern experience in which the new is everywhere. This furthermore explains why every impression must be registered and parried independently of its content. The shock is the mode of functioning of both reality and the psychic apparatus, which "shocks" reality in advance through its registration into distinct and well-defined events ("short experience").

Indeed, both film and the everyday are potentially shocking, but whereas the latter necessitates a parrying of the shock, the former is supposed by Benjamin to make the shock enter the apparatus and be processed, thus improving one's ability to handle shocks after the film ends and the everyday resumes. Film thus presents a unique combination of distraction and shock: the spectators must remain very attentive, due to the shock effect of the film (SW 4:267)—that is, all the new impressions and images it proposes to the eyes—but, on the other hand, they somehow let go and absorb the shock through distraction. The constant change of image in the film, isolated from any present circumstance of the spectators, enables them to reverse the direction of shock: instead of registering reality, the psychic apparatus can now allow itself to actually be shocked by it. Art, and particularly the art of cinema, appears as a possible way to absorb shocks through distracted attention, a form of perception that lets the shock in without registering it, exactly as in Freud's early theory of deferred retroaction. But if the shock really does enter the apparatus during film and waits for its deferred retroaction, when and where exactly does this retroaction take place? Indeed, "cult" films become so by being watched over and over again through a ritualistic retroaction, but this model does not seem to be valid for "regular" films. Does the film itself retroact something, or does it wait for its retroaction in the future?

We encountered ritualistic retroaction as illustrated by a film like *The Triumph of the Will*. But the contemporary spectator (or at least anyone who is not a fervent adherent of any fascist regime) could hardly stand the tedious repetition of old propaganda films. While watching *The Triumph of the Will* at home, I must admit that I found myself fighting against the temptation to press the fast-forward button—not because the film outraged me, but because I felt bored by its repetitive structure. One increasingly expects a film today not to repeat itself too much, and if it does, there must be a good reason for that; otherwise, one would just not watch it.[13]

According to Benjamin, films (other than propaganda films) do not repeat any origin in a way that would magnify and mystify them. This is why he sees in film the number one tool in giving up any idea of a "first-time-experience": origin, authority, tradition or aura. All these are rather chains to be broken and gotten rid of in favor of true political freedom. Indeed, from this freedom, from this acceptance of loss and integration of its shock, a new aura of the habitual may see the light of day. However (and here I only repeat a critique often addressed to Benjamin), the spectator—then and today—seems to have huge difficulties in giving up the origin and is rather pushed to look for it in illusionary places: the painted distance of a backdrop.

Perhaps we have become too used to film since Benjamin's time, such that film, too, offers a beautiful semblance and beautiful heroes who soon become auratic models for one's everyday behavior. Shocking as they might be, films today tend either to hide their shock or to accentuate it to the extreme, as in horror films or pornographic scenes, such that the combination of shock (nearness) and distraction (distance) is seldom achieved: one is either distracted or shocked, but rarely both. Is there a way to engage in a repetition that would retroact the film's shock and connect it to the everyday? Before I try to tackle this question, another reflection on the mechanism of deferred retroaction should be made, through Benjamin's last text, dedicated to the question of time.

THE ANGEL OF DEFERRED RETROACTION

In his 1940 *On the Concept of History*, Benjamin delineates three allegoric figures: the *automaton*, the *angel of history* and, mediating between the two, a *secret dwarf*. According to Benjamin, these figures represent different historical attitudes or forces: the automaton stands for *historical materialism*, the angel for *messianic history*, and the dwarf for *theology*. I do not intend to fully analyse Benjamin's highly elliptical and dense arguments, but rather to briefly show the different modes of temporality manifested by these figures. My main argument is that the angel of history is the figure in Benjamin that realises the mechanism of deferred retroaction, and as such it serves as an auratic model. However, the messianic character of the angel makes it difficult to understand how to implement this aura in the everyday. With a view to explaining this possibility, I propose to sketch an alternative angel: *the angel of the everyday*.

The automaton is depicted as a puppet imitating a Turkish chessplayer who always beats his rivals. Its mysterious force, however, stems from a secret figure: a "hunchbacked dwarf", a master at chess hidden inside the table in front of the automaton, guiding its moves.[14] This description implies not only that an always-winning figure is often nothing but an automaton, but also, and more importantly, that behind every automaton (mechanical repetition) stands a covert figure which enacts and governs it. Who could it be? Benjamin identifies the dwarf as *theology*, "which today, as we know, is small and ugly and has to keep out of sight" (SW 4:389). The dwarf guides the puppet similar to theology, which secretly guides historical materialism and makes it win each of its moves, for historical materialism can explain every situation through a dialectic of forces in which a defeat would be simply described as a preparation for victory. However (and here Benjamin's unique messianic interpretation of Marx is at work), the dialectic is guided by theology, which aims towards redemption: "The past carries with it a secret index by which it is referred to redemption. Doesn't a breath of the air that pervaded earlier days caress us as well? . . . If so, then there is a secret agreement between past generations and the present one. Then our coming was expected on earth. Then, like every generation that preceded us, we have been endowed with a weak messianic power, a power on which the past has a claim" (SE 4:390).

If we read these lines attentively, we can find in them the return of deferred retroaction, albeit on a social rather than personal level: every generation waits for its future retroaction, at the same time as it is in charge of retroacting the deferred past. This is the "secret agreement" between the different generations, realised by a "messianic power": the ability to awaken the dead and revive the past in the present. However, this messianic power is *weak*, since only redemption can revive all times. This would be the final stage, the end of history in which *everything is retroacted and nothing is deferred*. In Benjamin's words, "Nothing that has ever happened should be regarded as lost to history. Of course only a redeemed mankind is granted the fullness of its past— which is to say, only for a redeemed mankind has its past become citable in all its moments. Each moment it has lived becomes a *citation à l'ordre du jour*. And that day is Judgment Day" (SW 4:390).

Rather than speculating on the nature of Judgment Day, I propose to focus here on the moments that are supposed to be revived and recited. What are these moments and how can they be extracted as separate segments from the indifferent stream of Time? Here Benjamin returns to the question of *image*, and more precisely to the shock-image (*both* visual and tactile) as the only way to delineate a moment of past time. Time, he says, can only be grasped through shock-image, but this shock is precisely what makes time ungraspable: "The true image of the past flits by. The past can be seized only as an image that flashes up at the moment of its recognizability, and is never seen again" (SW 4:390).

The flashing/shocking moment of time is not experienced as such on the spot but rather retroactively—that is, in an attempt to seize a past moment. In other words, the shock does not "happen" in the present and can only be perceived and experienced as a "second time". Benjamin moreover describes the shock as characterising *memory*, which accentuates the similarity of this situation to the mechanism of deferred retroaction: "Articulating the past historically does not mean recognizing it 'the way it really was'. It means appropriating a memory as it flashes up in a moment of danger. Historical materialism wishes to hold fast that image of the past which unexpectedly appears to the historical subject in a moment of danger" (SW 4:391).

This situation is a classical case of deferred retroaction: a danger in the present brings about a shocking memory of the past that probably involved a danger as well, such that the past addresses the needs of the present and vice versa. The two moments of shock thus correspond to each other and act upon each other, making the moment of the past a part of the present and redeeming it from oblivion.

However, this redeeming work of deferred retroaction is not something that can be easily achieved on the level of either political or personal history. One rather tends to sink into a state of "acedia, which despairs of appropriating the genuine historical image as it briefly flashes up" (SW 4:391). This difficulty is probably what made Benjamin place Paul Klee's painting *Angelus Novus* on his desk (see figure 5), such that, I would suggest, he could be constantly reminded of the need for retroaction. Like Heidegger's anxiety, which is a "big" negativity intended to remind one of the "small" negativities of everyday life, the angel of history represents a "strong" messianic power that should remind one of the "weak" messianic power hidden in every moment of our life. This is how Benjamin famously describes the angel of history:

> There is a picture by Klee called *Angelus Novus*. It shows an angel who seems about to move away from something he stares at. His eyes are wide, his mouth is open, his wings are spread. This is how the angel of history must look. His face is turned toward the past. Where a chain of events appears before *us*, *he* sees one single catastrophe, which keeps piling wreckage upon wreckage and hurls it at his feet. The angel would like to stay, awaken the dead, and make whole what has been smashed. But a storm is blowing from Paradise and has got caught in his wings; it is so strong that the angel can no longer close them. This storm drives him irresistibly into the future, to which his back is turned, while the pile of debris before him grows toward the sky. What we call progress is *this* storm. (SW 4:392)

Many interpretations have been offered for this enigmatic description,[15] but my main concern here is the question of deferred retroaction and its possibility within the modern everyday. Benjamin describes two moments in this mechanism, but instead of taking them to be the past and the present, he moves forward and examines how the *future* retroacts the *present*. This future is incarnated by the angel, who is looking at *us*—his past, our present. His temporal position, however, entails a perception opposite to ours. Whereas we see the present as composed of successive events, and forget that they are all articulated upon the global movement of the everyday, the angel sees our time as holistic, and only then as separated into different moments. Since we

Figure 5. Paul Klee, *Angelus Novus*, 1920. The Israel Museum.

are dead for him and therefore no longer exist in his present, he necessarily sees our time as one big catastrophe, from which infinite wreckages are produced, with every moment—every "shock", every "immediate experience"—adding another wreckage to the pile ascending towards the sky.

The angel would have liked to repair the wreckages, to reconstruct the past and undo its catastrophic character; yet he cannot, since he, too, is located *in* time. Only a complete *halt* of the angel's movement would stop the catastrophe and give time the unity it deserves: the redemption of all its moments. But the angel is forced to keep moving backwards to the future behind him; consequently, he only faces more and more wreckages that continue to pile up, without being able to repair them, to integrate them into the global movement of the every-day. Rather than helping us, the angel himself seems to need help, because of the storm that puts him in danger. Yet isn't the dangerous storm precisely the second event which retroacts the first? And isn't this first event rather composed of numerous past events of danger— that is, of shock? The angel thus redeems the past only partially, retroacting it as a global catastrophe composed of different wreckages. In other words, the angel retroacts and exposes the global movement of the everyday, but he does not manage to integrate into it the different shocks or "immediate experiences" that took place upon it. Instead, he sees them as belonging to one big catastrophe—the catastrophe of their separation from each other, which causes them to be lost. Only a com-plete redemption would repair the wreckages—that is, would make them united again, integrated into a long experience, whereas the angel redeems the infinite gone moments merely as a continuous catas-trophe. [16]

The description of the angel might sound extremely abstract and irrelevant to our here and now everyday life, which is quite alien to terms such as "redemption" or "messianic power". However, I suggest that we, too, are the angels of our past, looking at it shocked, seeing it as something which is catastrophic—dead, gone, composed of infinite moments and wreckages of lost time. Is there a way for us to halt time and redeem the past? An example of such a redemption could be Proust's experience of involuntary memory, in which a "catastrophic" time (Combray before the madeleine, of which he remembers little) is united with its distinct moments ("wreckages") that can be told and redeemed. Proust thus succeeded in becoming the angel of his own history: his own angel of history. He did so not only thanks to the accidental experience of the madeleine but also through an everyday fight against the present experience—that is, a fight against the move-ment of time which carries the angel backwards to the future. Proust tried to halt, defer and suspend his present life, to give up any immedi-ate experience in order to transform his *past* immediate experiences into long experience. In this way he achieved what the angel failed to accomplish: to repair the wreckages and stop the catastrophe. To be an angel of history is thus to attempt to halt the movement of time, and the more one succeeds in it, the more one can repair the wreckages and give the past a new life, through giving up the present and avoiding the movement towards the future.

Benjamin's intention in the *On the Concept of History* seems to be similar to the halt of time conducted by Proust. Thesis X, which immediately follows the thesis on the angel of history, consequently begins with an almost Proustian declaration: "The themes which monastic discipline assigned to friars for meditation were designed to turn them away from the world and its affairs. The thoughts we are developing here have a similar aim" (SW 4:393). Benjamin tries to turn away from the present and redeem the past—yet not in order to create his own history, as Proust did, but rather in order to teach *us* what a writing of history might look like, a writing of history that turns its back to the future only in order to revolutionise it: "The French Revolution viewed itself as Rome reincarnate. It cited ancient Rome exactly the way fashion cites a bygone mode of dress. . . . The same leap in the open air of history is the dialectical leap Marx understood as revolution" (SW 4:395).

What is a revolution? Surprisingly, according to Benjamin, it is a *gaze upon the past* that cites and revives it, but it is a gaze that cannot turn backwards—that is, forwards, to the future. Like the angel, it is trapped in a storm from Paradise that carries it and prevents it from flying, as well as from looking in directions other than the past. According to this image, it is paradoxically the inability to look at the future that enables one to dream and change it. By turning upside down the usual direction of time, one can stop focusing on the here and now, the numerous everyday invisible repetitions, and embark upon a different kind of repetition that is much more dramatic, redeeming the past's heroic moments. But once the revolution has taken place, can one return to the normal direction of time and look at the future? Benjamin says that the revolution *explodes* time—not in order to halt it for good, but rather to inaugurate a new set of events to repeat, and above all the event of revolution itself considered as Day Zero: "What characterizes revolutionary classes at their moment of action is the awareness that they are about to make the continuum of history explode. The Great Revolution introduced a new calendar. The initial day of a calendar presents history in a time-lapse mode. And basically it is the same day

that keeps recurring in the guise of holidays, which are days of remembrance" (SW 4:395).

Benjamin tries to develop a new model both for understanding revolution and for enabling it, by enacting the force beneath revolution—
namely, theology, or messianic power. This historical materialism
could thus become revolutionary as well, aiming to redeem the past
through its retroaction. The figure of the angel, being placed in the
future, serves as a reminder of the constant need for retroaction, but
also of the necessary *incompleteness* of this retroaction. Only thus can
the continuation of time and the realisation of the revolution take place;
only thus can the pretension to seize and win *every* move of the past be
avoided—the pretension of the automaton and the dwarf (theology) that
guides it.

Once more, if we go beyond Benjamin's theological and revolutionary vocabulary, we can say that his new model of historical materialism
offers a *plastic* repetition—that is, a repetition which combines destruction and creation. It admits the catastrophe and the wreckages, the need
for immediate experiences in a modern world; yet it does not give up
the attempt to repair them precisely through their retroaction. Moreover, this attempt can be done only through a time-halt—that is, a
suspension of the everyday: "The historical materialist cannot do without the notion of a present which is not a transition, but in which time
takes a stand [*einsteht*] and has come to a standstill. For this notion
defines the very present in which he himself is writing history. . . . He
remains in control of his powers—man enough to blast open the continuum of history" (SW 4:396).

Similar to the way the phenomenological reduction functions, Benjamin proposes to start the historical retroaction by halting the global
movement of the everyday, such that one could acquire a substantial
power to control it. Nonetheless, this control, as we have now seen,
must remain partial, since even the angel himself cannot redeem the
past. The time-halt is rather an active response to reality's demands, a
response in the form of *shock*.

We saw in the previous chapter how the psychic apparatus reacts to
the shocking reality by shocking it in return, thus parrying its overwhelming capacities. In this way, isolated moments of time are created,
leading to immediate experience and voluntary memory. In his *On the
Concept of History*, Benjamin delineates a similar process of a shock-
wave that moves from the inside towards external reality, but since it is

now done *out of time*, through a momentary time-halt, the result is quite different:

> Thinking involves not only the movement of thoughts, but their arrest as well. Where thinking suddenly comes to a stop [*einhält*] in a constellation saturated with tensions, it gives that constellation a shock, by which thinking is crystallized as a monad. The historical materialist approaches a historical object only where it confronts him as monad. In this structure he recognizes the sign of a Messianic arrest of happening, or (to put it differently) a revolutionary chance in the fight for the oppressed past. (SW 4:396)

Benjamin speaks here of thinking rather than perception, since it is a question for him of the historian who analyses the past. However, the voluntary halt of time does much more than just thinking, and it is rather close to what Merleau-Ponty named "radical reflection". It is a process in which one creates "monads"—that is, isolated moments of time that are both the object of reflection and its effect. Reflection manages to extract past events that had been forgotten and repressed, liberating them through giving them a name. Similarly, historical materialism ought to create historical objects not in order to freeze them but rather in order to liberate them from the oppressing forces that did not allow them to be fully realised. Deferred retroaction is thus a process in which a shocking halt in time permits a past event to finally take place for the first time, which is always already second.

If we return to the angel of history, we may now say that the shocking/shocked gaze it directs at the past permits the wreckages to pile, wreckages which had so far been indistinct parts of a past catastrophe. The halt of time and the shocking/shocked gaze are a first step in repairing the past and integrating it in the present through deferred retroaction. But what kind of a time-halt does the angel present for our contemporary everyday life? Can his (our) gaze and movement of time ever be (re)turned *forwards*? Or in another direction?

SHERMAN'S ANGELS

To conclude this chapter, I would like to locate yet another angel, or rather *angels*. Not, this time, in painting or film, but in the work of American artist Cindy Sherman, who explores photography as a form of art.[17] One of Sherman's first series from the late 1970s has the curious title of *Untitled Film Stills*. Every photography in the series presents a different heroine in an everyday place and situation (walking in the street, standing in a kitchen, visiting a library, etc.), but something in the picture somehow transcends the everyday and gives it a cinematic allure, as indicated by the series' title (see figure 6).

What is it that makes the picture look as if it belonged to a film? What is it that makes the ordinary situation look somewhat extraordinary? The scene depicted in *Untitled Film Still 13* presents a usual visit to the library, and yet something about it does not look usual at all. The heroine (a librarian? a nurse?) is reaching for a book in the cinema books section (we can read at least one title—*Cinema of Horror: The Movies*). But curiously, instead of looking at the book, her gaze is turned back diagonally to the fore, to a point above and outside the frame. This turning of the gaze to an unexpected yet invisible point characterises most of the images of *Untitled Film Stills*. It is moreover one of the crucial elements in Sherman's technique of suspending the everyday and blurring the categories of the ordinary and the extraordinary. Sherman disconnects the eye and the hand, the visual and the haptic, the *Vorhanden* and the *Zuhanden*, not simply to oppose them, but also to put their relationship into question. An everyday situation thus becomes eventful, or, stated differently, an event takes root in the everyday, both (the event and the everyday) being defined through each other, overcoming their (modern) opposition.

This process is achieved not only in the way each photograph is constructed but also in the way they are to be exhibited: never individually but always in a series and in small, uniform format, densely hung on the museum or gallery wall. The spectator is confronted at once with dozens of photographs which sooner or later lead him or her to the uncanny discovery that it is always Cindy Sherman herself who appears in them, reproducing herself each time under another false identity. The pictures thus show infinite everyday possibilities that are true and false at the same time. These possibilities are produced and reproduced, exposing how various everyday surroundings, which normally would not draw particular attention, can be staged differently and consequently lead to different events.

The reproduction of photography (multiplication of images) and the reproduction of the everyday (multiplication of settings) are equaled by Sherman not in order to condemn reproduction or to point to the loss of aura it entails; on the contrary, Sherman shows how the modern aura can be erected *only* upon reproduced images, settings and identities.

Figure 6. Cindy Sherman, *Untitled Film Still 13*, 1979.

She cheats her spectators, as it were, but, unlike Benjamin's gambler, she is able to play out the lie and extract from it an experience that acquires a certain glamour and an aura. The aura is then revealed to be conditioned by the everyday: a meeting point of familiarity and strangeness, habituation and shock.

To return to the lost-and-found office, Sherman reverses Benjamin's order and starts from the second compartment ("found") in order
to arrive at the first ("lost"). She offers the spectators the "painted
distance of a backdrop"—that is, a ready-made aura achieved through a
calculated balance between distance (unusual aspect) and nearness
(everyday aspect)—yet the multiplicity of the images and their uniform
size in black and white oblige the spectator to move from one picture to
another, and, in a way, to be shocked over and over again by what is
actually the same protagonist (Cindy Sherman), each time presented in
a new version. In this way one engages in an immersed reflection
whose result would be an understanding of the essence of the everyday—that is, its dependence upon the event which it conditions.

This immersed reflection is soon discovered to be a process of
deferred retroaction, only that the direction of time is reversed. Let us
recall Benjamin's scheme of auratic deferred retroaction: (1) first encounter with the object; (2) repetitive practice and habituation; (3) an
auratic encounter with the object. Now, Sherman starts from phase 3—
that is, with an auratic image that is ready-made and isolated. But this
image is not alone: not only is it a reproduction, but it is also a part of a
series, such that the spectator must move to other similar yet different
images, both auratic and reproduced. This movement from one image
to another is already phase 2, the phase of practice that finally leads to
phase 1, retroacting the lost image which stands at the basis of all the
others: the image of "the" everyday, a global movement for events to
take place upon it, retroact it and transform it. Indeed, it is not the
different objects in the exhibition that receive the aura of the habitual,
since these objects are not ours, but rather the everyday of each spectator, an everyday which can be accessed only through a practice of its
reproduced possibilities.

Cindy Sherman thus offers a practice of everyday possibilities, a
practice that, according to Benjamin, is supposed to take place in the
cinema. It is precisely because she recognises the cinema's potential to
engage in such a practice of the everyday that Sherman chooses to halt
the movement of the film and to focus on one picture each time. She
thus assumes the role of the "historical materialist" or the phenomenologist, who halts the movement of time only to better understand it. This
is one of Sherman's most important insights: the film is supposed to
shock the spectator and make him or her practice the everyday experience of shock by viewing, touching and finally becoming habituated to
it. But the problem is that the film's movement attenuates the shock and

seduces one to escape or parry it, similar to what happens in the everyday itself. Every image of the film leads too quickly to another, making the movement of the film and the movement of the everyday too close to each other. Shock, let us recall, cannot be perceived in real time but only retroacted, such that the combination of shock and distraction, the visual and the tactile, is hardly achieved in today's cinema, which either hides or over-accentuates its shocking element. Therefore, new techniques must be invented to relaunch a practice that has been banned in modernity.

Sherman comes to propose such new technique for everyday practice, extracting from each imagined film one shock-image that captures the film "in a time-lapse mode". Every picture is both an auratic backdrop (found-articles compartment) and a façade (lost-articles compartment). However, rather than hiding its interior, the façade now invites one to explore it and discover the interdependency between seeing and dwelling. Each image retroacts numerous other images which stem from both our cinematic and our everyday imagery, exposing what Benjamin calls "the optical unconscious": all those images hidden in the everyday that need to be practiced and retroacted. These images are not static or isolated, but rather part of events: they condition events and are conditioned by them. Whereas in normal life all everyday details are taken for granted and are not seen as necessary elements of the event, Sherman shows how the event is composed of nothing but everyday elements, which, through an estrangement of the gaze, are suddenly seen as auratic as well.

To sum up, Sherman develops in *Untitled Film Stills* a double procedure of freezing a cinematic-yet-everyday image that invites one to explore and retroact its internal multiplicity, as well as its relation to many other images which are presented near it. She reproduces herself in order to achieve various reproduced images that send and refer to each other with no origin besides the everyday itself. They make one practice not only one "film" or one everyday possibility, but rather many such films and everyday possibilities. The result is an upheaval of the linear movement of time, starting from an auratic image and ending with an auratic everyday which encompasses all the images and all the everyday possibilities retroacted through this peculiar practice: that of *seeing* Sherman's exhibition and *dwelling* in it.

In a series of color photographs in large format printed in 1980, Sherman uses a slightly different technique. *Untitled 66* (see figure 7) shows a woman crossing a highway which probably leads to a grey, dilapidated American suburb. The woman is carrying what appears to be a bicycle. She is wearing a long, almost colorless coat, her hair is short and her face has little, if any, makeup. Her gaze is turning diagonally outside the frame. It is an everyday woman in an everyday situation, but once more, something in the picture makes it extraordinary from the outset. Is it the blue halo which encircles the woman? Is it the strong light shining on her right-hand side? Or is it the strange relationship between the figure and her background? This background, indeed, is soon revealed to be a projection, the photograph having been taken in the studio, staged by Sherman like all the other photographs in the series. The woman's aura thus stems from the combination of being imprisoned in a stereotyped grey everyday life while simultaneously transcending it. She crosses a road which leads to her miserable home, but she also remains in the studio, illuminated by various projectors, lights and images. She is a weary woman who has given up her youthful dreams, but she is also Cindy Sherman, a young artist who dreams of conquering the vibrant art scene of New York City.

In her photographs Sherman often plays on the history of art, and if we return to Klee's painting *Angelus Novus* (figure 5), we ought not to

Figure 7. Cindy Sherman, *Untitled 66*, 1980.

be surprised to notice some similarities between it and *Untitled 66*. Like Sherman's woman, the angel stands in the midst of a halo. Like her, he, too, stares at something in the corner of the picture, outside the frame.[18] "His eyes are wide, his mouth is open", writes Benjamin, and he adds that the angel is carried backwards by a storm from heaven, watching with horror his past—that is, us ourselves, in the present. The woman, however, does not appear to be going back, but is rather moving to her left as she crosses the street. Yet at the same time, and for reasons not disclosed, her gaze is turned towards something almost in the opposite side of her movement. What could it be?

My suggestion is that Sherman's feminine angel is no longer looking at the present or the past, but rather at the everyday, which is always located elsewhere, to the side of the frame.[19] The everyday cannot be looked at or retroacted directly, for it is never a matter of specific events but of their background and supportive elements. *Untitled 66* is a concentrated meditation on the everyday, and more particularly on the possibility of attaining the aura of the habitual in the age of technological reproducibility. Similar to *Untitled Film Stills*, the aura is first given directly—yet not as the aura of the habitual, but rather as a lure, in the form of the blue distance of the backdrop—the halo around the woman—which traps the spectators in the picture, enchanting them in order to soon deceive them. However, this deception, again, is only the first phase in the practice of the gaze. The different images in the series are both auratic and everyday, both artificial and natural, and through passing the gaze from one to another, the spectator practices them and is finally led to give up the aura of the backdrop in favor of the aura of the habitual. This cannot be achieved by the initial gaze, which is direct and therefore shocked by the picture, but rather through an oblique gaze that moves between the two compartments of the lost-and-found office—that is, between the façade, the interior and finally the blue distance.

Untitled 66 thus calls one to adopt a different gaze at the same time it demonstrates this gaze through the eyes of the woman. Indeed, Benjamin's very last definition of the aura, which I have not yet mentioned, is the ability to return one's gaze:

> What was inevitably felt to be inhuman—one might even say deadly—in daguerreotypy was the (prolonged) looking into the camera, since the camera records our likeness without returning our gaze. Inherent in the gaze, however, is the expectation that it will be returned by that on

which it is bestowed. Where this expectation is met . . . , there is an experience [*Erfahrung*] of the aura in all its fullness. (SW 4:338)

The experience of the aura is conditioned by returning one's gaze, but this returning cannot be an isolated event. Rather, it is a question of long experience, a process of practice and of immersed reflection that may lead to an aura, but not immediately. Modernity is characterised precisely by the inability to return the gaze, both that of the camera and those of everyday people in everyday situations. Benjamin gives the example of public transportation: you get on a bus and sit next to people who do not look at you, and whom you try not to look at in return, thus making the bus ride into an immediate experience which is registered and parried rather than fully lived.[20] Now, although Sherman's woman does not return her gaze either, she nevertheless returns it on a different level, at least to someone who is located outside the frame, in the direction she is looking. Who is this person? It is, of course, another picture of Sherman, hung just beside it in the gallery.

Rather than calling us to return the gaze and attain the fullness of the aura, Sherman shows that behind or in front of every modern gaze lies a series of reproduced gazes, identities and events, each similar to each other ("our likeness") without being completely the same. Any attempt to overcome the reproduction once and for all and attain "true" experience would therefore only lead to a false or fascist aura, pretending to achieve fullness where in fact absence reigns. However, the acknowledgement of reproduction is only the first step towards a retroaction of another kind of aura. This aura is achieved through a long practice combining shock and habituation, the visual and the tactile. This shock would stem not only from a full auratic image but also from the repetitive revelation that the images always imitate other images and other everyday yet eventful situations.[21] Every trauma and every shock, as we saw in Freud, stems from both fullness and absence, from reality which gives "too much" (the initial auratic image) and "too little" (the revelation of its reproduction). Sherman plays on these two dimensions of shock, and she forces the initial impression that pretends to seize the full aura to give way to a series of impressions, shocks and "immediate experiences". In this way one can now practice, connect to each other and appropriate rather than parry them.

The proposed practice of shock does not seek to attain a presumed origin, a total authority or a figure which might return a full gaze.[22] Rather, it encounters an oblique gaze referring to a backdrop that is neither blue nor magic, but rather grey and ordinary. The woman is looking to her right, where another photograph is hung on the wall, thus telling the spectator not to linger too much on one image, not to pretend to achieve a direct gaze within the everyday.[23] One must move on, it says, and continue to explore the multiplicity of reproduced images. Yet the woman's gaze also seems to tell us that the real aura is not to be found in any of the pictures but rather in the movement between them: the movement of the everyday, which must be relaunched and retroacted every minute of our lives.

NOTES

1. "By the interest it takes in technological phenomena, by the curiosity it displays before any sort of invention or machinery, every childhood binds the accomplishments of technology to the old worlds of symbol. There is nothing in the realm of nature that from the outset would be exempt from such a bond. Only, it takes form not in the aura of novelty but in the aura of the habitual. In memory, childhood, and dream" (AP, 461).

2. See Miriam Bratu Hansen, *Cinema and Experience* (Berkeley: University of California Press, 2012), 117.

3. Hansen, *Cinema and Experience*, 118. Hansen's proposal thus addresses Adorno's accusation of Benjamin's too hasty abandonment of the aura. See Theodor W. Adorno, *Notes to Literature*, 2 vols., ed. Rolf Tiedemann, trans. Shierry Weber Nicholsen (New York: Columbia University Press, 1991–1992), 2:326. On this issue, see also Rebecca Comay, "Materialist Mutations of the Bilderverbot", in *Walter Benjamin and Art*, ed. Andrew Benjamin (London: Continuum, 2005), 32–59.

4. For an original interpretation of loss in Benjamin's early work on theatre in the light of Freud's *Mourning and Melancholia* (SE 14:234–58), see Ilit Ferber, *Philosophy and Melancholy: Benjamin's Early Reflections on Theatre and Language* (Stanford, CA: Stanford University Press, 2013), esp. 16–66.

5. For the origin of the "blue distance" in Simmel and Klages, see Hansen, *Cinema and Experience*, 115.

6. In German the lost-and-found office (*Fundbüro*) is actually a merely "found office", which makes the existence of two different compartments in it even more unusual than it is in English.

7. Moreover, the opening lines of the section entitled "Combray", immediately after the madeleine experience, are very similar to Benjamin's description of the lost-articles compartment: "Combray at a distance, from a twenty-mile radius, as we used to see it from the railway when we arrived there in the week before Easter, was no more than a church epitomising the town, representing it, speaking of it and for it to the horizon, and as one drew near, gathering close about its long, dark cloak, sheltering from the wind, on the open plain, as a shepherdess gathers her sheep, the woolly grey backs of its huddled houses, which the remains of its mediaeval ramparts enclosed, here and there, in an outline as scrupulously circular as that of a little town in a primitive painting. To live in, Combray was a trifle depressing" (Marcel Proust, *Swann's Way*, trans. C. K. Scott Moncrieff and Terence Kilmartin [New York: Vintage Books, 1989], 52).

8. "The first volume consists of five-hundred-twenty pages of dense text. What is, then, the vast and grave subject that leads to such developments? Does Mr. Marcel Proust embrace in his grand work the history of humanity or at least the history of a

century? Not at all. He tells us his childhood souvenirs. Was his childhood, then, full
with extraordinary events? In no way: nothing special happened to him. . . . One
wonders how many volumes Mr. Marcel Proust would pile up to fill libraries if he came
to tell the story of his entire life". Paul Souday, "Du coté de chez Swann", *Le Temps*, 10
December 1913, reprinted in Marcel Proust, *Du coté de chez Swann* (Paris: Flammarion,
1987), 654–55 (my translation). The same impatient critic became, however, in the
course of time a fervent admirer of Proust and wrote his biography in 1927.

9. See Benjamin's two articles on toys, "Old Toys" (SW 2:98–102) and "The Cultu-
ral History of Toys" (SW 2:113–16). See also, on that theme, Susan Buck-Morss, *The
Dialectics of Seeing: Walter Benjamin and the Arcades Project* (Cambridge, MA: MIT
Press, 1991), 261–75.

10. This theme is further elaborated by Michel de Certeau, who describes various
everyday manners of walking in the city. See Certeau, *The Practice of Everyday Life*,
trans. Steven Rendall (Berkeley: University of California Press, 1984), 91–110.

11. Marshall McLuhan has developed this notion of an audile-tactile perception that
he attributes to TV images. See his *Understanding Media: The Extensions of Man*
(Cambridge, MA: MIT Press, 1994).

12. For an illuminating analysis of distraction and habituation in film, see Eli Friedlander, *Walter Benjamin: A Philosophical Portrait* (Cambridge, MA: Harvard University Press, 2012), 171–80. Significantly, Friedlander claims that film is able "to make
the ordinary a matter for distraction" precisely through its shock effect (178).

13. Harold Ramis's film *Groundhog Day* from 1993 is a good example of a film that
makes repetition its theme. The hero is trapped in the same day, which he unwillingly
repeats over and over again, so that no matter what happens, it restarts the next morning.
However, in a typical Hollywoodian maneuver, it is only when the hero truly falls in
love, thus attaining "experience", that he can get out of repetition—and out of the
everyday.

14. This description is based on Edgar Allan Poe's essay from 1836, "Maelzel's
Chess Player", in *Edgar Allan Poe: Essays and Reviews*, ed. G. R. Thompson (New
York: Library of America, 1984), 1253–76.

15. See, for example, Howard Caygill, "Non-Messianic Political Theology in Benja-
min's 'On the Concept of History'", in *Walter Benjamin and History*, ed. Andrew
Benjamin (London: Continuum Books, 2005), 215–26; Michael Löwy, *Fire Alarm:
Reading Walter Benjamin's "On the Concept of History"*, trans. Chris Turner (London:
Verso, 2006).

16. Benjamin declares in *Central Park* (1939), "Redemption depends on the tiny
fissure in the continuous catastrophe" (SW 4:185).

17. On Sherman's work in the context of modern art, see Laura Mulvey, "A Phantasmagoria of the Female Body: The Work of Cindy Sherman", *New Left Review* 188
(July–August 1991): 137–50. For a Lacanian analysis of Sherman as investigating the
"traumatic gaze", see Hal Foster, *The Return of the Real* (Cambridge, MA: MIT Press,
1996), 146–53.

18. Ariella Azoulay claims that whereas Benjamin depicts the angel as looking forward, he is actually squinting to the side. See Ariella Azoulay, *Once upon a Time:
Photography following Walter Benjamin* (Ramat Gan: University of Bar-Ilan Press,
2006), 89–101 (in Hebrew).

19. I thus reverse Lacan's analysis of Holbein's *The Ambassadors*, since it is not the
spectator who looks from the side in Sherman's works, but rather the protagonists of her
pictures. However, since Sherman is both photographer and protagonist, subject and
object of the gaze, the spectator-protagonist relationship becomes dialectical. On the
need to "look awry" in a Lacanian context, see Slavoj Žižek, *Looking Awry: An Introduction to Jacques Lacan through Popular Culture* (Cambridge, MA: MIT Press, 1992),
esp. 3–12, 88–122. On the diagonal gaze as going beyond and against the visual, see

Hagi Kenaan's insightful analysis of Levinas, in Hagi Kenaan, *The Ethics of Visuality: Levinas and the Contemporary Gaze* (London: Tauris, 2013), esp. 70–71, 135–36.

20. One of Sherman's very first series is indeed entitled "Bus Riders" (1976).

21. See Benjamin's essay from 1933 *On the Mimetic Faculty*, in which he states, "For clearly the perceptual world [*Merkwelt*] of modern man contains only minimal residues of the magical correspondences and analogies that were familiar to ancient peoples. The question is whether we are concerned with the decay of this faculty or with its transformation" (SW 2:721). Sherman would answer that the mimetic faculty has *changed* rather than *deteriorated*. It is through the reproduction of identities that one mimics in modernity; this faculty needs to be practiced through art and technology in order to be applied in the everyday.

22. In his early *The Origin of German Tragic Drama* (1925), Benjamin writes something very similar to what I have tried to convey here: "That which is original is never revealed in the naked and manifest existence of the factual; its rhythm is apparent only to a dual insight. On the one hand it needs to be recognized as a process of restoration and re-establishment, but, on the other hand, and precisely because of this, as something imperfect and incomplete" (Walter Benjamin, *The Origin of German Tragic Drama*, trans. John Osborne [London and New York: Verso, 1998], 45). I am grateful to Ilit Ferber for having referred me to this passage. See also Samuel Weber, "Genealogy of Modernity: History, Myth and Allegory in Benjamin's *Origin of the German Mourning Play*", *Modern Language Notes* 106, no. 3 (1991): 465–500.

23. The danger of the direct gaze upon a frozen image and the consequent shock it entails is told in E. T. A. Hoffmann's *The Sandman* and Freud's essay *The Uncanny* (SE 17:217–56), but although Freud relates the uncanny to the problem of repetition compulsion, he does not further elaborate the link between the two. This is precisely what I have tried to do throughout this book, considering Heidegger's anxiety, Merleau-Ponty's pathology, Freud's trauma and Benjamin's shock as more or less uncanny halt-moments in a process of deferred retroaction.

Concluding Remarks

Always there is World
and never Nowhere-without-a-Not.

—Rilke, *Eighth Duino Elegy*

My aim in this book has been to challenge the modern opposition between the everyday and experience, and it is now time to consider the results I have arrived at and the work that still remains to be done.

I began the book with a model of the everyday as consisting of a double movement of foundation: a global, repetitive movement, on the one hand, and a concrete founding action, on the other hand. I claimed that these two movements cannot be conceived independently of each other and that the key to the renewal of the global movement of the everyday is an integration of concrete actions and events into it by means of repetition. However, modernity tends to disconnect the two movements, and the challenge was therefore to understand both why it does so and how to reconnect these two movements. For this purpose, I located three everyday mechanisms—shock, deferral and repetition—and followed the way they interact with each other in different aspects of the everyday.

One of the figures that returns several times throughout the book is Charlie Chaplin as the protagonist of *Modern Times*. Whereas in the beginning of the film he is shocked by a situation he cannot control, he soon starts to shock it in return, sabotaging the factory—but this only leads him to a nervous breakdown. It seems that there is no way to integrate shocks into the everyday, such that only its complete annihilation can redeem one from alienating mechanical reality. Indeed, upon his release from hospital the doctor tells Chaplin, "Take it easy and avoid excitement"—but how can he take it easy when so many shocks and excitements are offered?

My proposal in this book is not to "take it easy", but rather to face the negativity of shocks through various forms of suspension and deferral. *Modern Times* was conceived as a parody and a critique of Fordian capitalism. The shocks of today are more subtle, at least for the middle class that can avoid brutality, such that one may wonder if the word *shock* is still appropriate. The examples of Houellebecq, Duras and Viola showed us, however, that the shocking element of the everyday is still there, although it tends to hide itself precisely because it is parried. The first step is thus to re-discover the shock, not as an extraordinary event, a shock-event conforming to the criteria of the mass media, but rather as a tacit phenomenon comprising all those impressions around us that we do not or cannot absorb, yet with which we must nonetheless deal. The question I have tried to develop in this book is therefore how to expose and suspend shock at one and the same time.

In the first two chapters I focussed on the role of suspension and immersed reflection within the everyday. I presented suspension as a deferral of the everyday or some elements in it, beginning with Husserl and his idea of phenomenological reduction as a methodological tool with which to suspend the everyday theoretically. However, Husserl was soon obliged to admit that this suspension can never be complete, as the everyday is in constant flux, and any attempt to freeze it is doomed to fail. The question is whether there is any possibility of suspending the everyday from within without halting it completely.

This is what I have tried to show with the help of Heidegger and Merleau-Ponty, indicating several modes of suspension that take place within the everyday itself. The first concerned a tool that is suddenly found unusable. I characterised this incident as a moment of *negativity*, in which the global movement of the everyday is somehow stopped, such that one reflects on how to relaunch it by repairing, replacing or removing the unusable tool. Only then can the movement be resumed, integrating into it the insights and changes brought about by reflection. Such reflection, I would argue, is immersed—that is, it poses a distance from the everyday while being a part of it as a founding act that returns to the everyday and is integrated into it. However, this ideal picture of the everyday must confront the Falling, which I have analysed as the difficulty in engaging in an immersed reflection, and a preference for external and ready-made categories.

Although the Falling remains largely unexplained in Heidegger, I attribute it to the modern reluctance to address the negativity of the everyday. Indeed, the global movement of the everyday gives the impression of stability, repeating over and over the same things (body, language, habits, actions, objects, etc.), but in reality nothing remains the same. As Heraclitus taught us, everything—including the everyday—is constantly changing in infinite but imperceptible ways. Reflecting upon these changes would be the key element in the renewal of the everyday, but the Falling seems to prevent this, looking only for dramatic, yet superficial, changes, such as, for instance, extraordinary and once-in-a-lifetime events. This is why a much more radical suspension of the everyday is called for, and this through *anxiety*. Anxiety is a moment of "big" negativity, forcing one to face the nothingness upon which the foundations of the everyday lie. In anxiety one fully understands Being and the way it relates to the everyday; yet its radical negativity does not allow the reflection brought by it to be immersed. Therefore no founding action takes place in anxiety, and it rather risks becoming itself an extraordinary event.

In the second chapter I turned to Merleau-Ponty and analysed the body as a central arena of the everyday. The body is characterised by an ontological ambiguity that corresponds to the double movement of foundation I have proposed. On the one hand, the body is active in that it touches, feels and reacts, and as such it is constantly engaged in numerous founding acts. But, on the other hand, the body is passive in that it is touched and felt, and as such everything that happens "outside" returns to it and is integrated into it. The body is thus both interior and exterior, subjective and objective, and it seems that this ambiguity allows us to maintain the right balance between renewal and stability, essential for the everyday.

I have given several examples of situations in which the ontological ambiguity of the body manifests itself—namely, dance, sex, drugs and football. The problem with these situations is that their ecstatic character makes it difficult to understand how the integration of a founding action into the global movement of the everyday concretely takes place. This is all the more puzzling if we confront these situations with a *psychological* ambiguity towards the body—that is, the difficulty to engage in embodied activity due to, for instance, feelings of shame. The body, so it seems, tends to be objectified in the everyday, such that one sees it solely as an object of the gaze, losing the ability to balance between the body's two aspects.

Merleau-Ponty therefore acknowledges, too, that most of the time it is external categories that reign in the everyday and affect its movement. In order to understand what leads to this situation, he analyses two pathological cases: the amputated person suffering from a phantom limb and the brain-damaged Schneider. In both cases one remains only with already founded and constituted categories that cannot be transcended and renewed. I would argue that what one lacks in these pathological cases is *embodied reflection*—that is, the ability to look at an everyday situation from a certain distance while remaining in it. Pathology thus manifests an extreme case of a frozen movement of the everyday, and as such it offers an important hint about the causes of this stagnation. Indeed, the refusal of the amputated persons to admit their mutilation often goes hand in hand with the appearance of a phantom limb. The body, I argue, is deficient by definition, and it is the inability to acknowledge its inherent negativity that leads to the immobility of the body and the slowing down of the movement of the everyday.

The phenomenological analysis of the everyday has thus given us important insights regarding both its "appropriate" functioning and its degradation. The latter is attributed to the use of ready-made categories that cover up negativity and prevent the work of immersed or embodied reflection as a momentary suspension of the everyday. However, phenomenology does not explicitly mention whether the ability to maintain an open enough everyday movement is related to a particular moment in history. For example, it does not link the difficulty to reflect upon a damaged tool to the easy possibility in Western culture of replacing the tool with a cheap new one, produced in a faraway country by anonymous workers: the contemporary brothers and sisters of Charlie Chaplin.

Furthermore, phenomenology considers negativity merely as the realm of deficiency, lack and finitude. My thesis, however, is that negativity stems not only from the realm of the "too little" but also from the "too much" in an age of infinite choice (for those who can afford it). To further study the negativity as that which both enables and impedes the founding movement of the everyday, I proposed to situate it in the context of modernity, with the help of Freud and Benjamin.

Indeed, the Freudian texts I have analysed do not mention modernity explicitly, but I have tried to show that the modern everyday is articulated in Freud's shift from a theory of a unique *trauma* to a theory of multiple *shocks*. Freud's early theory sees trauma as a stimulus that penetrates the psychic apparatus without arriving at consciousness. It is only through a mechanism of *deferred retroaction* that the traumatic event can be perceived, with a second event partly repeating the first and retroacting it. A trauma can thus take place only through its later repetition, which causes the trauma to burst out. However, Freud soon came to understand that if it is only repetition that gives access to the first event, then the very existence of the "primal scene" must be called into question. This is why he developed a second theory of trauma, in which it is either repeated immediately without deferral, as in the case of shell-shocked soldiers, or so much deferred that its origin can no longer be retrieved. The everyday implied by this second theory is ruled by a post-traumatic repetition of both immediate and indefinite shocks in the form of the symptom.

Freud thus ends up with a theory of a shocking and shocked everyday life, and in order to understand a way out of this situation, I examined Benjamin's theory of modernity. With him, I proposed to understand Freud as the discoverer of *consciousness* rather than of the unconscious. Consciousness is attributed the role of *parrying* the shocks of modernity—that is, the infinite external and internal stimuli that characterise an overwhelming reality. To parry the shocks, they must be registered and given specific time and place, such that every event in life becomes an "immediate experience" that is not integrated into the global movement of the everyday. It is moreover from this situation that the distinction between the ordinary and the extraordinary stems: everything is shocking and nothing is shocking; everything is registered but nothing is integrated, such that the shocking and "extraordinary" event is felt to remain outside the global movement of the everyday.

I finally proposed that the key for the integration of shocks lies in the mechanism of deferred retroaction, in which the shocking event is repeated by a second one that allows its further elaboration. However, in Freud it is only the *child* who is capable of a playful deferred retroaction that would not only prolong the shock but also bind and discharge it, gradually integrating it into the everyday. And indeed, Charlie Chaplin is often presented as a child who is not interested in the adults' rules. But remaining with this solution would make Chaplin into the "reverse image" of the adult everyday, as Lefebvre argues. This is why I have tried to locate an adult possibility of integration of shocks into the everyday, through Benjamin's notion of the aura of the habitual.

Contrary to the "old" aura that used deferred retroaction to give an object the allure of eternity, the aura of the habitual acknowledges the ephemeral character of the everyday. It does not hide negativity, but rather brings it to the fore. This aura of the habitual can be attained through a certain practice of deferred retroaction that I located in the work of Cindy Sherman, or, more exactly, in the experience of looking at her work. In this experience one retroacts various frozen images of the everyday that suspend and reflect it simultaneously. The spectator goes from one shock-image to another, revealing both their extraordinary allure and their dependence on ordinary, yet variable, surroundings. The result is an experience of the aura of the habitual that does not simply suspend the everyday but also enhances it. The aura of the habitual is thus finally revealed to be another version of the immersed or embodied reflection we found in phenomenology: a suspension of the everyday as a part of its practice.

However, immersed reflection should not be conceived outside its historical context. In other words, one cannot simply imagine an old-fashioned world with slow manual work that allows enough time for the integration of its different moments into the everyday. To avoid the romantic temptation and take modernity seriously, one should apply the notion of immersed reflection and deferred retroaction to contemporary situations, such as the flow of rapidly changing images that are reproduced daily on our computer screens. An immersed reflection of these would allow retroaction of other images and other everyday situations, thus leading to their integration into the everyday.

What new possibilities does modernity offer for the aura of the habitual and immersed reflection? Can these be enacted, for instance, by video games that make the virtual and the actual dialogue through special capsules, integrating the player's bodily movements into the game? Can networks such as Facebook or Instagram demonstrate the interdependency of the ordinary and the extraordinary, and this through the possibility of sharing small moments with other people? Or do they instead reinforce the objectification of the everyday and the attempt to make isolated moments look extraordinary? These questions should guide any future research on the everyday that aims not only to delineate its categories but also to challenge them.

Bibliography

Adorno, Theodor. *The Jargon of Authenticity*, trans. Knut Tarnowski and Frederic Will. Evanston, IL: Northwestern University Press, 1973.

———. "Letter to Walter Benjamin, March 18, 1936". In Theodor Adorno, Walter Benjamin, Ernst Bloch, Bertolt Brecht and Georg Lukács, *Aesthetics and Politics*, ed. Frederic Jameson, trans. Harry Zohn. 120–27. London and New York: Verso, 2007.

———. *Notes to Literature*, 2 vols., ed. Rolf Tiedemann, trans. Shierry Weber Nicholsen. New York: Columbia University Press, 1991–1992.

Agamben, Giorgio. *Infancy and History: The Destruction of Experience*, trans. Liz Heron. London and New York: Verso, 1993.

———. *Language and Death: The Place of Negativity*, trans. Karen E. Pinkus with Michael Hardt. Minneapolis: University of Minnesota Press, 1991.

Aho, Kevin A. *Heidegger's Neglect of the Body*. Albany: State University of New York Press, 2009.

Alloa, Emmanuel. *La Résistance du sensible: Merleau-Ponty critique de la transparence*. Paris: Éditions Kimé, 2008.

Askay, Richard R. "Heidegger, the Body, and the French Philosophers". *Continental Philosophy Review* 32 (1999): 29–35.

Azoulay, Ariella. *Once upon a Time: Photography following Walter Benjamin*. Ramat Gan: University of Bar-Ilan Press, 2006 (in Hebrew).

Backhaus, Gary. "Simmel's Philosophy of History and Its Relation to Phenomenology: Introduction". *Human Studies* 26, no. 2 (2003): 203–8.

Baldwin, Thomas. "Merleau-Ponty's Phenomenological Critique of Natural Science". *Royal Institute of Philosophy Supplement* 72 (2013): 189–219.

———. "Speaking and Spoken Speech". In *Reading Merleau-Ponty: On Phenomenology of Perception*, ed. Thomas Baldwin, 87–103. London and New York: Routledge, 2007.

Baranger, M., W. Baranger, and J. M. Mom. "The Infantile Psychic Trauma from Us to Freud: Pure Trauma, Retroactivity and Reconstruction". *International Journal of Psychoanalysis* 69 (1988): 113–28.

Barbaras, Renaud. *The Being of the Phenomenon: Merleau-Ponty's Ontology*, trans. Ted Toadvine and Leonard Lawlor. Bloomington: Indiana Univesity Press, 2004.

Barthes, Roland. "The Death of the Author". In *Image–Music–Text*, ed. and trans. Stephen Heath, 142–48. New York: Hill & Wang, 1977.

Bass, Alan. "The Problem of 'Concreteness'". *Psychoanalytic Quarterly* 66 (1997): 642–82.

Bauman, Zygmunt. *Liquid Life*. Cambridge: Polity Press, 2005.

———. *Liquid Modernity*. Cambridge: Polity Press, 2000.

Beauvoir, Simone de. *Memoirs of a Dutiful Daughter*, trans. James Kirkup. New York: Penguin Books, 1963.

Bégout, Bruce. *La Découverte du quotidien*. Paris: Allia, 2005.

———. *La Généologie de la logique*. Paris: Vrin, 1999.

Benjamin, Andrew. "The Decline of Art: Benjamin's Aura". *Oxford Art Journal* 9, no. 2 (1986): 30–35.

———. "Tradition and Experience: Walter Benjamin's 'On Some Motifs in Baudelaire'". In *The Problems of Modernity: Adorno and Benjamin*, ed. Andrew Benjamin, 122–40. London: Routledge, 1989.

———. "Translating Origins: Psychoanalysis and Philosophy". In *Discourse, Subjectivity, Ideology*, ed. Lawrence Venuti, 18–41. London and New York: Routledge, 1992.

Benjamin, Walter. *The Arcades Project*, ed. Rolf Tiedemann, trans. Howard Eiland and Kevin McLaughlin. Cambridge, MA: Belknap Press, 1999.

———. *The Correspondence of Walter Benjamin 1910–1940*, ed. Gershom Scholem and Theodor W. Adorno, trans. Manfred R. Jacobson and Evelyn M. Jacobson. Chicago: University of Chicago Press, 1994.

———. *Gesammelte Schriften*, Band I. Frankfurt am Main: Suhrkamp, 1991.

———. *Illuminations*, trans. Harry Zohn. New York: Shocken Books, 1968.

———. *The Origin of German Tragic Drama*, trans. John Osborne. London and New York: Verso, 1998.

———. *Selected Writings*, 4 vols., ed. Marcus Bullock, Howard Eiland, Michael W. Jennings and Gary Smith. Cambridge, MA: Harvard University Press, 1996–2003.

Bergson, Henri. *Matter and Memory*, trans. Nancy Margaret Paul and W. Scott Palmer. New York: Zone Books, 1991.

Berman, Marshall. *The Politics of Authenticity: Radical Individualism and the Emergence of Modern Society*. London: Allen & Unwin, 1971.

Bernet, Rudolf. *La Vie du sujet*. Paris: Presses Universitaires de France, 1994.

Blanchot, Maurice. "Everyday Speech". In *The Infinite Conversation*, trans. S. Hanson, 238–45. Minneapolis and London: University of Minnesota Press, 1993.

Bohleber, Werner. "Remembrance, Trauma and Collective Memory: The Battle for Memory in Psychoanalysis". *International Journal of Psychoanalysis* 88 (2007): 329–52.

Bollas, Christopher. *The Shadow of the Object: Psychoanalysis of the Unthought Known*. New York: Columbia University Press, 1987.

Breton, André. *Manifestoes of Surrealism*, trans. Richard Seaver and Helen R. Lane. Ann Arbor: University of Michigan Press, 1969.

Buck-Morss, Susan. "Aesthetics and Anaesthetics: Walter Benjamin's Artwork Essay Reconsidered". *October* 62 (Autumn 1992): 3–41.

———. *The Dialectics of Seeing: Walter Benjamin and the Arcades Project*. Cambridge, MA: MIT Press, 1991.

Buckly, R. Philip. *Husserl, Heidegger and the Crisis of Philosophical Responsibility*. Dordrecht: Kluwer, 1992.

Butler, Judith. "Sexual Ideology and Phenomenological Description: A Feminist Critique of Merleau-Ponty's *Phenomenology of Perception*". In *The Thinking Muse*, ed. J. Allen and Iris M. Young, 85–100. Bloomington: Indiana University Press, 1989.

Carbone, Mauro. *The Thinking of the Sensible: Merleau-Ponty's A-philosophy*. Evanston, IL: Northwestern University Press, 2004.
————. *An Unprecedented Deformation: Marcel Proust and the Sensible Ideas*, trans. Niall Keane. Albany: State University of New York Press, 2010.
Carel, Havi. *Illness*. Stockfield: Acumen, 2008.
Carr, David. *Interpreting Husserl*. Dordrecht: Martinus Nijhoff, 1987.
————. "Translator's Introduction". In Edmund Husserl, *The Crisis of European Sciences and Transcendental Phenomenology*, xv–xliii. Evanston, IL: Northwestern University Press, 1970.
Caruth, Cathy. "An Interview with Jean Laplanche". *Postmodern Culture* 11, no. 2 (2001): n.p.
————. *Unclaimed Experience: Trauma, Narrative and History*. Baltimore: Johns Hopkins University Press, 1996.
Cavell, Stanley. *In Quest of the Ordinary: Lines of Skepticism and Romanticism*. Chicago and London: University of Chicago Press, 1988.
Caygill, Howard. "Non-Messianic Political Theology in Benjamin's 'On the Concept of History'". In *Walter Benjamin and History*, ed. Andrew Benjamin, 215–26. London: Continuum Books, 2005.
Centonze, Diego, Alberto Siracusano, Paolo Calabresi and Giorgio Bernardi. "The Project for a Scientific Psychology (1895): A Freudian Anticipation of LTP-memory Connection Theory". *Brain Research Reviews* 46, no. 3 (2004): 310–14.
Cerbone, David R. "Heidegger and Dasein's 'Bodily Nature': What Is the Hidden Problematic?". *International Journal of Philosophical Studies* 8, no. 2 (2000): 209–30.
Certeau, Michel de. *The Practice of Everyday Life*, trans. Steven Rendall. Berkeley: University of California Press, 1984.
Comay, Rebecca. "Materialist Mutations of the Bilderverbot". In *Walter Benjamin and Art*, ed. Andrew Benjamin, 32–59. London: Continuum, 2005.
Critchley, Simon. *Very Little . . . Almost Nothing: Death, Philosophy, Literature*. London and New York: Routledge, 1997.
Critchley, Simon, and Reiner Schürmann. *On Heidegger's* Being and Time, ed. Steven Levine. London and New York: Routledge, 2008.
Dastur, Françoise. *Chair et langage: Essais sur Merleau-Ponty*. Paris: Encre Marine, 2002.
David-Ménard, Monique. *Hysteria from Freud to Lacan: Body and Language in Psychoanalysis*, trans. Catherine Porter. Ithaca, NY, and London: Cornell University Press, 1989.
Davis, F. B. "Three Letters from Sigmund Freud to André Breton". *Journal of the American Psychoanalytic Association* 1, no. 21 (1973): 127–34.
Debord, Guy. *The Society of Spectacle*, trans. Donald Nicholson-Smith. New York: Zone Books, 1995.
Deleuze, Gilles. *Cinema 1: The Movement-Image*, trans. Hugh Tomlinson and Barbara Habberjam. Minneapolis: University of Minnesota Press, 1986.
————. *Cinema 2: The Time-Image*, trans. Hugh Tomlinson and Robert Galeta. Minneapolis: University of Minnesota Press, 1989.
————. *Difference and Repetition*, trans. Paul Patton. New York: Columbia University Press, 1994.
Derrida, Jacques. "Différance". In *Margins of Philosophy*, trans. Alan Bass, 3–27. Chicago: University of Chicago Press, 1982.
————. "Freud and the Scene of Writing". In *Writing and Difference*, trans. Alan Bass, 196–231. Chicago: University of Chicago Press, 1978.
————. *The Post Card: From Socrates to Freud and Beyond*, trans. Alan Bass. Chicago: University of Chicago Press, 1987.

————. *Voice and Phenomenon*, trans. Leonard Lawlor. Evanston, IL: Northwestern University Press, 2011.

Dillon, M. C. *Merleau-Ponty's Ontology*. Bloomington: Indiana University Press, 1988.

Dorfman, Eran. "Freedom, Perception and Radical Reflection". In *Reading Merleau-Ponty: On Phenomenology of Perception*, ed. Thomas Baldwin, 139–51. London and New York: Routledge, 2007.

————. "History of the Lifeworld: From Husserl to Merleau-Ponty". *Philosophy Today* 53, no. 3 (2009): 294–303.

————. "Naturalism, Objectivism and Everyday Life". *Royal Institute of Philosophy Supplement* 72 (2013): 117–33.

————. "La Parole qui voit, la vision qui parle: De la question du Logos dans *Être et temps*". *Revue Philosophique de Louvain* 104, no. 1 (2006): 104–32.

————. *Réapprendre à voir le monde: Merleau-Ponty face au miroir lacanian*. Dordrecht: Springer, 2007.

Dreyfus, Hubert L. *Being-in-the-World*. Cambridge, MA: MIT Press, 1991.

————. "The Return of the Myth of the Mental". *Inquiry* 50, no. 4 (2007): 352–65.

Duras, Marguerite. *Hiroshima mon amour*, trans. Richard Seaver. New York: Grove Press, 1961.

————. *The Ravishing of Lol Stein*, trans. Richard Seaver. New York: Grove Press, 1966.

Durkheim, Émile. *Division of Labor in Society*, trans. G. Simpson. New York: The Free Press, 1947.

————. *Selected Writings*, ed. Anthony Giddens. Cambridge: Cambridge University Press, 1972.

————. *Suicide*, trans. John A. Spaulding and George Simpson. New York: The Free Press, 1951.

Duttlinger, Carolin. "Imaginary Encounters: Walter Benjamin and the Aura of Photography". *Poetics Today* 29, no. 1 (2008): 79–101.

Ehrenberg, Alain. *The Weariness of the Self: Diagnosing the History of Depression in the Contemporary Age*. Montreal: McGill-Queen's University Press, 2010.

Eickhoff, Friedrich-Wilhelm. "On Nachträglichkeit: The Modernity of an Old Concept. *International Journal of Psychoanalysis* 87, no. 6 (2006): 1453–69.

Eliade, Mircea. *The Myth of the Eternal Return: Cosmos and History*, trans. Willard Trask. New York: Harper & Row, 1963.

Farias, Victor. *Heidegger and Nazism*. Philadelphia: Temple University Press, 1989.

Faye, Emmanuel. *Heidegger: The Introduction of Nazism into Philosophy in Light of the Unpublished Seminars of 1933–1935*. New Haven, CT: Yale University Press, 2009.

Ferber, Ilit. *Philosophy and Melancholy: Benjamin's Early Reflections on Theatre and Language*. Stanford, CA: Stanford University Press, 2013.

Ferenczi, Sándor. "Confusion of the Tongues between the Adults and the Child—(The Language of Tenderness and of Passion)". *International Journal of Psychoanalysis* 30 (1949): 225–30.

Fink, Eugen. "The Philosophical Phenomenology of Edmund Husserl and Contemporary Criticism". In *The Phenomenology of Husserl*, ed. and trans. R. O. Elveton, 73–147. Seattle: Noesis Press, 2000.

Foster, Hal. *The Return of the Real*. Cambridge, MA: MIT Press, 1996.

Foucault, Michel. *The History of Sexuality*, vol. 1, *An Introduction*, trans. Robert Hurley. New York: Random House, 1978.

Franck, Didier. "Being and the Living". In *Who Comes after the Subject?*, ed. E. Cadava, P. Connor and J.-L. Nancy, 135–47. London: Routledge, 1991.

Freud, Sigmund. *The Standard Edition of the Complete Psychological Works of Sigmund Freud*. 24 vols., ed. James Strachey. London: Hogarth Press, 1953–1974.

————. "Beyond the Pleasure Principle" [1920]. In *Standard Edition* 18: 7–64.

————. "Extracts from the Fliess Papers" [1892–1899]. In *Standard Edition* 1: 175–282.

————. "Further Remarks on the Neuro-Psychoses of Defence" [1896]. In *Standard Edition* 3: 159–85.

————. "Inhibitions, Symptoms and Anxiety" [1926 (1925)]. In *Standard Edition* 20: 87–175.

————. *The Interpretation of Dreams* [1900–1901]. *Standard Edition* 4–5.

————. "Negation" [1925]. In *Standard Edition* 19: 235–39.

————. "A Note upon the 'Mystic Writing-Pad'" [1925 (1924)]. In *Standard Edition* 19: 227–32.

————. "Obsessive Actions and Religious Ceremonies" [1909]. In *Standard Edition* 9: 115–27.

————. "Project for a Scientific Psychology" [1895]. In *Standard Edition* 1: 283–397.

————. "The Psychopathology of Everyday Life" [1901]. In *Standard Edition* 6: 1–279.

————. "Remembering, Repeating and Working-Through (Further Recommendations on the Technique of Psycho-Analysis II)" [1914]. In *Standard Edition* 12: 145–56.

————. "Repression" [1915]. In *Standard Edition* 14: 146–58.

————. "Screen Memories" [1899]. In *Standard Edition* 3: 303–22.

————. *Studies on Hysteria* [1893–1895]. *Standard Edition* 2.

————. "Three Letters from Sigmund Freud to André Breton". *Journal of the American Psychoanalytic Association* 21, no. 1 (1973): 127–34.

————. "The 'Uncanny'" [1919]. In *Standard Edition* 17: 217–56.

Friedlander, Eli. *Walter Benjamin: A Philosophical Portrait*. Cambridge, MA: Harvard University Press, 2012.

Frisby, David. *Fragments of Modernity: Theories of Modernity in the Work of Simmel, Kracauer and Benjamin*. Cambridge, MA: MIT Press, 1988.

Fritsche, Johannes. *Historical Destiny and National Socialism in Heidegger's* Being and Time. Berkeley and Los Angeles: University of California Press, 1999.

Gardiner, Michael. *Critiques of Everyday Life: An Introduction*. London and New York: Routledge, 2000.

Gelb, Adhémar, and Kurt Goldstein. "Psychologische Analysen hirnpathologischer Falle auf Grund von Untersuchungen Hirnverletzer". *Zeitschrift für die gesamte Neurologie und Psychiatrie* 41 (1918): 1–142.

Goldenberg, Georg. "Goldstein and Gelb's Case Schn.: A Classic Case in Neuropsychology?". In *Classic Cases in Neuropsychology*, vol. 2, ed. C. Code, C. W. Wallesch, Y. Joanette and A. R. Lecours. Hove: Psychology Press, 2003.

Goldstein, Kurt, "Über die Abhängigkeit der Bewegungen von optischen Vorgängen". *Monatsschrift für Psychiatrie und Neurologie* 54 (1923): 141–94.

Haar, Michel. *The Song of the Earth: Heidegger and the Grounds of the History of Being*, trans. R. Lilly. Bloomington: Indiana University Press, 1993.

Hansen, Mark. *Embodying Technesis: Technology beyond Writing*. Ann Arbor: University of Michigan Press, 2000.

Hansen, Miriam Bratu. *Cinema and Experience*. Berkeley: University of California Press, 2012.

Harman, Graham. *Tool-Being: Heidegger and the Metaphysics of Objects*. Chicago: Open Court, 2002.

Hass, Lawrence. *Merleau-Ponty's Philosophy*. Bloomington: Indiana University Press, 2008.

Heidegger, Martin. *Basic Writings*, ed. David Farrell Krell. London and New York: Routledge, 1993.

————. *Being and Time*, trans. J. Macquarrie and E. Robinson. New York: Harper & Row, 1962.

————. *Being and Time*, trans. Joan Stambaugh. Albany: State University of New York Press, 1996.

————. *The Fundamental Concepts of Metaphysics: World, Finitude, Solitude*, trans. William McNeill and Nicholas Walker. Bloomington: Indiana University Press, 1995.

————. *History of the Concept of Time*, trans. Theodore Kisiel. Bloomington: Indiana University Press, 1992.

————. *Sein und Zeit*. Tübingen: Max Niemeyer, 1927.

————. *Zollikon Seminars: Protocols—Conversations—Letters*, trans. Franz K. Mayr and Richard R. Askay. Evanston, IL: Northwestern University Press, 2001.

Heller, Agnes. *Everyday Life*. London: Routledge, 1984.

Hesse, Hermann. *Demian*, trans. Michael Roloff and Michael Lebeck. New York: Bantam, 1968.

Highmore, Ben, ed. *Everyday Life and Cultural Theory: An Introduction*. London and New York: Routledge, 2002.

————. *The Everyday Life Reader*. London and New York: Routledge, 2002.

————. *Ordinary Lives: Studies in the Everyday*. London and New York: Routledge, 2010.

Houellebecq, Michel. "Approches du désarroi". In *Interventions*. Paris: Flammarion, 1998.

Husserl, Edmund. *Cartesian Meditations*, trans. D. Cairns. The Hague: Martinus Nijhoff, 1960.

————. *The Crisis of European Sciences and Transcendental Phenomenology*, trans. David Carr. Evanston, IL: Northwestern University Press, 1970.

————. *Experience and Judgment*, trans. J. S. Churchill and K. Ameriks. Evanston, IL: Northwestern University Press, 1973.

————. *Ideas: General Introduction to Pure Phenomenology*, trans. W. R. Boyce Gibson. London: Allen & Unwin, 1931.

————. *Ideas Pertaining to a Pure Phenomenology and to a Phenomenological Philosophy*. Second book: *Studies in the Phenomenology of Constitution*, trans. R. Rojcewicz and A. Schuwer. Dordrecht: Kluwer, 1989.

————. *Logical Investigations* I, trans. J. N. Findlay. New York: Humanities Press, 1970.

————. *On the Phenomenology of the Consciousness of Internal Time (1893–1917)*, trans. John Barnett Brough. Dordrecht: Kluwer, 1991.

————. "The Origin of Geometry". In Maurice Merleau-Ponty, *Husserl at the Limits of Phenomenology*, ed. and trans. Leonard Lawlor and Bettina Bergo. Evanston, IL: Northwestern University Press, 2002.

————. "Philosophy as a Rigorous Science", trans. M. Brainard. *New Yearbook for Phenomenology and Phenomenological Philosophy* 2 (2002 [1910–1911]): 249–95.

Ihde, Don. *Bodies in Technology*. Minneapolis and London: University of Minnesota Press, 2002.

————. *Technology and the Lifeworld: From Garden to Earth*. Bloomington: Indiana University Press, 1990.

Illouz, Eva. *Cold Intimacies: The Making of Emotional Capitalism*. Cambridge: Polity Press, 2007.

————. *Why Love Hurts: A Sociological Explanation*. Cambridge: Polity Press, 2012.

Jameson, Frederic. "The Theoretical Hesitation: Benjamin's Sociological Predecessor". *Critical Inquiry* 25, no. 2 (1999): 267–88.

Kenaan, Hagi. *The Ethics of Visuality: Levinas and the Contemporary Gaze*. London: Tauris, 2013.

Killen, Andreas. *Berlin Electropolis: Shock, Nerves, and German Modernity*. Berkeley, Los Angeles and London: University of California Press, 2006.

Kirchhoff, Christine. *Das psychoanalytische Konzept der "Nachträglichkeit": Zeit, Bedeutung und die Anfänge des Psychischen.* Gießen: Psychosozial, 2009.

Krauss, Rosalind. *The Optical Unconscious.* Cambridge, MA: MIT Press, 1993.

Krell, David Farrell. *Daimon Life: Heidegger and Life-Philosophy.* Bloomington: Indiana University Press, 1992.

Lacan, Jacques. "Homage to Marguerite Duras". In *Writing and Psychoanalysis: A Reader*, ed. John Lechte, 136–42. London and Sydney: Arnold, 1996.

———. "The Mirror Stage as Formative of the Function of the I as Revealed in Psychoanalytic Experience". In *Écrits: A Selection*, trans. Alan Sheridan, 1–7. London: Tavistock, 1977.

———. *The Seminar of Jacques Lacan.* Book 1: *Freud's Papers on Technique, 1953–1954*, trans. John Forrester. New York and London: Norton, 1988.

LaCapra, Dominick. *Writing History, Writing Trauma.* Baltimore: Johns Hopkins University Press, 2001.

Laplanche, Jean. *Life and Death in Psychoanalysis*, trans. J. Mehlman. Baltimore: Johns Hopkins University Press, 1985.

———. *New Foundations for Psychoanalysis*, trans. D. Macey. Oxford: Blackwell, 1989.

———. *Problématiques VI: L'après coup.* Paris: Presses Universitaires de France, 2006.

Laplanche, Jean, and J.-B. Pontalis. "Fantasy and the Origin of Sexuality". *International Journal of Psychoanalysis* 49 (1968): 1–17.

Lefebvre, Henri. *Critique of Everyday Life*, vol. 1, trans. John Moore. London and New York: Verso, 1991.

Levinas, Emmanuel. *Totality and Infinity: An Essay on Exteriority*, trans. A. Lingis. The Hague, Boston and London: Martinus Nijhoff, 1969.

Leys, Ruth. *Trauma: A Genealogy.* Chicago: University of Chicago Press, 2000.

Löwy, Michael. *Fire Alarm: Reading Walter Benjamin's "On the Concept of History"*, trans. Chris Turner. London: Verso, 2006.

Luft, Sebastian. "Husserl's Phenomenological Discovery". *Continental Philosophy Review* 31 (1998): 153–70.

Lukacher, Ned. *Primal Scenes: Literature, Philosophy, Psychoanalysis.* Ithaca, NY: Cornell University Press, 1986.

Malabou, Catherine. *What Should We Do with Our Brain?*, trans. Sebastian Rand. New York: Fordham University Press, 2008.

Marder, Elissa. *Dead Time: Temporal Disorders in the Wake of Modernity (Baudelaire and Flaubert).* Stanford, CA: Stanford University Press, 2001.

Marucco, N. C. "Between Memory and Destiny: Repetition". *International Journal of Psychoanalysis* 88 (2007): 309–28.

Marx, Karl. *Capital: A Critique of Political Economy*, vol. 1, trans. Ben Fowkes. London: Penguin Books, 1976.

Masson, Jeffrey Moussaieff. *The Assault on Truth: Freud's Suppression of the Seduction Theory.* New York: Farrar, Straus & Giroux, 1984.

McDowell, John. *The Engaged Intellect.* Cambridge, MA: Harvard University Press, 2009.

McLuhan, Marshall. *Understanding Media: The Extensions of Man.* Cambridge, MA: MIT Press, 1994.

Merleau-Ponty, Maurice. "Eye and Mind". In *The Primacy of Perception*, ed. James E. Edie, trans. Carleton Dallery, 159–90. Evanston, IL: Northwestern University Press, 1964.

———. *Institution and Passivity: Course Notes from the Collège de France (1954–1955)*, trans. Leonard Lawlor and Heath Massey. Evanston, IL: Northwestern University Press, 2010.

————. *Phenomenology of Perception*, trans. Donald A. Landes. London and New York: Routledge, 2012.

————. *Phenomenology of Perception*, trans. Colin Smith. London: Routledge, 2002.

————. "The Primacy of Perception and Its Philosophical Consequences". In *The Primacy of Perception*, ed. James E. Edie, trans. Carleton Dallery, 12–42. Evanston, IL: Northwestern University Press, 1964.

————. *The Prose of the World*, trans. John O'Neill. Evanston, IL: Northwestern University Press, 1973.

————. *The Structure of Behavior*, trans. Alden L. Fisher. Boston: Beacon Press, 1963.

————. *The Visible and the Invisible*, trans. Alphonso Lingis. Evanston, IL: Northwestern University Press, 1968.

————. *The World of Perception*, trans. Olivier Davis. London and New York: Routledge, 2004.

Moran, Dermot. "Husserl's Transcendental Philosophy and the Critique of Naturalism". *Continental Philosophy Review* 41 (2008): 401–25.

Moran, Joe. *Reading the Everyday*. London and New York: Routledge, 2005.

Mulhall, Stephen. *Heidegger and* Being and Time. London and New York: Routledge, 1996.

————. *Philosophical Myths of the Fall*. Princeton, NJ: Princeton University Press, 2005.

Mulvey, Laura. "A Phantasmagoria of the Female Body: The Work of Cindy Sherman". *New Left Review* 188 (July–August 1991): 137–50.

Nancy, Jean-Luc. *The Birth to Presence*, trans. Brian Holmes et al. Stanford, CA: Stanford University Press, 1993.

————. "The Intruder". In *Corpus*, trans. R. A. Rand. New York: Fordham University Press, 2008.

Pink, Sarah. *Situating Everyday Life: Practices and Places*. London: Sage, 2012.

Poe, Edgar Allan. "Maelzel's Chess Player" [1836]. In *Edgar Allan Poe: Essays and Reviews*, ed. G. R. Thompson, 1253–76. New York: Library of America, 1984.

Pold, Soren. "An Aesthetic Criticism of the Media: The Configurations of Art, Media and Politics in Walter Benjamin's Materialistic Aesthetics". *Parallax* 5, no. 3 (1999): 22–35.

Proust, Marcel. *Swann's Way*, trans. C. K. Scott Moncrieff and Terence Kilmartin. New York: Vintage Books, 1989.

————. *Time Regained*, trans. Andreas Mayor and Terence Kilmartin. New York: Modern Library, 2003.

Rabinbach, Anson. *The Human Motor: Energy, Fatigue, and the Origins of Modernity*. New York: Basic Books, 1990.

Ramachandran, V. S. *The Tell-Tale Brain: Unlocking the Mystery of Human Nature*. London: Windmill Books, 2012.

Ricoeur, Paul. *From Text to Action*, trans. K. Blamey and J. B. Thompson. Evanston, IL: Northwestern University Press, 1991.

Rimbaud, Arthur. "A Season in Hell". In *A Season in Hell and The Drunken Boat*, trans. L. Varèse, 3–91. New York: New Directions, 1961.

Roberts, John. *Philosophizing the Everyday: Revolutionary Praxis and the Fate of Cultural Theory*. London and Ann Arbor, MI: Pluto Press, 2006.

Rockmore, Tom. *On Heidegger's Nazism and Philosophy*. Berkeley: University of California Press, 1997.

Roff, Sarah Ley. "Benjamin and Psychoanalysis". In *The Cambridge Companion to Walter Benjamin*, ed. David Ferris, 115–33. Cambridge: Cambridge University Press, 2004.

Rogozinski, Jacob. *The Ego and the Flesh: An Introduction to Egoanalysis*, trans. Robert Vallier. Stanford, CA: Stanford University Press, 2010.

Royle, Nicholas. *The Uncanny*. Manchester: Manchester University Press, 2003.

Rushkoff, Douglas. *Present Shock: When Everything Happens Now*. New York: Current, 2013.

Russell, Matheson. "Phenomenological Reduction in Heidegger's 'Sein und Zeit': A New Proposal". *Journal of the British Society for Phenomenology* 39, no. 3 (2008): 229–48.

Samuels, Maurice. "2000: Trauma on the Boulevard". *Romanic Review* 101, no. 1/2 (2010): 115–22.

Sartre, Jean-Paul. *Being and Nothingness*, trans. Hazel Barnes. New York: Simon & Schuster, 1956.

Sayeau, Michael. *Against the Event*. Oxford: Oxford University Press, 2013.

Schutz, Alfred, and Thomas Luckmann. *The Structures of the Life-World*, trans. Richard M. Zaner and T. Engelhardt. Evanston, IL: Northwestern University Press/London: Heinemann, 1973.

Sheringham, Michael. *Everyday Life: Theories and Practices from Surrealism to the Present*. Oxford: Oxford University Press, 2006.

Simmel, Georg. *The Philosophy of Money*, trans. Tom Bottomore and David Frisby. London: Routledge, 1978.

———. *Simmel on Culture: Selected Writings*, ed. David Frisby and Mike Featherstone. London: Sage, 1997.

Sluga, Hans. *Heidegger's Crisis: Philosophy and Politics in Nazi Germany*. Cambridge, MA, and London: Harvard University Press, 1993.

Smith, Nicholas. *Towards a Phenomenology of Repression: A Husserlian Reply to the Freudian Challenge*. Stockholm: Stockholm University, 2010.

Sokolowski, Robert. *Introduction to Phenomenology*. Cambridge: Cambridge University Press, 2000.

Souday, Paul. "Du coté de chez Swann". *Le Temps*, December 10, 1913. Reprinted in Marcel Proust, *Du coté de chez Swann*, 654–55. Paris: Flammarion, 1987.

St. John of the Cross. *The Collected Works of St. John of the Cross*, trans. K. Kavanaugh and O. Rodriguez. Garden City, NY: Doubleday, 1964.

Stoessel, Marleen. *Aura: Das vergessene Menschliche: Zur Sprache und Erfahrung bei Walter Benjamin*. Munich and Vienna: Carl Henser Verlag, 1983.

Strötgen, Stefan. "'I compose the Party Rally . . .': The Role of Music in Leni Riefenstahl's *Triumph of the Will*", trans. Anita Ip. *Music & Politics* 2, no. 1 (2008): 1–14.

Taminiaux, Jacques. *Metamorphoses of Phenomenological Reduction*. Milwaukee, WI: Marquette University Press, 2004.

Taylor, Charles. *The Malaise of Modernity*. Toronto: House of Anansi Press, 1991.

Teuber, H.-L. "Kurt Goldstein's Role in the Development of Neuropsychology". *Neuropsychologia* 4 (1966): 299–310.

Toffler, Alvin. *Future Shock*. New York: Random House, 1970.

Tönnies, Ferdinand. *Community and Civil Society*, trans. José Harris and Margaret Hollis. Cambridge: Cambridge University Press, 2001.

Tutté, J. C. "The Concept of Psychical Trauma: A Bridge in Interdisciplinary Space". *International Journal of Psychoanalysis* 85, no. 4 (2004): 897–921.

Valéry, Paul. "The Conquest of Ubiquity". In *Aesthetics*, trans. Ralph Manheim. New York: Pantheon Books, 1964.

Van Haute, Philippe, and Tomas Geyskens. *The Confusion of Tongues: The Primacy of Sexuality in Freud, Ferenczi and Laplanche*. New York: Other Press, 2004.

———. *From Death Instinct to Attachment Theory*. New York: Other Press, 2007.

Visker, Rudi. "Dropping: The 'Subject' of Authenticity". In *Deconstructive Subjectivities*, ed. Simon Critchley and Peter Dews, 59–83. Albany: State University of New York Press, 1996.

Weber, Samuel. "Genealogy of Modernity: History, Myth and Allegory in Benjamin's *Origin of the German Mourning Play*". *Modern Language Notes* 106, no. 3 (1991): 465–500.

Weigel, Sigrid. *Body- and Image-Space: Re-Reading Walter Benjamin*, trans. Georgina Paul. London and New York: Routledge, 1996.

Weinstein, Deena, and Michael A. Weinstein. *Postmodern(ized) Simmel*. London and New York: Routledge, 1993.

Wolin, Richard, ed. *The Heidegger Controversy: A Critical Reader*. Cambridge, MA: MIT Press, 1993.

Zahavi, Dan. *Husserl's Phenomenology*. Stanford, CA: Stanford University Press, 2003.

Zimmerman, Michael E. *Eclipse of the Self: The Development of Heidegger's Concept of Authenticity*. Athens: Ohio University Press, 1981.

Žižek, Slavoj. *Looking Awry: An Introduction to Jacques Lacan through Popular Culture*. Cambridge, MA: MIT Press, 1992.

Index

drives, 104, 109, 110, 111, 123n2, 124n14, 125n20–125n21, 137, 138. *See also* death, drive; desire
drugs, 70, 73, 81
Duras, Marguerite, 186; *Hiroshima mon amour*, 23, 112, 113–114, 116, 117, 118, 121; *The Ravishing of Lol Stein*, 23, 26n20, 112, 116–119, 126n40, 156n42
Durkheim, Émile, 10, 19, 53, 91, 129; *The Division of Labor in Society*, 15–16; "malady of infiniteness", 16, 17, 20, 53, 91; *Suicide*, 16

Ehrenberg, Alain: *The Weariness of Being Oneself*, 20
emotion, 17, 18, 20, 47, 78, 106, 122, 130, 147
epoché. *See* phenomenological reduction
Erfahrung. See experience, long
Erlebnis. See experience, immediate
event, 1, 4, 6, 7, 8, 14, 17, 22, 25n15, 31, 54, 59, 74, 78, 82, 100, 105–106, 120, 121, 133, 136, 140, 153n9, 168, 171, 173, 174, 176, 179, 180, 185; auratic, 148–149, 150, 151, 159, 160–161, 162–163, 177; extraordinary/ordinary, 3, 8, 9, 18, 41, 73, 112, 117, 118, 139, 141, 143, 161, 181n8, 186, 187, 189; shocking, 3, 5, 127–128, 135, 139–140, 145, 150, 151, 162, 164, 170, 186, 189; traumatic, 102, 103–104, 105, 107, 108, 109, 110, 112, 113–114, 115–116, 118, 119, 121, 122, 125n26, 127–128, 151, 164, 189
the everyday: ambiguity and, 6, 7, 8–9, 36, 66–67, 72; anonymity and, 6–7, 8, 25n7; crisis of, 5–6, 12, 20, 47, 127, 142; extraordinary and, 9–10, 11–12, 13, 14–15, 17, 18, 19, 27n39, 73, 86, 90–91, 112, 115, 120, 127, 136, 139, 141, 153n13, 160, 161,

174, 178, 189, 190; foundation of, 1–5, 12, 22–23, 38, 39, 43, 45, 46, 48, 55, 56–57, 59, 63n48, 71, 72, 73, 75, 76–77, 79, 80, 82–86, 90, 99, 185, 187, 188; modernity and, 1, 5, 6, 7, 10, 11, 12, 13, 14, 15, 16, 18, 19, 20, 21, 23, 24, 25n9, 31, 49–50, 61n29, 82, 86, 91, 97, 98, 104, 117, 119, 120, 123, 128, 129, 136, 139, 140, 150, 162, 168, 174, 180, 185, 187, 188–189, 190; movement of, 1, 2–5, 6, 7, 8, 9, 22, 23, 24n3, 33, 45, 46, 47, 51, 54, 58, 61n28, 74, 75, 76, 77, 79–80, 82, 83, 86, 90, 100, 139, 153n9, 160, 161, 162, 168–170, 172, 177, 180, 185, 186, 187–188, 189; ordinary and, 1, 9, 12–13, 14, 19, 27n39, 86, 90–91, 114, 117, 120, 127, 128, 139, 153n13, 160, 161, 174, 181, 189; renewal of, 22, 23, 27n39, 37, 46, 48, 59, 76, 79, 86, 90, 185, 187
experience: ecstatic, 23, 73, 187; immediate, 24, 137–141, 142, 144, 162, 169, 170, 172, 180, 189; lived, 34–36, 37, 60n11, 134; long, 24, 133, 137–141, 142, 143, 145, 153n9, 162, 170, 171, 180; opposed to the everyday, 1, 5, 7, 9, 12, 13, 21–22, 25n11, 34, 36, 71, 73, 86, 89, 128–132, 135, 136, 139, 142, 152, 162, 180, 182n13, 188

fantasy, 11, 94n19, 104, 131, 137
fascism, 57, 63n50, 73, 129, 145–146, 147–149, 155n33, 157, 165, 180
finitude, 23, 59, 74, 77, 84, 91, 162, 188
Fink, Eugen, 38
Flaubert, Gustave, 9, 14, 130, 153n6, 153n8; *Madame Bovary*, 12, 13, 26n20
flesh, 69–70. *See also* body
football, 70
fort-da game, 105, 114, 117, 120, 152
Foucault, Michel, 28n44, 98